STAY UP-TO-DATE on the LATEST in ePHILANTHROPY

We know that you need the most up-to-the-minute information
to succeed online.

Yet, the world of Internet fundraising and relationship building is constantly changing.
So, to keep you informed, we will provide occasional **FREE e-mail updates**
on new resources, changes, and the latest ideas
in the ever-changing world of fundraising on the Internet.

If you would like to receive these periodic updates, please register at:

www.josseybass.com/go/internetfundraising

or

www.ephilanthropyfoundation.org/epfbook.asp

Thank you,

Mal Warwick   Ted Hart   Nick Allen

Neither the editors nor the authors endorse any specific vendors identified in this book. We encourage readers to assess all vendor options carefully and to make independent decisions based on their own organizations and needs.

To find more information about fundraising online please visit us at:

Mal Warwick & Associates, Inc.
2550 Ninth St., Suite 103
Berkeley, California 94710
Phone: (510) 843–8888
Fax: (510) 843–0142
www.malwarwick.com

ePhilanthropyFoundation.Org
1101 15th Street, NW
Washington, DC 20005
Phone: (877) 536–1245
Fax: (202) 478–0910
www.ephilanthropyfoundation.org

Donordigital
182 Second Street
San Francisco, California 94105
Phone: (415) 278–9444
www.donordigital.com

Fundraising
on the
Internet

Fundraising on the Internet

The ePhilanthropyFoundation.Org's Guide to Success Online

SECOND EDITION

MAL WARWICK | TED HART | NICK ALLEN

Editors

PREFACE BY **Paulette V. Maehara**, CFRE

JOSSEY-BASS
A Wiley Company
www.josseybass.com

Published by

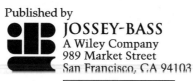

JOSSEY-BASS
A Wiley Company
989 Market Street
San Francisco, CA 94103

www.josseybass.com

Jossey-Bass books and products are available through most bookstores. To contact Jossey-Bass directly, call (888) 378-2537, fax to (800) 605-2665, or visit our website at www.josseybass.com.

Substantial discounts on bulk quantities of Jossey-Bass books are available to corporations, professional associations, and other organizations. For details and discount information, contact the special sales department at Jossey-Bass.

We at Jossey-Bass strive to use the most environmentally sensitive paper stocks available to us. Our publications are printed on acid-free recycled stock whenever possible, and our paper always meets or exceeds minimum GPO and EPA requirements.

Credits are on page 292.

Library of Congress Cataloging-in-Publication Data
Fundraising on the Internet: the e-PhilanthropyFoundation.org's
guide to success online / Mal Warwick, Ted Hart, Nick Allen, editors;
preface by Paulette V. Maehara.—2nd ed.
        p.   cm.—(The Jossey-Bass nonprofit and public management series)
Includes index.
    ISBN 0–7879–6045–4 (alk. paper)
    1. Fund raising—Computer network resources. 2. Nonprofit organizations—
Computer network resources. 3. Internet. I. Warwick, Mal. II. Hart, Ted, date-
III. Allen, Nick, date- IV. ePhilanthropyFoundation.org. V. Series.
    HV41.2 .F87 2002
    658.15'224'02854678—dc21   2001004868

SECOND EDITION

HB Printing   10 9 8 7 6 5 4 3 2 1

The Jossey-Bass
Nonprofit and Public Management Series

CONTENTS

PREFACE
The Internet Evolution: Online Fundraising Works

Remember when it was OK to say the words *Internet revolution?* As late as autumn 2000, you could create a new buzzword just by adding the letter *e* in front of any word. Imagine . . . e-business . . . e-marketing . . . even ePhilanthropy! With the Internet, the world was ours for the taking. Or rather, the e-taking.

Now, of course, all those notions sound naïve. Say the words *Internet revolution,* and you're likely to meet with reactions ranging from apathy to scorn. The failure of many dot-com businesses—and the crash of technology stocks—have reinforced the notion that the Internet, for all its opportunity, is out of favor.

The Internet revolution is over, ultimately a victim of expectations that exceeded reality. In the end, this may be a good thing. The hype can die down, the expectations can be adjusted to reflect reality, and the real work—the Internet *evolution*—can begin.

If your organization is like many charities, you're probably not sure what to do with the Internet. You know there's potential online. In the United States alone, the number of adults with Internet access has surpassed a hundred million. That's far too large an audience to ignore.

But challenges remain. Some of the excuses we hear for why charities are not getting on the Internet have validity. It *is* unpredictable. Effective and efficient business models *are* few and far between, and many new ideas get taken out for a test spin and are just as quickly put back on the shelf. A lot of organizations don't know what they're doing or how to harness their potential online. And how do long-standing ethical guidelines, such as the Association of Fundraising Professionals' Code of Ethical Principles, or those of other organizations, apply to the online environment?

This is where the second edition of *Fundraising on the Internet* comes in. This volume contains the blueprints and guidelines your organization needs to get started—and succeed—on the Internet. It will speak to you in plain language about what you can expect to get from the Internet, the challenges you'll face, and why charities need to be online.

The introduction from the first edition, published in 1996, perhaps said it best: "Fundraising on the Internet is a pioneer adventure." Five years later, the statement is still true. Given the changes that continue to occur on the Internet, this volume, like the earlier edition, is a work in progress. But charities have found success on the Internet, and business models and practices have been developed from which your organization can learn. There is a growing body of evidence that proves what we have thought all along: Online fundraising works. It takes effort, and you probably won't see substantial revenue overnight, but online fundraising is working for charities that take the time to invest in and cultivate their online users. After all, that's what fundraising is all about anyway!

As you explore the new opportunities online, take the time to become familiar with the ePhilanthropyFoundation.Org, a foundation set up to foster ethical online philanthropy. The Foundation is developing standards, information, models, and types of assistance for charities getting started online. The writers of this book constitute a Who's Who of Internet fundraising experts—they really know their stuff, and they come at the Internet environment from a variety of perspectives.

Part One, "The Big Picture," reviews the current landscape of Internet fundraising and where this new medium is headed. The chapters on professional standards, best practices, evaluation of online fundraising success, and government regulation will be of great interest to all practitioners, whether your organization is just getting started on the Web or has had a site for several years.

Part Two, "Online Fundraising Fundamentals," covers the essentials of Internet fundraising, ranging from electronic newsletters and special events online to donation portals and shopping malls. So much has happened in the last couple of years with online fundraising that individuals of all experience levels will find this section compelling and informative.

Next, Part Three, "Technology and Your Organization," explores behind-the-scenes efforts involved with a charity's online fundraising, including donor research and managing donors and volunteers in the Internet environment as well as the complexities involved in online fundraising for multichapter organizations.

Part Four, "Tapping into Outside Resources," will be especially helpful, given most charities' current technical limitations. The chapter on outsourcing online services (Chapter Nineteen) is perhaps the most exciting part of the book, covering new developments and advances the online landscape has experienced over the past several years.

Part Five, "Beyond the Basics" explores some of the many ways that nonprofit organizations can maximize their online presence. Six chapters cover topics such as Web site design, viral marketing, and advocacy campaigns and plumb the future of fundraising with a look at building one-to-one relationships through technology.

With a new communications medium such as the Internet, a section on "Case Studies" is always invaluable. What worked—and what didn't—can be a real eye-opener.

An extensive resource section rounds out the book, with source documents that illuminate vital topics such as ethical online fundraising practices and effective e-mail marketing techniques.

In a society that can be as cynical and apathetic as ours, it may be difficult to remain enthusiastic about the Internet. But I firmly believe, and I don't say this lightly, that the future of philanthropy lies on the Internet. Yes, the axiom that "people give to people" will remain, but the Internet provides incredible opportunities for charities to recruit new donors and volunteers, energize their constituents in action, and develop an entire new generation of—here's the new buzzword—*e-donors*. Like any other fundraising initiative, the online campaign will require a lot of effort and groundwork before the results are seen, but it will happen.

So yes, maybe the Internet revolution is over, and the cynics won the first round. But the Internet evolution—the real work of creating a philanthropic landscape online, step by step—is just beginning. It's time to get started.

September 2001
Alexandria, Virginia

Paulette V. Maehara, CFRE
President and CEO, Association
of Fundraising Professionals

INTRODUCTION
Five Years of Online Fundraising

NICK ALLEN

"Fundraising on the Internet is a pioneer adventure. There are few experienced guides, the trails are rough and unmarked, and the technology can be as creaky as a wooden wagon wheel." That's what we wrote in 1996 in the first edition of Fundraising on the Internet: Recruiting and Renewing Donors Online. *By 2001, there are dozens of experienced guides (and we recruited some of them to write chapters for this book). The trails are better marked, thanks to the experiences of thousands of organizations that have toiled to acquire and cultivate donors online. The ongoing improvement in Internet technology and the creation of many new online service providers have improved the technology itself and made it more widely and cheaply available.*

WHAT'S CHANGED MOST DRAMATICALLY, however, is the number of donors around the world who are online—and who increasingly depend on the Internet to communicate with loved ones and strangers, find information, do business, and deal with the nonprofit organizations that enrich their lives. Twenty to thirty million Americans were online when we edited the first edition of this book; today more than a hundred million Americans (and fifteen million Canadians) are active users of e-mail and the Web. North Americans alone exchange more than eight billion e-mail messages a day!

These numbers mean that the Internet—the World Wide Web and e-mail—has the potential to reach more donors than ever. Every organization that has invested in an ambitious presence on the Internet is seeing the number of visitors to its site—and new donors—increase month after month. Although this book focuses on fundraising and donor relationship management, the Internet serves many other purposes for organizations: branding, marketing, organizing, advocating, distributing information, selling products, collaborating, and communicating.

Many organizations expected that the Internet would reduce their staff loads by automating information delivery, donation processing, and other tasks. But it turns out that as you communicate with more people (online or off), there's more work. Web site visitors or donors who would seldom take the time to write a letter or call on the phone (even with a toll-free number) think nothing of sharing their opinions in e-mail. The good news is that although these exchanges require staff time (and resource planning), they will certainly increase donor loyalty if properly managed.

A Lag in Achievement

Despite the dramatic rise in Internet use in the last five years, revenue from online fundraising is still a minor contributor even to organizations who have invested millions of dollars in expanding their Internet presence. When we wrote the first edition, the American Red Cross was not yet taking online credit card donations (although 30 percent of the donors calling its toll-free donation number said they found the number on the Web). In fiscal year 1999, the Red Cross raised $2.6 million online from almost 22,000 donors (average gift: $118). That's a lot of money and a lot of donors—but still less than 2 percent of the $172 million the Red Cross raised for disasters (and its over $800 million in total public support). Before the Internet, these donors would have seen the news about hurricanes or Kosovo but few would have taken the trouble to find the Red Cross's toll-free number or look up its mailing address. Now they just type in www.redcross.org.

Hundreds of national organizations are each bringing in hundreds of thousands of dollars a year in online credit card donations—many from new donors who either haven't received their direct mail or haven't given by mail. To make this happen, these organizations have generally invested in building effective Web presences, building large e-mailing lists to bring supporters (donors and prospects) back to their sites, and actively promoting their sites online and off-line; many have several staff members dedicated to the Internet.

At the same time, only a few smaller organizations have seen comparable increases in their online income. Most have not invested enough in staff or Web and e-mail development; others simply can't offer the compelling case and the urgency that would prompt individual donors—online or in the mail—to give. However, some small organizations whose mission is really vital to their supporters have made the Internet work. For example, Cure Autism Now, a Los Angeles-based organization that offers in-depth information and advocacy options to people with autistic children, raised $60,000 via an end-of-year 2000 e-mail campaign that reached thousands of people.

As Internet use increased, hundreds of for-profit companies were launched—many with the same venture capital invested in other dot-coms—to provide fundraising services to nonprofits. As George Irish discusses in Chapter Twenty-Four, some were portals where visitors could go to research and choose a charity, then make a donation on the spot. Others were shopping sites, where you could send your donors to shop online for books or clothes or laptops; your organization would get a small commission. Some enabled you to organize an online auction; others allowed your supporters to download a computer program that would show them banner ads and send you a commission.

The largest category, known as application service providers, or ASPs, enable an organization to "rent" complex applications for such tasks as accepting online credit card contributions or managing sophisticated e-mail programs, while leaving the installation, maintenance, and upgrading to the ASP. The most ambitious ASPs offer plug-and-play platforms where organizations can manage the content of their Web sites (without HTML or programming) and use an integrated suite of services, including donation processing, event registration, e-mail messaging, and donor tracking.

Although the majority of all these new companies have closed, some—especially the ASPs—will survive and eventually prosper.

Online Fundraising: Taking It to the Next Level

As development and communications professionals at thousands of nonprofits added online fundraising to their portfolios, the organizations that bring nonprofits together for learning and policymaking also embraced online fundraising. The national and local conferences of the Association of Fundraising Professionals (AFP, formerly NSFRE) presented dozens of workshops on the topic (as did the Direct Marketing Association's Nonprofit Federation, the Council for Advancement and Support of Education [CASE], and the Association for Healthcare Philanthropy [AHP]).

The ePhilanthropyFoundation.Org was established in 2000 by nonprofit organizations and for-profit companies to promote ethical online philanthropy and help nonprofits build trust with online donors (see Lisa Aramony, Chapter Two, on ethics and Ted Hart and Michael Johnston, Chapter One, on building trust). At the same time, the U.S. states' attorneys general began to discuss a common standard for regulating online philanthropy (see Michael Johnston, Chapter Six, on regulation) and the Internal Revenue Service, in its request for comment (Announcement 2000–84, IRS Bulletin 2000–42), began a review of how current laws and regulations should be interpreted in relationship to Internet fundraising.

With the crash of many dot-coms in 2001 and the realization that raising money online involves the same rules and relationships as it does off-line, many organizations went back to basics. They learned that raising money online requires building and maintaining a Web site or sites that provide donors and other supporters with information, action, and involvement. Raising money online also demands obtaining the e-mail addresses of everyone—current mail donors, Web site visitors, and others—and regularly communicating with them to keep them informed about the organization's work and drive them to its Web site to learn more, take action, or make contributions. After all, acquiring donors is more about building a relationship with someone who cares about a charitable mission and a nonprofit's good work than about sending someone to shop at Amazon.com or buy Britney's sneakers on eBay!

In the five years since the first edition of this book, ePhilanthropy has come a long way. We hope this book and the accompanying Web site will help you take online fundraising to the next level for your organization—and so provide us with your success stories for the next edition of this book.

THE CONTRIBUTORS

Mal Warwick in 1979 founded Mal Warwick & Associates, Inc., a fundraising and marketing agency in Berkeley, California, specializing in direct mail. He serves as chairman and CEO. He is also cofounder (with Nick Allen) of donordigital.com LLC, which assists nonprofit organizations in online fundraising and advocacy campaigns, and is a cofounder of the telephone fundraising firm Share Group, Inc., in Somerville, Massachusetts. Mr. Warwick has written or edited twelve books for nonprofit managers, including *The Five Strategies for Fundraising Success* and *How to Write Successful Fundraising Letters.* With Nick Allen and Michael Stein, he coedited the first edition of this book in 1996.

Ted Hart is founder and president of the international ePhilanthropy-Foundation.Org [www.ePhilanthropyFoundation.org], created to foster the use of the Internet for philanthropic purposes. An Internet and fundraising strategist with over fifteen years of experience in communications, fundraising, and nonprofit management, he is also a president of the fundraising consulting firm, Hart Philanthropic Services Group, and serves as an international board member for the Association of Fundraising Executives (AFP) and as treasurer of the Open Philanthropy Exchange (OPX) Initiative. Mr. Hart frequently lectures throughout North America on fundraising, nonprofit management, ethics, and the Internet.

Nick Allen is president of donordigital.com, the digital direct marketing company that helps nonprofits use the Internet for fundraising, advocacy, and marketing. Based in San Francisco, donordigital.com develops online donor acquisition and relationship management programs for leading nonprofits across the United States, as well as other Internet fundraising, advocacy, and marketing programs.

Among donordigital.com's clients are the American Lung Association, United Jewish Communities, Earthjustice Legal Defense Fund, Planned Parenthood Federation of America, Rainforest Action Network,

National University, the National Council of La Raza, and the Jewish Community Federation of San Francisco.

Allen was co-editor of the first edition of *Fundraising on the Internet* (1996) and is former director of the Internet Solutions Group at Mal Warwick & Associates, Inc. He has twenty-five years of experience in building nonprofit organizations, raising money, organizing, and media and public relations. He has worked as executive director (and founder) of Neighbor to Neighbor and as Washington director of the Fenton Communications public interest PR firm. In the early 1990s, he spent three years based in Prague, training environmental activists across Central and Eastern Europe.

Allen speaks frequently about the Internet at conferences, seminars, and workshops, including the international conferences of the Association of Fundraising Professionals (formerly NSFRE) and the Direct Marketing Association (DMA).

He is the father of Alexandra and Jacob.

Lisa Aramony, vice president of the AOL Time Warner Foundation and AOL Time Warner's senior director of corporate relations, focuses on building capacity for nonprofits through the effective and strategic use of interactive technology and on integrating philanthropy into the Internet. During the last two years, Aramony led the creation and management of Helping.org, the premier online philanthropy portal. She and her team have provided strategic direction to America's Promise, the Starbright Foundation, the National Mentoring Partnership, and dozens of other nonprofits. Previously, in her nine-year tenure with AOL, Aramony was responsible for the company's first direct mail efforts and the launch of AOL's e-commerce and shopping channel. She began her career in the nonprofit sector, working in the United Way system.

Michael Cervino is a seasoned strategy and marketing consultant for nonprofit organizations, serving as an expert on the use of technology for fundraising, relationship marketing, and e-business transformation. He has worked on behalf of nonprofits with Commerce One, AppNet, and New Media Publishing. Prior to focusing on Internet strategy and implementation consulting, Cervino developed Relationship Marketing programs for Fortune 500 clients such as Time Warner Communications, the Dreyfus Service Corporation, and Bancomer. During this same period, he worked at Craver, Mathews, Smith and Company, where he was responsible for guiding the integrated marketing strategies for humanitarian and public interest organizations.

Todd Cohen is editor and publisher of Nonprofitxpress, an online newspaper at [www.npxpress.com] that reports on philanthropy. He is a columnist for the *NonProfit Times*. He is the founder and was editor of the Philanthropy News Network and the *Philanthropy Journal* of North Carolina, and was business editor of the *News & Observer*, the daily newspaper in Raleigh, North Carolina.

Graham Francis is the editor and creator of www.hitdonate.net, a Web site dedicated to providing the philanthropic community with advice on online fundraising. Touching on both technical and theoretical aspects of site building, hitdonate.net demonstrates how e-fundraising is far more than just designing a "Donate Now" button (and hoping for the best). Graham has written and designed print and Web publications for organizations including Amnesty International, the United Nations Association, and the government of the United Kingdom.

Lee Hoffman is president of PhilanthroTec, Inc., a company specializing in the development of planned giving software. He is also president and CEO of Planned Giving Design Center, LLC, and Going Virtual, LLC, the Internet company behind the development of the Planned Giving Design Center network of Web sites. Over the years, Hoffman has trained thousands of planned gift specialists in the use of the PhilanthroTec's software and planned giving techniques. He has lectured at many industry conventions across the country and is coauthor of *Harnessing the Power of the Charitable Remainder Trust* (PhilanthroTec, 1999).

George Irish is director of Internet Services for HJC New Media (Toronto). He has produced award-winning Web sites for nonprofit organizations such as Greenpeace, the Body Shop Canada, University of Toronto, Amnesty International, and numerous others. Irish is a board member of eCommons.net, a hub for developing online civic space, citizen engagement, and e-governance tools, and a member of the ePhilanthropy Foundation's education committee.

Aleta Jeffress is the director of product management and quality assurance at eTapestry, where she manages all the application changes made to the product. This includes gathering suggestions from customers and prospects, designing and implementing new features, and ensuring that high-quality products are delivered on a continuing basis.

Michael Johnston is the president and founder of HJC Consultants and HJC New Media. He has worked with over a hundred nonprofit organizations in Canada, the United States, and the United Kingdom. He is an expert in fundraising and the use of the Internet by nonprofit agencies and has written three books on these topics: *The Fund Raiser's Guide to the Internet, The Nonprofit Guide to the Internet,* and (as editor) *Direct*

Response Fundraising, all published by John Wiley & Sons and all endorsed by the Association of Fundraising Professionals. Johnston currently sits on the board of directors of the ePhilanthropy Foundation and is the chair of its education committee. He is also a past board member and current member of the Association of Fundraising Professionals.

Laura Kujawski is editor and publisher of the free daily news Web site for nonprofits, PNNOnline. She has also worked there on producing regional conferences around the country aimed at helping nonprofit organizations learn how to develop technology plans. Kujawski has over twenty years of experience in the nonprofit sector. She honed her fundraising and membership development skills while at the Alcohol-Drug Council and the New Jersey and North Carolina Centers for Nonprofits. While at the Centers for Nonprofits, she was responsible for providing management technical assistance to 501(c)(3) tax-exempt organizations throughout the state.

Alison Li is director of Internet projects for HJC New Media. She is a researcher, educator, Web developer, and programmer. As a professor of science and technology studies at York University, she promoted the critical evaluation of science and its implications for society. Now as a project leader, Li works with clients such as the Multiple Sclerosis Society of Canada, Save the Children Canada, and the Parkinson Foundation of Canada.

Jay B. Love, president and CEO of the application service provider eTapestry, previously served in a sales and marketing consulting capacity to one of largest database software vendors in the nonprofit world, Target Software. There he worked with fifty of the largest nonprofit organizations in North America, handling databases of multimillion names. Prior to Target, Love served as president and CEO of Master Software Corporation. MSC provided the most widely used family of database products for the nonprofit sector. During his thirteen years at MSC, Love was responsible for the implementation of nearly six thousand nonprofit database systems all over the world.

Steve Love is vice president and creative director of Commerce One Design Center, which he founded. His thirty-five-member team has helped build award-winning, intelligent user experiences for a variety of clients, including the United Nation's International Children's Emergency Fund (UNICEF), United Nations Foundation, World Wildlife Fund, Greenpeace USA, NARAL, Association of Fundraising Professionals, MCI Worldcom, and Cablevision's the WIZ. Previous to joining Commerce One, Love served as a marketing specialist and strategic planner at the fundraising agency Craver, Mathews, Smith and Company, where he helped develop and analyze fundraising programs for Planned Parenthood Federation of America, Families USA, and Susan G. Komen Breast Cancer Foundation.

Jim McGee is the founder and CEO of Target America, Inc. His company has rapidly emerged as a leading prospect research firm. He has been in the field of database marketing for over twenty-five years. Starting at Xerox and then later at Saachti & Saachti Direct, Jim's career focused on harnessing emerging database technologies with marketing strategies for many different clients.

Brian Murrow leads the PricewaterhouseCoopers ePhilanthropy practice. This practice works with nonprofits, dot-coms, and large multinational organizations. Murrow and his team of over fifty consultants work with their clients to develop and implement Internet strategies, create customized Web-based applications, and encourage and foster inter- and intra-sector collaboration of Web-based tools and standards. In addition to consulting, Brian managed a $150 million private client stock and bond portfolio that earned recognition in the *New York Times* for high returns relative to its peer group. He speaks at industry conferences on e-business and ePhilanthropy, and has appeared on business-oriented television programming on CNBC and ABC.

John Parke serves as senior vice president of sales at MyAssociation. Prior to joining MyAssociation, he was with Marriott International for eighteen years, most recently as the vice president of national accounts. He focused on understanding and addressing customer needs to increase customer satisfaction. Parke managed more than $1.3 billion in sales and helped lead Marriott to become one of the nation's top twenty-five rated sales forces for four consecutive years. He currently serves on the boards of the Convention Liaison Council and Meeting Professionals International and on the advisory board for the Internal Association of Exposition Managers.

Jerold Pearson is director of market research, Stanford University. All research for this chapter was designed, written, analyzed, and reported by him. More information can be found on the Web at [www.stanford.edu/~jpearson/].

Phil Richmond is the national director of sales for eTapestry. He began his IT career as a software developer and has spent the last fourteen years in senior-level positions at companies providing computer and networking solutions to all types and sizes of organizations. Prior to eTapestry, Phil was General Manager at WorkNet Communications, an Internet and networking provider to small and medium businesses, and business development manager at Powerway. Phil has presented numerous seminars and lectures focusing on the integration of technology into everyday business processes.

Martin Schneiderman is founder and president of Information Age Associates, Inc., a consulting firm that specializes in providing strategic planning, project management, and technical consulting services to corporations, foundations, and nonprofit organizations throughout North America, Europe, Africa, and Asia. Schneiderman is technology editor and a regular contributing writer for *Foundation News & Commentary.*

Shirley Sexton is an Internet strategist with over fourteen years of experience in communications, marketing, and nonprofits. As director of nonprofit services at Commerce One, Sexton has directed online efforts for clients including the American Civil Liberties Union, Association of Fundraising Professionals, Common Cause, the Democratic Leadership Council, Heifer Foundation, League of Women Voters, NARAL, National Safe Kids Campaign, Pew Center on Global Climate Change, the Pew Charitable Trusts, and U.S. Committee for Refugees. She provides expertise and guidance on Internet initiatives, with an emphasis on customer relationship management and brand integration.

Eric Lee Smith is the chief product architect behind GivingCapital, having conceived the idea, developed the product design, and led the product development effort. Prior to founding GivingCapital, Smith had his own consulting firm, Future Performance, which specialized in the design and implementation of Internet-based financial services sites. His clientele included firms such as Reuters and Vanguard. Before that, he was a member of the founding team at Reality Technologies (later Reality Online). He is a professional game designer and has won a number of awards.

Michael Stein has over a decade of experience working with nonprofits, foundations, labor unions, and socially responsible businesses. He is the coauthor of two books about the Internet, including the first edition of this book. Stein specializes in Internet strategy, online marketing, and e-fundraising. He works as an Internet strategist with CompassPoint Nonprofit Services, donordigital.com, and the Management Center, and as a guide on online fundraising with TechSoup.org. He is a frequent speaker and workshop presenter to nonprofits nationwide, and his opinion and analysis have been featured in major online and off-line media.

Shaun Sullivan is chief technology officer of Blackbaud, Inc. He has been building, designing, and supporting software solutions for non-profits for more than twelve years. Since joining Blackbaud in 1989, he has played a key role in every major release of the company's flagship product, the Raiser's Edge. Most recently, Shaun designed and co-developed RE:NetSolutions, Blackbaud's ePhilanthropy suite of products. As CTO of Blackbaud, Shaun focuses on the company's technical direction and on emerging technologies.

Tom Watson is a New York Silicon Alley pioneer and serves as CEO of Changingourworld.com based in New York City. He cofounded Changing Our World Inc., an Internet, fundraising, and philanthropic services company that helps not-for-profit and corporate clients achieve their goals in philanthropy. Before joining Changingourworld.com, Watson was cofounder and co-managing editor of atNewYork.com and Silicon AlleyJobs.Com. He is a member of the board of directors of the New York Software Industry Association and of Weblab.org.

Ken Weber leads Commerce One's Global Nonprofit Practice, a leading provider of comprehensive Internet solutions to innovative nonprofits. Ken holds a B.A. in English Literature from Guelph University, Ontario, Canada. He is nearing completion of an M.A. in journalism and telecommunications from Indiana University, Bloomington. Prior to joining CommerceOne in 1995, Ken worked extensively in traditional media, primarily in print and broadcast, in Toronto, Canada.

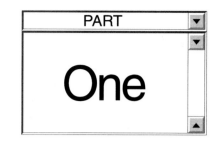
The Big Picture

CHAPTER ▼
▼
1
▲
▲

Building Trust Online

Years of experience in the off-line world have taught fundraisers that attention to ethics, privacy, security of information, honesty in reporting, and building a case for support will yield success in fundraising—because they help build trust. Building trust in the Internet is equally vital, although the medium is in its infancy in terms of philanthropy. It's essential that professional fundraisers pursue clear, ethical principles for the use of the Internet. To fulfill the promise of the ePhilanthropy revolution, the Internet must be viewed as a way to enhance the philanthropic experience. The greatest value of this important new communications channel lies in its ability to provide donors with increased access to information and more consistent, timely details regarding the stewardship of their charitable support.

EVERY FUNDRAISER KNOWS that the most important element in building a relationship with a prospective donor is trust. In some instances, years are spent cultivating prospects to draw them closer to the mission of the organization. Throughout that effort, trust is the most basic element: trust in the mission, trust in the people, trust that the donor will be treated fairly, and trust in the integrity of organization. In fact, trust is the foundation of *all* successful relationships.

However, the use of the Internet for philanthropic purposes raises a number of special challenges for fundraisers who seek to foster trust among their donors. We need to learn how to build trust *from a distance*. We do that in direct mail, so we can do it online, too.

Before embarking on any ePhilanthropy efforts, take a moment to review the ePhilanthropy Code of Ethical Online Philanthropic Practices (see Resource A). If you follow the principles within this code, you can be confident that your organization's online efforts are consistent with ethical practices. What's more important, you'll send a signal to your donors that you're serious about strengthening relationships with them and providing options and opportunities to fulfill their philanthropic intent.

Design, content, maintenance, and follow-up all work hand in hand in creating an image of your organization on the Internet. The issues surrounding donor trust online are not isolated from the off-line reality of your organization—both aspects must be addressed together in a holistic approach to donor trust.

In examining the issues related to donor trust and confidence, several themes come to mind:

- Avoiding intrusive governmental action
- Strengthening the reliability and predictability of the online philanthropic experience
- Preserving and strengthening donor options online
- Promoting donor education related to giving on the Internet
- Using technology to enhance relationships, not as a substitute for them
- Avoiding misuse of the Internet by those who (even in the off-line world) seek to take advantage of good-hearted supporters who wish to give

This chapter, and much of this book, should help any organization meet these issues head-on and counter the challenges that it will inevitably meet when trying to build trust online.

First Impressions

The layout and design of your Web site can have a direct impact on people's impressions of your organization. You can have the most far-reaching and inspiring mission on the planet, but if you fail to display that mission in an understandable and pleasing way on the Web, you could cause confusion and potentially create a negative impact on your organization. Keep the following two guidelines clearly in mind at all times:

- Make a good first impression.
- Your book *will* be judged by its cover.

When people visit your Web site, they make judgments about it (and therefore your organization) in the first few seconds. If your site is slow to load, if its navigation is less than intuitive, if it contains broken or out-dated links, if it has features that visitors and donors find hard to under-stand, they will leave—in most cases *never* to return.

If there's anything we have learned about the Internet, it is that everyone has options. Like it or not, your visitors and donors will leave if they find your Web site less than impressive.

The Internet, and other new technologies, give all donors wider phil-anthropic choices and easier access to those choices. Donors are one click away from changing their allegiance! If they take away the impression that you have a bad Web site, they'll forget about your mission and con-tinue their search. It's all too easy for them to find another, similar organ-ization that has put more thought and care into its online presence.

As ePhilanthropy continues to build steam, more and more people will expect to be able to give online to their organization of choice.

Outdated content on your Web site indicates that you don't have anything new to share—that your organization has remained static. Your Web site needs to demonstrate that your organization keeps up with the changes affecting your mission and your community. Help your visitors and donors see you as the "go to" resource for all infor-mation related to your mission.

Six Ways to Build Trust

Here are six, already proven ways a nonprofit organization can build trust online: Ensure online security with seals of approval, match online content with the organization's mission, provide for easy site naviga-tion, maintain stewardship of online gifts and online donors, appreciate the needs and expectations of donors first, and provide effective tech-nology that enables donors to find the information they need.

Ensure Online Security with Seals of Approval Symbols such as VeriSign, BBB Online, and TRUSTe are designed to reassure visitors that sites have established measures ranging from security to privacy of data. These seals testify to the safety of the Web site and the commit-ment the organization has to the principles promoted by the particular trust mark provider.

An organization can also take matters into its own hands and craft a statement that explicitly states how it has taken steps to make any online donation safe and trustworthy. For example, you might consider the following language to help build trust and confidence: "[Name of organization] takes the confidentiality of your information very seri-ously. For this reason, we use the highest level of security that technol-ogy provides when dealing with your credit card information. To guard against fraud, your information is securely encrypted and automatically passed directly to the financial network for processing. At no time is this information made available to anyone else."

Any organization that wants to build trust in online philanthropy needs to post a similar statement to remind online donors that it's taking this medium seriously.

Match Web Site Content to the Organization's Mission Your organization has built a reputation of service in your community. Based on your reputation and previous experience with you, visitors will be predisposed to trust what you convey on your Web site. The experience they then have online will either enhance or diminish that trust.

For instance, the Canadian National Institute for the Blind (CNIB) has built a reputation for providing excellent service to citizens with visual impairment. Its advocacy and program services are top-notch. Its Web site is equally helpful for individuals who are visually impaired. The organization has worked long and hard to build a Web site that can be accessed by such individuals. Following on that tradition of excellent service to clients, CNIB has decided to introduce an "online ombudsman." That ombudsman can be reached by any online visitor or donor who had problems or inquiries about online activities (including donations) to CNIB.

Provide for Easy Site Navigation It's essential that visitors or donors easily find what they're looking for. You can increase the odds they'll do so by using easy-to-understand terms, consistently placing navigational buttons, writing clear instructions to help donors make their gifts online, and providing them with easy ways to search the site's content.

Maintain Stewardship As we all know, there's nothing more important than providing good stewardship for the gifts donors make to our organizations. All donors demand this—online donors especially so. Ask yourself these questions:

- How clear is the procedure on your site for making an online contribution?
- How well do you respond to concerns or comments?
- Is there assurance that personal information will be kept secure and private?

These questions are central to good stewardship, both of the gift and the relationship. At a minimum, every nonprofit organization should post its privacy statement on its home page (and on any forms or giving areas) to ensure that donors understand and trust what you'll do with their contact information if they make online donations.

Appreciate the Needs and Expectations of Donors First When building a Web site, give a good deal of thought to the needs and expectations of the constituents closest to your organization. Taking into account the needs of your donors and key visitors will help you identify the elements you need to build into the site first and those you'll bring online over time.

For example, Greenpeace USA has created an online form that takes into account donors' needs and expectations to deal with a human voice when they can't get everything they need from its Web site (Exhibit 1.1). This form provides donors, visitors, or prospective donors with the opportunity to fill in an online form and specify times when they would like to receive telephone calls from the organization. This is a wonderful way to put the donor first.

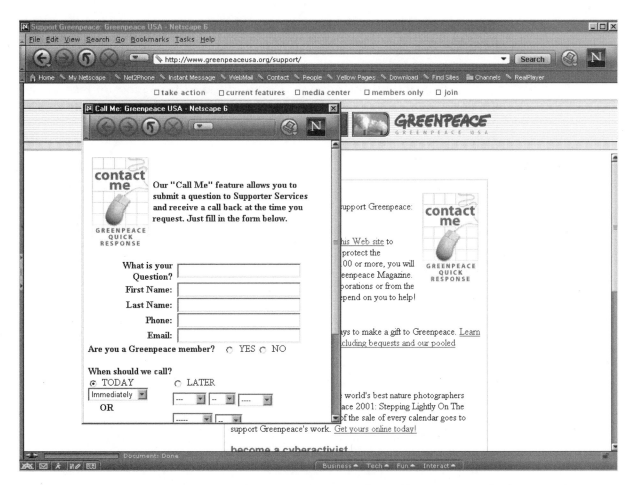

Exhibit 1.1. Putting Donors First Online by Meeting Their Expectations for Human Contact.

Provide Effective Technology It's not necessary to deploy the latest and greatest technology on your Web site (not that there's anything wrong it either). What's important is to understand that most people will judge your Web site by its speed and ease of use. Ask yourself

- Do your pages load quickly?
- Can donors easily find what they're looking for?
- Do they have the opportunity to communicate and provide feedback?
- Can they make secure gifts online?

Greenpeace again—but this time Greenpeace International in Amsterdam—wanted to provide online donors with a *free* technological tool that would help them find what they were looking for, offer another method of feedback, and make individuals feel more secure in giving online.

To do that, Greenpeace International attached a live chat button to its giving form. This button employs a piece of free chat software called ICQ. If prospective donors want to know exactly how to give online, they can click on the ICQ channel and use the software to chat live with the support services staff (Exhibit 1.2).

A live chat button works. This simple, and free, piece of technology helps Greenpeace build trust among online donors—and any other non-profit organization can do the same.

Paying attention to these six ways of building trust will give your organization a competitive advantage. If you also pay close attention to the ePhilanthropy Code of Ethical Online Philanthropic Practices (Resource A) and the Ten Rules of ePhilanthropy Every Nonprofit Should Know (Resource B), you enhance your efforts to build trust among your visitors and donors and begin building stronger relationships with them.

Relationship-Building at the Speed of the Internet

Think of who in your life you trust the most. Your spouse? Your friend? Your mom or dad? Chances are it's someone you communicate with on a regular basis. This is no less true with your online relationships. In development work, it's relationships that are the key to success, and building trust is the key to building relationships.

People visiting your site and potentially making gifts to your organ-

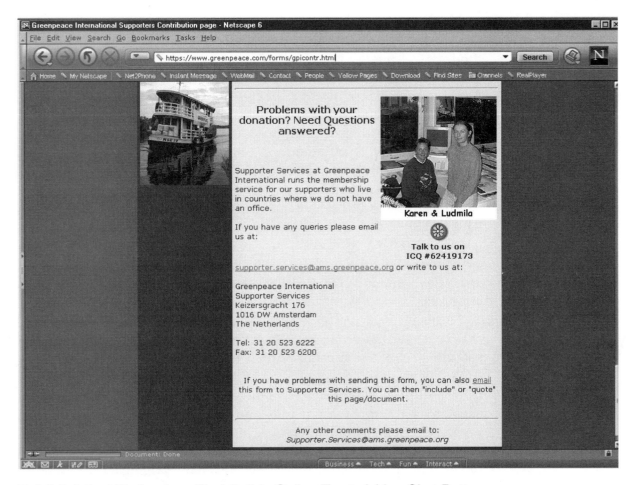

Exhibit 1.2. A Technology That Builds Online Trust: A Live Chat Button.

ization do so because they're interested in what you do. Because of that interest, they'll surf your site for all sorts of information, focusing on answers to questions that interest them. The Internet allows Web site visitors and donors to request more information at any time of the day. It's your responsibility to ensure that those requests for information are dealt with in a timely manner. If visitors don't feel good about you because it took a long time for you to respond to their inquiries, it will take more effort on your part to make them trust you.

As Bill Gates says, everything is moving "at the speed of the Internet"—and that's *fast*. Online donors have different expectations than do many off-line contributors.

The easily transferable allegiance the Internet enables means that you have to ensure that every online donor receives immediate service. Keep in mind that in most cases, online contributors will begin to distrust you if they don't receive direct responses to their inquiries within forty-eight hours. In most cases, automatic e-mail responses are most appropriate.

Understanding your donors and online visitors and providing excellent customer service builds the trust you need to be a successful e-fundraiser. Though it requires careful planning and intelligence in execution, it's not brain surgery. What is more important, however, fundraising online requires *commitment*—the very same level of commitment you invest in your off-line relationships.

Happy visitors become happy donors, and they can provide lots of word-of-mouth referrals and repeat visits that will benefit your organization over the long haul. Paying attention to building trust will pay off for your organization in many ways.

This is not the first time that nonprofit organizations and fundraisers have had to adapt to new technologies. The radio, television, newspapers, telephone, fax machine, and direct mail have all affected how we raise money. Some of the new methods that have evolved are more successful than others, and not all of them have been used with equal success by all nonprofits.

Each new communications technology has created a particular set of challenges for nonprofits and their donors; each has triggered a corresponding set of fundraising norms. The Internet is quickly reaching a stage where serious thought must be given to the mechanisms that will help build the level of donor confidence and trust that will equate to substantial growth of online philanthropy.

As nonprofit organizations use the methods and approaches outlined in this book, they will find donors approaching their Web sites with a mixture of wonder and apprehension. By placing an emphasis on relationships and the trust to drive those relationships, nonprofits will dramatically increase the chances of avoiding the missteps that could be devastating to the long-term success of ePhilanthropy.

The Ethics of Online Fundraising

In the 1990s, the emergence of e-commerce brought with it a myriad of questions and concerns over security and consumer privacy. The online industry muddled through. Security technologies were developed, and standards were set. Consumer confidence was slowly won over, for the most part, and e-commerce continues to increase.

The expansion of ePhilanthropy promises to raise the same questions, confusion, and ongoing debate about the "right" and "wrong" way to practice online fundraising.

As fundraising professionals, we can help pave the way to build consumer confidence in online fundraising. We can create trustworthy online fundraising tools and Web sites, and we can demonstrate that online fundraising activities will be held to high ethical standards. If we do not take these steps, if we allow online fundraising to develop without the benefits of universally applied ethical standards, we run the risk of permanently losing donor confidence and wasting the incredible potential of the Internet to expand philanthropy.

IF YOUR ORGANIZATION has integrated online donation collection into its Web site—or is planning to—you have the responsibility to understand and embrace the emerging standards and new tools that will contribute to consumer trust.

To help guide you through the complexities and confusion of this fast-changing new realm of fundraising, the ePhilanthropy Foundation has developed the ePhilanthropy Code of Ethical Online Philanthropic Practices. This code reflects the Foundation's mission to promote high ethical standards in online fundraising and to build trust among online contributors.

In this chapter, I'm reproducing the code in its entirety, along with practical examples for its use and interpretation. If you follow the general guidelines provided here, your efforts will be better received and more widely accepted by your donors, prospects, and all those who visit your Web site.

The ePhilanthropy Code of Ethical Online Philanthropic Practices

To promote ethical practices in online fundraising, the Foundation recommends that nonprofit organizations follow these guidelines:

Section A: Philanthropic Experience

1. Clearly and specifically display and describe the organization's identity on the organization's Web site.
2. Employ practices on the Web site which exhibit integrity, honesty, truthfulness, and seek to safeguard the public trust.

Seems a bit obvious, you say? Well, what may be obvious to you might completely escape your Web visitor's attention.

Here's a little exercise to see just how well you embrace these ideals. Pick three people you trust, but who have no vested interest in your organization or your Web site. Ask them to spend five minutes reviewing your site. (Even better, if you know the actual "average time spent per visitor" on your site, give them that much time.) After they've reviewed the site, ask them these questions:

- What is the primary mission of this organization?
- Does the Web site clearly describe the audience served by the organization?
- Does the Web site give you the impression that this is a well-established, trustworthy organization?
- Would you know how to contact this organization?
- Do you know who's in charge of this organization?

You can add questions of your own, but you get the idea. Though you may think that your identity, mission, and values are perfectly clear on your Web site, it may not be so obvious to the casual visitor. Make sure your Web site clearly displays the same values of honesty, integrity, and trustworthiness you bring to your off-line communications.

Section B: Privacy and Security

1. Seek to inspire trust in every online transaction.
2. Prominently display the opportunity to have donors' names removed from lists that are sold to, rented to, or exchanged with other organizations.

3. Conduct online transactions through a system that employs high-level security technology to protect the donor's personal information.

4. Provide either an "opt in" or "opt out" mechanism to prevent unsolicited communications or solicitations by organizations that obtain e-mail addresses directly from the donor, and require the "opt in" mechanism before the donor's e-mail address may be sold, transferred, or otherwise distributed to a third party for communication, advertising, or promotion purposes.

5. Protect the interests and privacy of individuals interacting with their Web site.

Section B guidelines 2 through 5 deal with the data related to privacy and security in online fundraising. You must protect the privacy of your visitors, be it their names, addresses, or even their usage patterns when they visit your Web site; and you must ensure that the online transaction tools used on the site protect information such as their credit card numbers. If you cover both, then you've also covered guideline 1 on this list: You will inspire trust in every online transaction on your site.

Whether you build it yourself—and it requires sophisticated programming skills—or you use a service provider, there are plenty of options available to nonprofits who want to offer a secure online fundraising environment but who do not have the budget to build their own tools.

In fact, there are so many options that choosing the right one for your organization can be daunting, but providing this type of secure environment will be essential to the success of your online fundraising efforts. So take some time reviewing your options, compare tools, and determine which one best meets your needs. For a complete listing of application service providers (ASPs) that offer online donation and other services to nonprofit organizations, visit The Nonprofit Matrix at [www.nonprofit-matrix.com]. Also, check the discussion boards at techsoup.org.

At The Nonprofit Matrix you'll find a comprehensive list of *giving portals* that connect donors to organizations they care about. Some of these portals, such as Helping.org and JustGive.org, provide information on all 501(c)(3) charities listed in the IRS database. (See Chapter Twenty-Four for a detailed discussion of giving portals.)

The Nonprofit Matrix also lists for-profit companies offering philanthropy services. These vendors will charge you a fee—sometimes a percentage of the transaction, sometimes a monthly minimum fee—but they generally provide more services than the nonprofit portals. In choosing an e-transaction vendor, make sure that you understand the cost structure and that you disclose that relationship to your donors. (See Section C.)

Some fundraisers are concerned that "opt in" or "opt out" messages can frighten away prospective donors or deter them from providing their e-mail address through a registration or similar process. On the contrary, if you don't specify to a Web user how their information will be used, you will probably invite suspicion as to your motives.

Web users are generally savvy enough to know that nothing in this world is free. If you're asking for their information, you're going to use it in some way. By providing them specifics, and giving them the opportunity to tell you how to and how not to use their name, you will gain their trust.

Exhibit 2.1 shows a screen from within one site's registration process. Note the clearly worded options giving the registrant the opportunity to indicate how their name should be used.

Section C: Disclosures

1. Disclose the identity of the organization or provider processing an online transaction.

If your organization uses a third-party provider to process donations generated from your Web site, you should disclose this information to your donors. Donors have a right to know who has access to their infor-

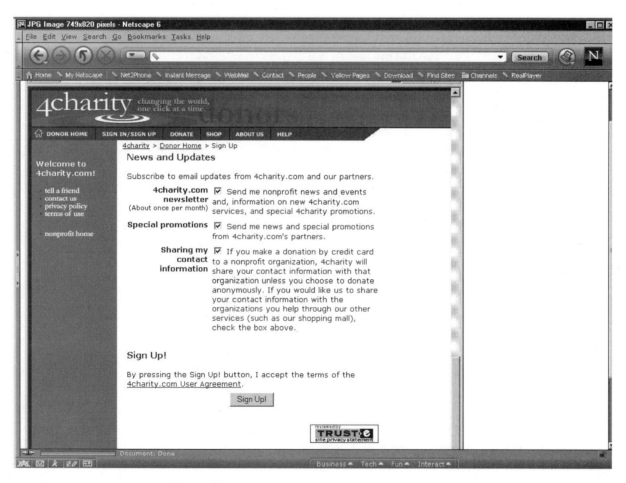

Exhibit 2.1. Effective Use of "Opt in, Opt out" Messages.

mation, where it's going, and how it will be used. By providing this information directly on your site, you will build trust in your donors.

The Association for India's Development provides a good example of a Web site that uses a third-party provider, Helping.org, to process its online donations. They use the opportunity to gain trust by disclosing some information about Helping.org and how it works (Exhibit 2.2).

> 2. Guarantee that the name, logo, and likeness of all parties to an online transaction belong to the party and will not be used without express permission.

This guideline requires nonprofit organizations to ensure that any transaction processing service provider will not make unauthorized use of its logos, organization name, and associated images. In the worst case, it speaks to the problem of the fraudulent use of logos or names of charities to raise money, with no intention to pass the money on to that charity. A more innocent example might be if an organization legiti-

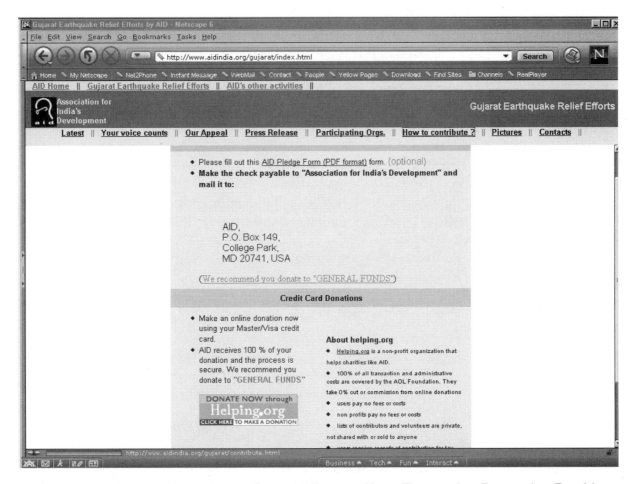

Exhibit 2.2. Disclose Information to Potential Donors About Transaction Processing Providers.

mately raising funds for animal protection displayed the logos of People for the Ethical Treatment of Animals (PETA) and the American Society for the Prevention of Cruelty to Animals (ASPCA) on its site without having any relationship with those organizations. As they do in the off-line world, nonprofits have the right to protect the use of their logo and likeness on the Web.

3. Maintain all appropriate governmental and regulatory designations or certifications.

The same government designations and certifications that exist in the off-line world also apply to nonprofits that practice online fundraising. In fact, since the Web will probably increase your visibility and reach, your best bet is to have your regulatory ducks in a row.

Nonprofits who qualify under IRS guidelines are required to file a Form 990. If you have any questions about the tax returns or reports required by tax-exempt organizations, visit the IRS's *Exempt Organizations Technical Guidelines Handbook,* in particular Chapter 48 regarding reports and returns, at [www.irs.gov/prod/bus_info/tax_pro/irm-part/part07/36082.html].

Philanthropic Research, Inc. (PRI) publishes these 990 forms for every organization filing them on their GuideStar Web site [www.guidestar.org]. Nonprofits are encouraged to visit their page in the GuideStar database and update their information if necessary. The Guidestar site also offers the ability for nonprofits to enhance their GuideStar listing with information about mission, programs, accomplishments, and so forth. PRI supplies their database to both Helping.org and JustGive.org, so it's worth the time to make sure your listing accurately reflects your organization's good works.

For Canadian organizations, the government has published Form T3010, the Registered Charity Information Return for 2001 on the Internet. You can find it at [www.ccra-adrc.gc.ca/E/pbg/tf/t301001eq/README.html]. Organizations that need to register can get the forms to do so at the Web site [www.ccra-adrc.gc.ca].

Section D: Complaints

1. Provide protection to hold the donor harmless of any problem arising from a transaction conducted through the organization's Web site.
2. Promptly respond to all customer complaints and employ best efforts to fairly resolve all legitimate complaints in a timely fashion.

This section addresses simple, commonsense customer service. The problem is that too often organizations neglect customer service needs generated online and don't consider their online visitors "real" customers.

Visitors making donations on your Web site are in no way at fault if your site is hacked into because it doesn't incorporate good security measures. You must be ready to provide restitution if something goes wrong with their donations. (Credit card companies cover anything over $50.) Before you hang out your online fundraising shingle, you should have a plan of action in place for dealing with such emergencies. You should also be prepared to respond to customer inquiries and complaints on a timely basis. Donors who use your Web site have a right to expect the same level of service they receive when they contact you by phone or the U.S. mail. Incorporate the Web into your existing customer service practices.

Section E: Transactions

1. Ensure contributions are used to support the activities of the organization to which it was donated.

Philanthropy portals—sites that collect donations for many organizations—must direct contributions directly to the organization designated by the donor, if such a designation is supplied. Nonprofit organizations should not solicit funds for a specific program or organization, then use them for something else. Donors need to trust that their money is going where they intended it to go.

2. Ensure that legal control of contributions or proceeds from online transactions are transferred directly to the charity or expedited in the fastest possible way.

It shouldn't take more than a few weeks for a third-party provider to deliver a donation to the intended nonprofit. And nonprofits have a right to know when the donation was made so that they can respond to the donor appropriately. Portals and third-party providers that adhere to this principle provide protection to both the donor and the nonprofit.

Nonprofits might also want to determine whether the processing provider they are using is making money on "the float" or the interest collected while the third-party holds the donation. If you object to this business practice, find a new provider.

3. Companies providing online services to charities will provide clear and full communication with the charity on all aspects of donor transactions, including the accurate and timely transmission of data related to online transactions.

As noted above, nonprofits have a right to comprehensive information regarding the donations designated for them through a third-party provider. This includes name, address, amount of donation, and any specific directions provided by the donor. This should be provided on a timely basis. If you aren't receiving this kind of service from an ASP, consider changing services. Otherwise, your relationships with your donors will suffer.

> 4. Stay informed regarding the best methods to ensure the ethical, secure, and private nature of online ePhilanthropy transactions.

One of the great things about the technology revolution is that it drives the continued creation of better, more efficient, more secure, easier-to-use technology. A nonprofit or ASP has the responsibility to stay informed and incorporate these new technologies where appropriate and feasible.

Several acceptable security software tools are available. When you choose a vendor to build your donation tool or review ASP tools to use, ask the company about the security measures they have in place to ensure private, protected transactions through their system.

Increasingly, consumers will look for "seals of approval" to show that your site adheres to high privacy standards. If you manage your own donation processing system, look into securing a seal from VeriSign, TRUSTe, BBB Online, or another provider.

> 5. Adhere to the spirit as well as the letter of all applicable laws and regulations, including but not limited to charity solicitation and tax laws.

The laws surrounding online fundraising and the tax implications resulting from it are still being developed and debated. As a nonprofit, you must of course maintain your registrations in the states where you operate. Your requirements as an online fundraiser are a bit less clear, but there are steps you can take to give your best-faith efforts in adhering to appropriate laws and regulations, as they are applied to the Internet.

The National Association of State Charity Officials (NASCO) created the Charleston Principles to provide guidance to state charity officials regarding charitable solicitations on the Internet. The principles were a result of a dialogue with nonprofit officials that started at the 1999 NASCO meeting in Charleston, North Carolina. Visit the NASCO Web site [www.nasconet.org] for a complete list of the principles. You will also be able to comment on the principles via the Web site.

> 6. Ensure that all services, recognition, and other transactions promised on a Web site, in consideration of gift or transaction, will be fulfilled in a timely basis.

When I talked about customer service, I stressed the importance of treating your online customers with the same respect and responsiveness you provide your off-line audience. The same holds true for the delivery of services—in this case, the processing of donations or the fulfillment of a request. Internet users have high expectations for the delivery of online services. E-mail is instantaneous in most cases; most online stores process your order within twenty-four hours.

As a nonprofit using the Web to reach new and existing donors, you must live up to the standards that users have come to expect. Your organization doesn't necessarily have to process donations every twenty-four hours but it won't do to check your online e-mail box every two months, either. Think about the standards you apply to your off-line contributions, then use the same, or higher, standards on the Web.

7. Disclose to the donor the nature of the relationship between the organization processing the gift or transaction and the charity intended to benefit from the gift.

Security and privacy continue to be issues that online users care deeply about. Most of the time, it's what the donor or online consumer doesn't know that scares her most. Who has access to my credit card information? For what purpose are you using my personal information?

One way to allay these fears and answer donors' questions about online fundraising is to provide easily accessible, comprehensive information about the donation process. Nonprofits who let donors know when they employ the services or products of a third party to process and manage online donations will instill trust in their donors. In all likelihood, donors will be more inclined to give through sites that disclose the nature of their giving processes and their vendor relationships, because they will have fewer questions or concerns about where their information and their money are going.

Ethical Practices Are Good Business

Most nonprofit organizations go to great lengths to instill confidence and trust in their donors and prospects. To abandon or overlook that important principle when integrating ePhilanthropy into an organization's operating structure would be a grave mistake. Instead of expanding its reach and raising new funds, an organization could irreparably damage its reputation. The ePhilanthropy Code of Ethical Online Philanthropic Practices (Resource A) provides some easy guidelines that nonprofit organizations and the vendors that support them can follow to ensure that online fundraising systems and communications maintain the faith and trust a donor has placed in an organization. If you're just starting out in ePhilanthropy, you may find these concepts a bit overwhelming, but rest assured they will all make sense as you explore your ePhilanthropy options, develop a technology integration plan, and begin to market your online offering. The organization that takes the time to incorporate these ideals into its online offerings will have gone a long way toward getting the most out of what the Internet has to offer.

The Emerging Gold Standard of Integrated Fundraising

Although some have predicted that fundraising on the Internet will eventually replace more traditional approaches to soliciting support, that's not likely to happen within our lifetimes, if ever. Today, fund raising on the Internet is rarely effective as a stand-alone operation. It works best when combined with other, proven fundraising techniques—particularly direct mail—through a multichannel strategy known as integrated fundraising. *However, to make this new approach yield its full potential, you'll need to follow eight rules: (1) Always consider the donor's point of view. (2) Focus on the big picture. (3) Keep your message clear and consistent. (4) Segment your audience for maximum impact. (5) Pay greater attention to cost-effectiveness rather than to cost. (6) Build on the success of direct mail. (7) Use the tools of marketing and public relations. (8) Set your schedule in advance—and stick to it.*

IT WAS MAY 2000, the high-water mark for the gun-control movement in America. Nearly one million people, most of them women, had marched on Mother's Day to demonstrate their commitment to ending the gun violence that had taken the lives of so many children.

The Million Mom March, the organization that hastily came together out of the euphoria and passion of the Mother's Day 2000 events, possessed several key assets other than this widely shared passion as it set out to build activist grassroots chapters across the country: talented and energetic staff leadership, a high-traffic Web site—and a list of approximately seventy thousand names and addresses that had been gathered either through the Web site or at Mother's Day marches, chiefly at the main event in Washington, D.C. About 40 percent of those people, or nearly thirty thousand, had also supplied e-mail addresses.

For Million Mom March staff, then, the challenge was clear: to convert as many as possible of those seventy thousand marchers, T-shirt buyers, and (in a few cases) donors into dues-paying members of the new Million Mom March organization. Normally, even the strongest direct mail letter sent to such a list would be unlikely to persuade more than a very small proportion—say, 3 or 4 percent at most—to enlist as members. Subsequent letters might enroll another 2 or 3 percent. However, taken together, the two or three direct mail efforts would very likely generate more expenses than revenue. That wasn't good enough for the Million Mom March. The organization needed to build its membership faster—and generate more dues money.

The answer to this challenge was an integrated, multichannel fundraising effort involving e-mail, the Web site, telemarketing, and direct mail. The Million Mom March used each of these channels to deliver much the same message. Everyone on the list received a letter; thirty thousand of them received e-mail messages before the letter was mailed; and about forty thousand later received telephone calls. The majority of these "warm, qualified prospects" (to use direct mail jargon) thus received at least two contacts. The results? Some 10 percent of them became dues-paying members, and the effort generated $300,000 for the Million Mom March at a cost of less than half that amount.

That's what an integrated fundraising program can accomplish!

Why Do We Need Integrated Fundraising?

Think back. The first time you read or heard about "fundraising on the Internet," did you react in one of the two following ways?

- Oh, sure! When pigs fly—*that's* when we'll be raising money online!
- Wow—what a concept! Pretty soon we'll be able to forget all about direct mail!

OK, the world's not that simple. Chances are, your initial response fell somewhere in the middle of this spectrum.

In fact, what we've learned in recent years is that fundraising on the Internet is rarely effective as a stand-alone operation. It works best when combined with other, proven fundraising techniques—particularly direct mail.

What Integrated Fundraising Means

Today, integrated fundraising is a goal for most nonprofit organizations, not a reality. In fact, the concept of integrated fundraising is generally better known in the abstract for the benefits it's thought to bring as well as its drawbacks. In theory, integrated fundraising reduces inconsistencies in communicating an organization's message, strengthens donor relationships, and yields increased revenue, especially over the long haul. The price that's paid for these considerable benefits includes heavy capital requirements, greater demands on management, and sophisticated skills to operate the more complex systems entailed in the process.

In the future, when integrated fundraising is a reality for most nonprofit organizations, fundraising will no longer take place in separate campaigns with separate measures of success. The Internet will loom large in this picture, providing multiple new giving opportunities. A prospect who picks up a membership brochure may later join online. A donor who receives an annual renewal letter may elect to make his gift online. A donor interested in a capital campaign may log on to view construction photos on the organization's Web site. Someone who previews auction items in a charity's newsletter may decide to enter a bid online. An individual who receives a planned giving brochure in the mail may go online to use a gift planning calculator on the organization's Web site. In this fashion, integrated fundraising, by seamlessly incorporating online communication and transaction tools, will offer new opportunities and increase the convenience of giving.

Meanwhile, however, to describe what integrated fundraising is, it's best to examine the idea from the ground up, by cataloging the eight assumptions that must be built into any effort to implement it.

Always Consider the Donor's Point of View It's a cliché that fundraising is about building relationships with donors, but precious few direct response fundraising programs put this wisdom into practice in more than a perfunctory way. An integrated approach to fundraising offers hope that donors' unique interests and behaviors will form the basis of the relationships that develop between them and the causes they support.

In practice, this means that the donors' point of view must prevail. If they want to contribute only once per year; if they don't want to receive your newsletter; if they're interested only in cats, not dogs; if they don't want to get your e-mail (or visit your Web site)—then those must be the rules of the relationship. Within the limits of feasibility, all donors must have the opportunity to define their own do's and don'ts.

Focus on the Big Picture Integrated fundraising puts special demands on nonprofit executives. Every donor counts; every relationship is precious. But a successful fundraising program rests on thousands, or hundreds of thousands, of donors; a broad array of fundraising techniques via diverse communications channels; management by a large number of staff persons, usually divided among several offices or departments; and year-round activity maintained over decades.

Integrated fundraising involves all the elements of a resource development program: direct mail, telemarketing, online communications, direct solicitations, capital campaigns, major donor fundraising, planned giving—from the bottom of the donor pyramid to the top. To succeed in integrated fundraising requires that the organization's leadership keep all this in perspective by orchestrating all these elements in an artful fashion so that the whole becomes greater than the sum of its parts.

Keep Your Message Clear and Consistent In recent years, fundraisers have begun to absorb the lessons that successful marketers in the private sector have learned about *branding*. This widely misunderstood buzzword is actually a variant on the fundraising concept of relationship building. To establish a brand is to create a total experience—for the customer and donor alike—that's consistent and comforting. For a nonprofit fundraiser, the goal of this effort is to entice, retain, and upgrade donors.

Effective branding programs are designed to break through the media clutter and fix simple ideas firmly in the minds of the audiences for whom they're intended. These programs possess the following characteristics:

- They're based on shrewd and accurate positioning for the brand— that is, they stake out at least one unique benefit.
- They are reduced to the simplest ideas boiled down to their emotional core.
- They place greater emphasis on benefits to the donor or customer rather than on the features of the product or service.
- They employ distinctive themes and images that remain unchanged over a long period.
- They make effective use of every available communication channel to repeat the same themes and images.

Segment Your Audience for Maximum Impact The ultimate goal of integrated fundraising is to build one-to-one relationships with donors. Sadly, one-to-one fundraising is a long way off.

Although Internet technology could enable one-to-one fundraising, few nonprofits have put their donor data online—or can make use of it for tailored offers. The big catalogers, such as Land's End, are integrating their customer databases; they know what you've ordered, when, and for whom, whether you ordered by calling an 800 number, mailing an order form, or visiting their Web site. If you log in at their site (or they use cookies to identify return visitors), they can access all this information in real time to present offers to you. However, only a handful of nonprofits have made the investment to put their off-line data online. And, in any case, it's the unusual organization that stores data deep enough to offer donors much more than gift-level options as part of the online experience.

For us mere mortals working for the majority of nonprofits, the best that we can hope for these days—with only rare exceptions—is intelligent donor file segmentation.

Effective segmentation requires using varying *marketing concepts*. For instance, it's not often effective to solicit high-dollar donors with the same message sent to the rest of the file (albeit in a fancier package or by exercising more patience on the phone). A donor who contributes $250, $500, or more at a time typically has a different sort of relationship with the cause he's supporting than does one whose highest gift never tops $30. Similarly, a long-lapsed donor is likely to feel very differently about a charity than an active one. The messages in direct mail packages, telephone scripts, or e-mail communications all need to reflect those differences.

In fact, the economies of communicating online make that far easier to do in e-mail or on a Web site. It's considerably cheaper to refer to the date of a donor's first gift or the cumulative amount of her contributions in an e-mail appeal than in a letter.

When nonprofits begin to integrate online activity into their donor databases, they will eventually be able to refer to online advocacy activity, what pages of a site were viewed, and even what reports were downloaded. *Then* the promise of one-to-one fundraising will be much closer to reality.

Pay Greater Attention to Cost-Effectiveness Than to Cost Fundraisers must take into account at least four factors in addition to efficiency (the sheer cost of raising a dollar): growth, donor involvement, visibility, and stability. (See Mal Warwick's *The Five Strategies for Fundraising Success,* Jossey-Bass, 2000.) To some degree, these five strategic goals are mutually exclusive; emphasizing any one of the four latter goals is likely to reduce efficiency—that is, raise the cost of fundraising. This lowered efficiency (or, in other words, higher investment) may be desirable in the long-term strategic interest of the organization.

Understanding these trade-offs is critical. For example, it's likely that a big current investment in online fundraising will not yield huge dividends in the short run. Strictly from the perspective of (short-term) fundraising efficiency, it's probably more advantageous to spend the same money on major donors, direct mail, or telefundraising. However, it seems equally likely that to do so would be disadvantageous to the organization in the long run, as returns from online fundraising efforts continue to climb.

Build on the Success of Direct Mail Like it or not—despite fast-evolving technology, demographic shifts, and changing popular attitudes—most donors still prefer, most of the time, to communicate with the causes and institutions they support by mail.

Currently, it's imprudent to expect substantial returns online. It's unusual for a nonprofit to be able to secure telephone numbers for even 75 percent of its donors. E-mail addresses are typically even more difficult for fundraisers to obtain; because people must give permission to an organization to use their e-mail addresses, virtually the only way to collect them is to ask donors directly. Today, only the rare organization has collected current e-mail addresses for even one-third of its donors. Nor is it merely a matter of securing phone numbers or e-mail addresses: Given the chance, significant numbers of donors decline to be solicited by either medium.

However, direct mail can be used to help drive traffic to a Web site where donors can learn more, see more, and become more involved with the mission of the organization. This combination of online and offline communication will provide for a deeper experience—and a stronger relationship—than can be built with periodic direct mail efforts alone.

As time goes on, donors may more readily volunteer their e-mail addresses. In any case, it's essential that fundraisers place a high priority on obtaining them. Eventually, the organizations that doggedly pursue such an effort will be rewarded with the key to harnessing a renewable resource in Internet fundraising.

Meanwhile, there is an important reason to communicate with donors and prospects through all available channels. As the world of commercial advertising and marketing has proven beyond a doubt, there is a multiplier effect in multichannel communications that frequently causes the response to a coordinated campaign to exceed the sum total of responses to uncoordinated efforts through each individual channel. This phenomenon of mutual reinforcement is one of the strongest arguments for integrated fundraising programs.

Use the Tools of Marketing and Public Relations Whether or not your organization has a marketing or public relations department, someone within your organization is responsible for the creation of newsletters, annual reports, and other forms of written communication with the public.

Your organization's Web site address or Uniform Source Locator (URL) should be included anyplace the address or phone of the organization is printed. Integrating the URL into all forms of communication, fundraising or otherwise, will help drive traffic to your site. Getting supporters in the habit of using your Web site as an important source of information is essential to the long-term success of an integrated fundraising effort.

Set Your Schedule in Advance—and Stick to It Success in fundraising results from persistence and timeliness as much as it does from wisdom or creativity. After all, the fundamental law of fundraising is *if you don't ask, you won't get the gift*. However, timing becomes triply important in an integrated fundraising program. In a large-scale effort that involves multiple departments and possibly multiple vendors as well, the demands on management can be huge. Slippage of a week or two in a fundraising appeal in January or February could well result in reducing the total number of fundraising opportunities—and thus the revenue—during the balance of the year.

Lessons for Today

There are five steps you can take today to speed up your organization's movement toward a future when integrated fundraising may be widespread and online gifts represent a goodly share of your revenue:

1. Offer donors the opportunity to make secured credit card contributions via your Web site.

2. Include your URL in all your communications, including your fundraising appeals.

3. Create a regular and frequent electronic newsletter or bulletin and send it to all your donors for whom you have e-mail addresses.

4. Use every available medium and every opportunity to coax an e-mail address from every prospect and every donor.

5. Whenever you plan a fundraising campaign, think carefully about how you might use e-mail and the Internet to strengthen your appeal.

Taking these five baby steps will cost you very little. Over the long haul, the return on that modest investment could well be considerable. Integrated fundraising—making the greatest possible use of online communication tools—is still a buzzword and a dream today. Tomorrow it may be our shared reality.

Promoting Your Organization Online

The first step toward building your organization's revenues, volunteer base, or programmatic initiatives through the Internet must be to identify who you want to reach, what you want them to do, and what will compel them to take those actions. You will achieve greater success if you develop an audience-driven strategy that will guide you in the selection of the online and traditional marketing tactics most appropriate for promoting your organization. You can achieve this by following the REACH approach, which covers five critical areas for online success: Refine your audience approach, Extend your message through outreach, Activate audience response, Cultivate after action, and Hone your approach based on results.

SO, YOU WANT TO PROMOTE your organization online? Fantastic. I have only one question: Why?

If you're thinking the Internet will open the spigot of cash flow for your organization, think again. Although the American Red Cross and Heifer Project International recently reported they each raised more than $2 million online in calendar year 2000, most organizations are seeing only a trickle of revenue—if any at all—from their online efforts.

Beyond fundraising, the online channel provides a new means to convert interest from more traditional channels into direct engagement across a variety of fronts. Forrester Research defined e-mail as one of the lower-cost and higher-impact marketing approaches in a study conducted in 1999 (see Figure 4.1). The online route provides an additional means through which interest generated by brand-building activities (for example, television and print advertising or public relations activities) can be channeled. As the new models emerge, organizations are discovering that strategically driven promotion of their online presence yields significant results.

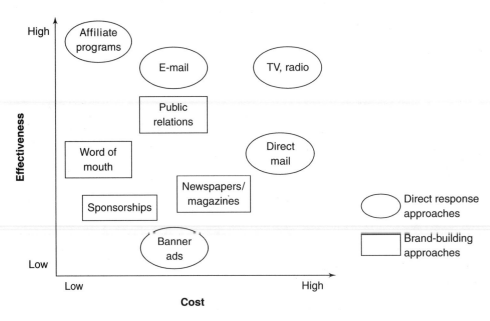

Figure 4.1. Effectiveness of Marketing Approaches.

Source: Forrester Research, Inc., April 1999.

Sound familiar? It should be. These audience imperatives are at the heart of all marketing. The Internet introduces new tools, techniques, and rules to this age-old dynamic. *Online* means *far more* than just your Web site presence. Internet technologies now permit an organization to communicate and engage not only through a Web site, but also directly through e-mail via rich media formats where the e-mail contains both the multimedia content and the fill-in form for taking action. It is now possible for organizations to engage in successful online promotions without the recipient of that promotion ever having to visit a Web site.

Getting Started: Your REACH Plan

You will achieve greater success in using the online channel for promotion if you develop an audience-driven strategy to guide you in the selection of the marketing tactics most appropriate for promoting your organization. Getting started begins with a well thought out REACH approach. The REACH approach covers the following five critical areas for online success: Refine, Extend, Activate, Cultivate, and Hone.

The REACH approach will assist you in targeting who you want to attract and identify the best means to reach them, spur them to action, sustain those relationships through cultivation, and evaluate your results.

Refine Your Audience Approach

In any marketing effort, the most important step is identifying your target audience and understanding what will motivate them to engage with your organization. To refine your audience approach, begin by addressing the strategic questions about your audience concerning their interests, motivations, and current proclivities. Table 4.1 outlines some of these questions.

Fact-based answers to questions such as these will assist you in refining the audiences who are most likely to be engaged online. The current perceptions, interests, and behaviors of these groups—especially their Internet activities—will provide insights into options for messaging and potential online avenues for reaching these audiences.

Table 4.1. Questions to Help Refine Your Audience Approach.

Audience definition	Who are my primary audiences for online engagement? What are the demographics and psychographics of these groups? How are they the same or different from my traditional (or off-line) audiences? How do they think and feel about my organization? How do I want them to think or feel?
Desired outcomes	What is the single most important action I want them to take? What other actions do I want them to take?
Current behavior	What are the current online behaviors of my primary audience?
	• How Web-savvy are they?
	• What sites do they visit?
	• What discussion groups or other forms of community do they belong to?
	• What are their current patterns for online giving, volunteering, advocacy, etc.?
	• How do they currently engage with my organization online?
	• What do they say about how they would like to engage with my organization online?
Organizational strong suits	What do these target audiences value most from my organization? What programs, projects, and messages spark the greatest interest?

Extend Your Message Through Outreach

The next area for exploration for your REACH plan is extending your message through the myriad outreach vehicles available to your organization. You should consider the breadth of possibilities but narrow your outreach efforts to a select few and execute them as well as possible. Your plan should focus on online *and* traditional activities that can drive traffic for your organization online.

Industry research for both commercial and nonprofit organizations indicates that traditional forms of marketing—television, radio, and direct marketing promotions—drive the majority of online activity.

Activate Audience Response

Your organization will be most successful when you use the Internet in ways that draw your audience into the organization through a combination of content and interactivity. This is the greatest strength of Internet technologies. The advent of rich media e-mail and multimedia Web site capabilities permits your organization to tell its story through audio, video, and text while providing a *direct action channel*. Leveraging this powerful capability requires that your story be compelling and the call to action interesting for the audience.

The direct actions you put in front of the audience can be multidimensional. You can make the fundraising "ask" while you reinforce the importance of donors' involvement by asking them to subscribe or to submit questions about the program through e-mail or a bulletin board.

This is where the intelligence you have gathered about your audience's online habits and interests in your organization comes into play. Your creative approach should focus on what the audience finds most exciting and positive about your organization. Your calls to action should be targeted to activities that are most likely to engage your audience based on their current behaviors.

Cultivate After Action

From the very beginning, you should have a plan in place for ongoing communications with individuals who have taken action through your promotion and have given you permission to recontact them. Your REACH plan for cultivation should include details on data capture, a calendar for ongoing communications, and a plan for follow-up calls to action. Table 4.2 provides a framework for your plan.

Like any good relationship, an online relationship must be cultivated. By establishing a cultivation plan early on as part of your overall REACH plan, you will ensure that your organization turns that first contact into a long-term relationship.

Hone Your Approach Based on Results

The final area of the REACH plan is crafting a strategy for the collection and use of the data you will need to hone your future approaches. The Internet is a new medium and highly experimental. Unlike direct mail, telemarketing, or other established channels for fundraising and communications, the online medium does not have mature and broadly accepted standards for data collection and metrics for measuring success.

This doesn't mean we should toss our analytical mores out the window as we flirt with the new technology. On the contrary, the highly seductive nature of the Internet's newest "bells and whistles" should require more analytical scrutiny rather than less.

The evaluation criteria and the data that support the analysis should be determined based on the objectives for your online efforts. Fundraising can be an integral part of the your online goals, but it may not be the only purpose. Education, advocacy, press outreach, and communications are just a few of the others that should be measured. Table 4.3 provides some effective metrics for evaluation. Preparing in advance to collect the data you will need to evaluate your program based on the metrics you have established will ensure that you make the most of the lessons to be learned.

Table 4.2. Cultivation Planning.

Data Capture	Communication Calendar	Call to Action Plan
Basic Data:	*Plan for:*	*Prepare for:*
Full name	Frequency	Upcoming online and off-line events
E-mail address	Timing with other communications	
Mail address		Seasonal or cyclical asks (e.g. holidays)
Contact permission	Message themes	
Action history	Creative testing for message length and number of stories	Opportunistic responses (e.g., action plan for emergency response messages)
Advanced Data:	Timing for calls to action	
Areas of interests		Immediate acknowledgment of action taken
Preference on channels and frequency for contact	*Baseline Plan:*	
	Semi-monthly contact	
Demographic profile		

Table 4.3. Measuring Success.

Fundraising	Advocacy	Media Reach	Subscribers	Cost Savings
Forms accessed	E-mails	Press sessions	E-mail list names	Downloads versus print materials
Forms submitted	Faxes	Downloads	Click-throughs	
Conversion rates	Post cards	Contact names	Pass along subs	FAQ versus phone
Average gift	Send articles	Story pick-ups	User sessions	Address changes
Costs and fees	Calls	Click-throughs	Conversions	E-mailing versus mail
ROI and COF	Petitions			
Value per user	Download action			Gift processing
Value per donor	Alert subscribers			Web action versus canvass or mail

Abbreviations: COF, cost of fundraising; FAQ, frequently asked questions; ROI, return on investment.

Promoting Your Organization Online: Tactical Options

This chapter would be incomplete without an overview of the tactical approaches you might consider for marketing your organization online. But providing a comprehensive overview of the tactics currently being used is impossible. Online marketing tactics are being created and evolving at a dizzying pace as new technologies and tools are unveiled on a seemingly daily basis.

Integrated Marketing Approaches

Traditional off-line activities are major sources from which users find out about Web sites. Even though most nonprofit organizations do not have the marketing and advertising budgets of major commercial players, you can use a number of traditional channels effectively to promote your organization online.

Public Relations and Media Events Press conferences, television and radio appearances, and public speaking engagements are prime opportunities to promote your Web site URL and spotlight your online programs. Coupling the public appearances with physical materials you leave behind provides the audience with a concrete reminder for how to find you online when they get home or back to their office.

Your Organization's Literature Business cards, stationery, fax forms, newsletters, annual reports, and other publications should include your Web site URL. If your organization has a regular publication, such as a newsletter, consider adding a regular article about your online offerings.

Integrated Promotional Opportunities Many organizations are fortunate enough to secure public service announcement (PSA) space on television or radio programs. Others have budgets for paid placement through these channels. The Internet provides a means to turn these brand-building activities into online engagement by directing viewers or listeners to visit your Web site or sending you an e-mail and by telling them what specific action they can expect or engage in when they do.

Integration with Direct Mail and Telemarketing Though still highly experimental, some organizations have been testing the use of direct mail and telemarketing to promote online giving or activism. The results have been mixed. Some organizations see as much as 50 percent of their online donations coming from individuals who report that a direct mail promotion drove them online. Others have not seen any significant traffic.

Online Outreach Approaches

Selecting the most appropriate online outreach approaches requires a solid understanding of the online habits of your target audience. Most organizations do not have the budgets for paid placements of banner advertising, e-mail lists, or keyword buys from search engines. But for those that do, knowing the audience will be essential for targeting these paid efforts. Knowing the habits of your audience becomes even more important to target your outreach efforts to press outlets, affinity Web sites, and discussion communities.

Search Engines Registering your organization with search engines—and regularly optimizing your registrations—is the most important way to promote your organization online. It is so important that an entire chapter of this book is dedicated to it.

E-Mail Communications E-mail outreach continues to be a powerful tool in the online promotional arsenal. As part of your reach plan, develop a communications calendar for which ongoing e-mail communications will be a central component. Entice the visitors to your site to sign up in the most trafficked areas, and regularly communicate with these subscribers. Other means of building your e-mail list include

- Collect e-mail addresses as part of all online data collection efforts (for example, as part of a donation or volunteer form) and provide an opt-in offer for your newsletter.

- Make sure everyone in your organization includes your URL in their e-mail signature lines. If you're running an online promotion or have a new or unique offering on your Web site, be sure to include a call-to-action in the signature line. A call-to-action can take many forms, such as "click to donate now" or "click to e-mail your Congressman."

- Don't overlook the hidden in-house list. Every staff member of your organization has friends, family, and colleagues in their e-mail address book. Use viral marketing (see section following this list) to leverage these contacts.

- Use your acknowledgment, direct mail, and telemarketing programs and your one-on-one contacts with supporters to collect e-mail addresses. Be sure to obtain permission before adding these names to your opt-in subscriber list.

Viral Marketing Viral marketing, also known as pass-along marketing, is a method of asking the recipient of an e-mail to send the message along to other people they know who might be interested. Some tactical approaches include

- E-mail based petition campaigns
- Rich media promotions (in which multimedia content is included in the e-mail message)
- Cyber-stickers that are banner ads used as a footer in an individual's e-mail message
- E-mail-to-a-friend feature that permits the user to send the content of a Web site or e-mail message along to a friend

For more information on viral marketing, see Chapter Twenty-Two.

Interactive Public Relations Half of all journalists report that they now use the Internet for story pitches and ideas, according to the Sixth Annual Middleberg-Ross Media in Cyberspace Study, March 2000. You can reach the press through online media kits, targeted e-mails to beat reporters covering your issues, and press-release distribution services.

Affinity Community Networking Use your knowledge of where your audience "lives" on the Web to identify Web sites, discussion forums, newsgroups, and other community hang-outs that will mention your organization's online program. Keep in mind that other sites and discussion forums are often hungry for new content and willing to share your news with their visitors and subscribers.

Partnerships More and more, companies are interested in partnering with nonprofits online to promote philanthropic initiatives, which opens new doors of opportunity for your organization online. Some of the most effective online promotions have been the result of partnerships between nonprofits and commercial entities. During the height of the Kosovo crisis in 1999, organizations such as CARE, UNICEF, and the American Red Cross partnered with search engines and news portals to highlight their relief efforts. Another form of partnership is content sharing and dissemination in which one organization's content is used in a partner organization's newsletter or Web site. Your message can reach a much broader audience this way, but be certain to negotiate for good branding and prominent display of your URL. Other forms include cause-marketing campaigns, public service announcement (PSA) banner advertising, or e-mail newsletter ad space.

Planning for Success

Successfully promoting your organization online requires you to be thoughtful and disciplined in your approach to marketing through this channel. The first step toward building your organization's revenues, volunteer base, or other programmatic initiatives through the Internet must be to identify who you want to reach, what you want them to do once you have their attention, and what will compel them to take those actions. Developing a REACH plan ensures these priorities will be addressed.

MICHAEL JOHNSTON

Evaluating Online Fundraising Success

The Internet is no different from any other fundraising channel: There are costs, response percentages, average gifts, and other measurable slices of reality. Evaluating the return on any investment in online fundraising is straightforward, as it is in direct mail, telemarketing, or any other field. The evaluation process entails four steps: (1) setting benchmarks and goals; (2) defining what is to be measured and putting measurement tools in place; (3) testing online fundraising tactics under controlled conditions and using measurement tools to collect empirical results; and (4) measuring success by comparing actual results with goals and benchmarks. Only by rigorously following such procedures can the nonprofit sector learn to take full advantage of this promising new medium.

IMAGINE. Your direct mail acquisition campaign is costing $2.00 to raise a dollar, but your online e-mail acquisition is costing only $1.00 to raise a dollar. Logically, you would be wise to invest more heavily in acquisition by e-mail, but if you don't know how the comparison stacks up, you may miss the opportunity to move more of your limited acquisition budget into online activities.

However, those measurements don't fall from the sky. To gain the benefit of information like that, you need to put in place—carefully and thoughtfully—an evaluation process. That process entails four steps:

1. Setting benchmarks and goals
2. Defining what is to be measured and putting measurement tools in place
3. Testing online fundraising tactics under controlled conditions and using measurement tools to collect empirical results

4. Measuring success by comparing actual results with goals and benchmarks

Setting Benchmarks

The key statistics to measure the fundraising performance of your Web site include the following:

Number of Visitors to the Web Site The conversion rate of visitors to donors is an important benchmark and will vary hugely from one site to another. For example, the international Web site for one multinational nonprofit converts only 0.004 percent of its visitors into donors, while fully 0.8 percent of the visitors to one of the organization's individual country Web sites become donors online. It's obvious that the national site is doing a far better job converting visitors to donors. With that knowledge in hand, the international organization can take steps to incorporate some of the features from that national site into its international operations online—and continue collecting data to track its progress toward a new, conversion rate.

Number of Visitors to Different Sections of the Web Site Analyzing where people go on your site (for example, home page, giving pages, key program pages, and so forth) can help you fine-tune your site to drive higher traffic to the key giving pages.

Length of Each Visit to the Web Site In an informal study of ten nonprofit Web sites, my firm discovered that visitors stayed an average of seven minutes on site and that the longer the visit time, the higher was the donor conversion rate (informal review by HJC New Media of ten nonprofit organizations, 1999–2000). Tracking your own site's staying power can help you determine whether you need to add or expand features to involve visitors more deeply.

Number and Types of Online Gifts (Which Could Be Tiny) Once you understand how people are currently giving online (or did so in the past), you'll be in a better position to set benchmarks and goals for the future. For example, you may have a small number of online donors who give *single* credit card gifts online but you may want to set the goal of capturing more *monthly* online donors in the future.

By treating measurements such as these as benchmarks, you can evaluate the performance of future online fundraising activities. For instance, you might determine that the number of visitors to the principal giving page on your site is too low and take steps to increase traffic there. By measuring that number on a continuing basis, you can gauge the relative success of any activities you're pursuing toward that goal: a banner campaign, for example, or an e-mail marketing campaign. To succeed in online fundraising, you will need to set measurable objectives so that you can test and evaluate the effectiveness of your work.

Setting Goals

An online fundraising plan is often determined by the maturity of the online fundraising program as a whole. If your organization has been fundraising online for two years, your goal may be to increase revenue—or the average gift, or the conversion rate—in your current online fundraising efforts. By contrast, for a newly launched online fundraising program, your goal may simply be to get any donations at all.

Goals help provide vision and inspiration to those who are responsible for the day-to-day execution of an online fundraising plan. Your goals might include any of the following:

- Find new supporters
- Build increased donor satisfaction
- Increase cost-effectiveness
- Stay ahead of the competition

Once you've chosen your goal or goals and determined benchmarks against which to measure your progress, it will be much easier to determine the ultimate success, or failure, of your online fundraising program.

Determining Success or Failure

Once you've set goals and benchmarks, it's time to put in place the functions that will allow you to capture data and perform analysis. Keep in mind that this data capture is not only about recording the right information about your visitors or supporters, it's also about being able to manipulate and *interpret* those data in a meaningful way. To ensure that that is possible, you'll need to set the parameters for data capture at the outset in two main areas: determining what financial data you'll need, and putting in place a site log reporting facility.

Financial Data

The data you'll need to capture include the following:

- Number of donations (single, monthly, total)
- Revenue (single, annualized monthly, total)

- Number of names collected (If your online fundraising campaign is a two-stage campaign, in which you first gather e-mail addresses and then send solicitations, calculating the number of e-mail addresses collected is vital to gauge your success in the first stage of the campaign.)

- An estimate of lifetime donor value based on normal off-line attrition rates (until experience teaches us specifically about online lifetime values)

All these numbers will be important when you attempt to calculate the success or failure of an online fundraising campaign. For example, you might invest $5,000 in an online banner campaign that results in the following: A hundred donors make sixty single credit card donations totaling $1,800; and forty donors make monthly credit card donations totaling $1,600 (with an average monthly amount of $40). During the month of the campaign, that would provide an immediate financial return of $3,400 for the initial $5,000 investment. However, the value of those forty monthly donors over the next twelve months would be $19,200—so the return on your investment will look very different if you distinguish between single-gift and monthly donors. That's why it's especially important to know the number of monthly donors as opposed to single-gift donors. Those numbers can make the difference between understanding whether your online fundraising efforts are a success or a failure.

Site Log Reporting

You'll need to capture four main types of data in this area.

Overall Number of Unique Visitors to the Site By analyzing increases and decreases in the level of traffic to your site, you can begin to understand how much traffic you need to generate significant income and when the best times are to run online campaigns or post requests for funds. This measurement should also give you an indication of the public's general awareness of your organization and whether the peaks in activity on your site match significant off-line events, such as big press coverage around a particular issue. To permit you to answer such questions on more than an anecdotal basis, you need to measure the increase or decrease in traffic on your site on a weekly basis (stated as a percentage). As you track this benchmark over time, you'll be able to spot trends, such as a big spike in activity during the Christmas holiday.

Number of Visitors to the "Join" or "Give" Page Compared to the Number of Gifts that Result You should track how often attempted donations fail, because you'll want to lower the failure rate. This is especially important because commercial studies have shown that up to 60 percent of online "shopping carts" are abandoned (*Revolution* magazine survey, 2000). By understanding the failure rate for the organization's giving area, you can set goals for improvements. You'll need to clock these numbers on a weekly basis and examining trends over time.

Breakdown of Visitors to the "Join" or "Give" Form by the Paths that Brought Them There By comparing where visitors last alighted on your site before they reached the giving form, you can spot opportunities for promotions in particular areas on your site. These numbers, too, should be tracked on a weekly basis.

URLs That Are Driving Donors to Your Site Perhaps you're running a banner campaign or you've established hypertext links with other Web sites. By tracking where visitors to your site come from, you can determine which sites yield better donation conversion rates. With this information in hand, you can try to bolster the more productive links and reduce or eliminate those that are only marginally useful.

Once you have set benchmarks and goals and you have the machinery in place to capture the necessary data to calculate success or failure, you'll need to create a testing schedule—a deliberate plan to determine the relative effectiveness of techniques and features you might add to the site to help you meet the goals you've set. Among the very first features to test are those that might help you strengthen your relationships with your donors.

Testing Relationship Building

One of the most important pieces of any online fundraising initiative are the tools you put into the back end to ensure that your organization is delivering exceptional service to all its constituents. Assuming you've covered all the basics and have begun work on improving your visitor conversion rates, you should begin introducing automated relationship tools and test whether they're cost-effective in strengthening your relationships with supporters online.

For example, you might decide it's time to solicit funds from two thousand e-mail addresses that have accumulated through a lead-generation form on your home page. You go online, enter your password, and select or craft an e-mail appeal to send those two thousand prospects.

You then program the e-mail messaging system to follow up, depending on how each individual responds to the solicitation. Those who don't even open the e-mail might automatically be sent a hard-hitting, premium-based second e-mail solicitation. Those who click on the hypertext giving link in the first solicitation but *don't* give could be sent a slightly more aggressive reminder e-mail. Finally, those who did click through and gave gifts would receive personalized acknowledgments.

An e-mail relationship-building program of this sort can be pre-programmed for a year in advance, automating responses to donors based on their behavior and stated preferences. For instance, if someone indicates an interest in planned giving, the program would automatically send them the electronic newsletter for your legacy society (Figure 5.1).

Any such program must be carefully and consistently evaluated. It's vital that you test continuously to analyze whether an automated, self-personalized, electronic correspondence with your donors and prospects will lead to greater customer loyalty, awareness, and satisfaction.

Conducting Surveys

To judge the success of automated relationship tools for online fundraising, you'll find customer satisfaction surveys essential. Such surveys are typically conducted in two stages over a set period of time (frequently one year); identical questionnaires are sent to the same people at the beginning and again at the end of the period. In the "terrestrial" (non-

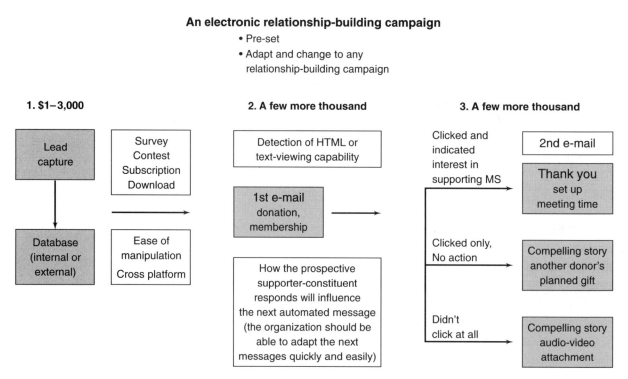

Figure 5.1. Sample Relationship Management Tools That Need to Be Tested.

electronic) world of more traditional fundraising, it's typical to collect information in both beginning and ending surveys for each of several important segments: special-event donors, for instance, as distinct from direct-mail donors and telemarketing respondents. Comparing the data from the first survey with those from the second will permit you to determine whether communications such as newsletters, phone calls, or face-to-face visits increased or decreased donor satisfaction with the organization. A survey of electronic constituents is similar. You'll find it useful to conduct one with the prospects you acquire in each lead-generation campaign, thereby allowing you to measure whether more personalized and empowering online relationship-building tools really lead to more customer satisfaction. By also including in your survey (and measuring separately) those direct mail, telemarketing, or special-events donors for whom you have e-mail addresses, you can also determine the relative effectiveness of online and off-line fundraising communications—and shape your recruitment budget accordingly. (A recent Stanford University study found that alumni who received electronic correspondence (an e-newsletter call @Stanford) gave 175 percent more to the annual fund campaign, and renewed at a higher rate, than alumni who received paper correspondence.)

Evaluating Online Fundraising Techniques

Off-line, we test a myriad of different techniques in fundraising to evaluate success. In a direct mail acquisition campaign, for example, we may test a picture and an outer envelope teaser to learn what effects they may have on the rate of response generated by a package. In a telephone fundraising campaign, we might change the caller script to emphasize the importance of making a monthly gift over a single gift. All this testing is part of an ongoing effort to improve the results of our work. It should be no different in online fundraising.

Testing should be an integral part of every online fundraising campaign. If you're going to run a banner campaign, for example, you need to make sure that you test multiple versions of the banner and evaluate at regular intervals the comparative performance of those different versions in drawing visitors to your site. Obviously, the objective is to abandon the poor performers and make wider use of the winning banners. All successful direct response fundraising is (or should be) based on the incremental improvements that testing enables.

When sending out e-mail solicitations, you'll be better able to measure how well you're doing—and plan for the future—by testing various techniques and approaches in your solicitations.

For example, say you want to solicit the two thousand prospects whose e-mail addresses you've accumulated through a lead-generation program. If you send out a simple text message asking the prospect to visit your Web site and make a credit card gift there, you can calculate performance very simply: If your investment in time and money is less than the resulting financial return, the solicitation was successful. Let's just say, for the sake of argument, that this text message returned $5.00 for every $1.00 invested. However, if you learn—through testing—that a more colorful Hypertext Markup Language (HTML) version of the solicitation yields $8 for every $1 spent, you'll clearly want to think about using HTML in future e-mail solicitations.

Success is relative in fundraising. One technique may be successful in that it was profitable but a failure in comparison to other techniques that could have been used. Only by testing—rigorously and often—can you learn which techniques perform the best for your organization.

Figure 5.2 illustrates how some nonprofit organizations are testing multiple techniques in online (e-mail) fundraising. In the example depicted, an e-mail solicitation is separated into four equal parts: the first group receives a simple text solicitation, the second an HTML version, the third a text message with an accompanying premium (for example, a screensaver), and the last an e-mail message that doesn't even ask for money in the body of the text. (This last option was included at the insistence of a staff person at the nonprofit who thought that netiquette demanded that they not ask for money so directly). After this initial, four-way test determined the strongest approaches, the organization would very likely conduct a second, two-way test to compare the two strongest techniques with each other. Finally, the winning approach would be adopted in future e-mail solicitations.

If these procedures strike you as onerous, all I can say is, welcome to the wonderful world of direct response fundraising! Careful measurements and continuous testing are the stuff of which success is made in direct response. Only by rigorously following such procedures can the nonprofit sector learn to take full advantage of the exciting new online channel.

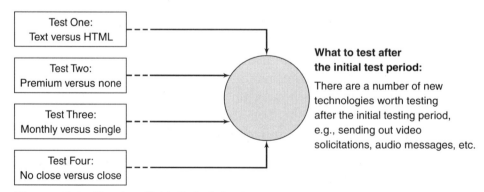

Figure 5.2. Testing E-Mail Solicitations.

CHAPTER

6

Regulating Online Fundraising

Lawmakers are only now coming to grips with the legal ramifications of Internet tools such as e-mail and the Web. It's inevitable that they'll play increasingly close attention to these ramifications, since there are genuine issues of privacy and security for regulators to consider. Inevitably, too, online fundraising will come under closer scrutiny as it evolves.

This chapter does not constitute legal advice; the author is not an attorney. Rather, it's included to help you understand the regulatory issues important to online solicitation and offer you the resources to find solutions.

CITIZENS IN NEW YORK, New York, who are concerned about saving Amazon rainforests can as easily donate online to Greenpeace in Brazil as they can to the local chapter of Greenpeace USA. They're likely to have no particular interest in understanding the complex organizational structure of Greenpeace International or how their money will get to where it's supposed to go. They're just interested in the cause.

But Greenpeace *does* have to be concerned with these issues. To comply with the complex laws concerning fundraising and taxation, especially as these laws pertain to Internet activities, Greenpeace must have in place the technology and procedures to sort out these issues cleanly and quickly.

This is just one example of how Internet technology is rapidly testing the notion of political borders and how nonprofit activities are governed. Nonprofits have traditionally worked within defined geographical boundaries. They draw support from within these boundaries and most often serve local needs. A multilevel nonprofit organization might span many different jurisdictions, but each of its local, regional, national, and international divisions has defined relationships to other divisions and to the laws of its own jurisdiction.

The Internet complicates these relationships by making interactions across political boundaries as easy as within them. Moreover, the fact of a relationship being interjurisdictional is often completely invisible (and of little significance) to the participants.

Internet users can access resources on computers from diverse geographical locations without any awareness of where the information is coming from in the physical world. Moreover, the computers serving up resources are also indifferent to the whereabouts of those accessing their files. Dan Burk argues, "So insensitive is the network to geography, that it is frequently impossible to determine the physical location of a resource or user. Such information is unimportant to the network's function or to the purposes of its creators" (Dan L. Burk, "Jurisdiction in a World Without Borders," *Virginia Journal of Law and Technology*, volume 3, Spring, 1997), and the network's design thus makes it difficult to determine the physical origin of any message.

The geographical indifference and indeterminacy characterizing online activities stand at odds with legal traditions, most of which presuppose that legal jurisdiction is defined by physical location. An e-mail sent to a recipient at, for example hotmail.com, could be received in any country in the world, and the sender would have no way of determining where the recipient was located. A Web site published by a small local charity can potentially be forwarded many times to anyone in the world, even though it might not be the intention of the organization to address its content and its solicitations to the world.

Current Regulation

Prior to the advent of the Internet, the majority of fundraising campaigns had a limited scope, with organizations targeting specific areas that were in their local jurisdiction. It was primarily the larger organizations that implemented national campaigns, as they had the means to support such efforts and could afford to follow the required registration regulations.

This new medium has created a national stage for even the smallest of nonprofit organizations and has rendered the present regulatory environment inadequate. The current laws were primarily put in place to protect the common citizen from fraud—an even more urgent need now, with the advent of online fundraising. Most jurisdictions require registration by the charity prior to soliciting gifts.

But the pervasive nature of the Internet poses challenges to that strategy for both would-be regulators and the nonprofits themselves. Even if an organization knew its site was being viewed in every state or province, the cost and the staff time required make it unlikely to register the site everywhere. Similarly, a state or provincial charitable registration office is unlikely to have the resources to pursue a large number of fundraisers operating at distances of thousands of miles.

As a result, regulating online fundraising will have to be different from regulating fundraising conducted through other media. The Internet transcends local, national, and international borders, thus making jurisdiction impossible to establish. For example, if a charity based in California posts a Web site that is viewed in Connecticut, which state has the authority to regulate its activity—and can Connecticut require this charity to register with their state?

At the time this chapter was written there were thirty-nine states with official legislation regarding charitable solicitations, with most regulating telephone or direct mail fundraising campaigns. Many states are applying the current laws to online activities. However, when surveyed, seven out of ten state officials did not think their fundraising laws adequately covered the Internet. (As part of the research associated with this chapter, state officials in the fifty states were sent a survey regarding the regulation of online charitable solicitation. Many were hesitant to respond to the survey, as this is an area of significant debate with no clear solution by any one state. Of the fifty states we contacted, only ten responded with completed surveys.) From a government perspective the utility of the present system is called into question, as the task of maintaining registration for these organizations is arduous. For instance, Section 13–22–5 of the *Utah Charitable Solicitations Act* states: "It is unlawful for any organization that is not exempt under Section 13–22–8 to knowingly solicit, request, promote, advertise, or sponsor the solicitation in this state of any contribution for a charitable purpose, unless the organization is registered with the division" (Utah Charitable Solicitations Act).

This provision notwithstanding, a Web site purporting to represent a charity can easily appear inside Utah without the charity's knowledge. If an individual in Utah finds a Web site for a group in Massachusetts, is it not the individual donor who knowingly made the first form of contact? This issue perplexes nonprofits and state regulators alike, but there is no clear path to resolving it.

The sheer amount of work involved in keeping track of online solicitations may provide the answer. Currently, most state regulators do not have the capacity to keep track of all the organizations that pass through their jurisdiction in the terrestrial world, let alone the Internet. According to Geoffrey Peters, "if only 10 percent of charities maintain a Web site that 'passively' asks for donations, the typical state will see an increase from 1,500 to 62,000 in the number of charities which must register. The resources which could otherwise be devoted to detection and prosecution of charitable fraud would thus be devoted to registration compliance" (taken from a memo distributed at the National Federation of Nonprofits Annual Conference entitled, "Critical Issues Facing Non-profits in the 21st Century: How Will Fundraising on the Internet Be Regulated?" November 1999).

You can easily see that if 62,000 charities were required to register in every state, the speed and scope that the Internet offers would be stifled, if not lost, in a "paperwork" system that is not conducive to this technology. The cost in both money and time to maintain registration in all applicable jurisdictions is more than some nonprofits can afford. A smaller organization that simply wants to communicate with its constituency through a cheap, new medium is suddenly prevented from doing so because it cannot afford to fit into a regulatory regime that was originally designed to deal with large, out-of-state solicitors.

A 1995 study conducted by Geoffrey Peters outlines the cost for non-profits of running an out-of-state direct response campaign. In this study Peters refers to four main areas of costs for organizations: the federal government and its agencies, such as the Internal Revenue Service; state government and its agencies, such as consumer protection divisions; city and county registration fees; and finally registration professionals. (To comply with the demands placed upon charities, Peters reports, many have had to hire for-profit companies to assist in the registration process. Peters argues that organizations may have to pay an additional $6,000 per year in registration services. In his study, Peters also discusses the additional indirect costs of fundraising and projects that given these direct and indirect costs imposed on nonprofits, the cost of maintaining a campaign could range from $25,000 per year for small organizations to $150,000 per year for larger charities.) The cost of registering alone for some organizations would thus significantly outweigh the cost of developing a basic online campaign—another reason to question the appropriateness of the current regulatory system.

Despite the realization that changes need to be implemented, most states, and nonprofit organizations too for that matter, are taking a wait-and-see approach and applying the standard solicitation regulations to the Internet until "someone tells them otherwise." In many cases that "someone" has become the courts. Organizations and state governments are now bringing cases to court as a way to determine who has jurisdiction over Internet activities and whether applying the existing laws to online practices violate basic constitutional rights.

Self-Regulation

The concept of self-regulation by the nonprofit sector is one of the possible reforms being considered in the debate over online campaigns. Organizations would voluntarily agree to abide by standards set by the sector, such as in ethical codes published by the Association of Fundraising Professionals or the ePhilanthropyFoundation.Org (see Resource A).

Registration as Professional Solicitor

Registration in every state (and maybe every county and municipality, too) may not be enough. Many charities use some kind of third-party service provider for some part of their online fundraising program. At the very least, they will use an application service provider (ASP) of some sort. Be aware that states define the term *professional solicitor* very broadly, and any service provider that specializes in serving charities, or even provides special programs or assistance to charities, may find itself subject to state professional solicitor regulation.

Some of the services that may be covered by these regulatory provisions are charity auctions, online donation pages or "buttons," or any other service specifically for charities. These services may be subject to professional solicitor regulation and may need to be registered properly in every state that requires it. Before contracting with such a provider it may be a good idea to ask whether they are registered as a professional solicitor, and if they say no then ask the reason. (It might be a good idea to have this reviewed by legal counsel before a final decision to register or not is made.)

In many cases it will be important to determine whether the appeal for donations is coming from the charity or from the ASP for the charity (the latter usually indicates a professional solicitor), and how much control over the fundraising process is exerted by the ASP or managed by the charity. If you have any doubt, discuss this with a lawyer.

Charleston Principles

The National Association of State Charity Officials (NASCO) released the Charleston Principles in 2000 [www.nasconet.org/stories/storyReader$10] as a nonbinding, suggested set of regulatory guidelines to determine when a nonprofit in one state must register in another state in order to raise funds on the Internet.

Those who raise money in multiple states with nationwide direct mail and telemarketing campaigns already have to register as fundraisers in all the states that require registration. The growth in Internet fundraising threatens to impose similar requirements on thousands of other nonprofits that *don't* cast their fundraising nets so widely but *do* raise money online. All of a sudden, many local and statewide nonprofit organizations that have Web sites with the capability to request gifts may be out of compliance with a variety of state registration laws and regulations.

The Charleston Principles attempt to offer a reasonable set of guidelines for when a nonprofit organization must register. A key distinction in NASCO's principles is that between *active* and *passive* fundraising. Any charity that's actively sending out e-mail solicitations to a state that requires registration should register if it's targeting donors there.

However, if that charity receives a contribution online from an interested supporter in another state *without having actively solicited the support,* the Charleston Principles make clear that the charity needn't worry about registering in that state.

However, if the charity's public profile rises to the point where it receives many donations from another state, it may need to register even if it has done no "active" fundraising in that state. The Charleston Principles suggest that a hundred individual donations or a total of $25,000 in contributions is the appropriate level where registration should be triggered.

Unified Registration

The current regulatory environment regarding interstate online charitable solicitations is unworkable. Even the smallest municipalities can (and some do) impose regulations on charitable solicitations. Such municipalities can then argue (in court) that when anyone residing in their jurisdiction visits a nonprofit Web site and makes a donation, they have the right to regulate that activity. It's unreasonable to expect charities to register in thousands of jurisdictions simply because the potential exists that a gift could someday be made from someone from those jurisdictions. Requiring this level of microregulation will seriously damage the ability of nonprofits to engage in any online fundraising activities.

You can help minimize the effort by using the Unified Registration Statement (URS) for Charitable Organizations, which is accepted by many states in lieu of their own registration form. To access this form, go to [www.nonprofits.org/library/gov/urs].

The URS is already accepted by thirty-two states within the United States. With unified registration, all information that is required by individual states is consolidated into one standardized form for registration. Although this does not replace individual state registration, it does remove the complexity of following requirements that vary among jurisdictions.

States That Currently Require Charitable Registration and Accept the Unified Registration Statement

Alabama	Massachusetts	Ohio
Arkansas	Michigan	Oklahoma
California	Minnesota	Oregon
Connecticut	Mississippi	Pennsylvania
Georgia	Missouri	Rhode Island
Illinois	Nebraska	South Carolina

Kansas	New Hampshire	Tennessee
Kentucky	New Jersey	Virginia
Louisiana	New Mexico	Washington
Maine	New York	Washington, D.C.
Maryland	North Dakota	West Virginia
		Wisconsin

**States That Require Charitable Registration
and *Do Not* Accept the Unified Registration Statement**

Alaska	Florida	Utah
Arizona	North Carolina	

The best summary of state requirements for charitable solicitors, with contact information for the office that regulate charitable solicitation in each state, is available for purchase from the AAFRC Trust for Philanthropy. Go to [www.aafrc.org/giving], and ask for the report entitled "Annual Survey of State Laws Regulating Charitable Solicitations."

Unwarranted Regulation Will Hinder Philanthropy

Everyone agrees, I think, that accountability is an important matter for nonprofits and that states have the right to regulate fundraising activities in their jurisdictions. But the borderless aspects of the Internet and the relative ease with which nonprofit organizations can appeal to everyone with a computer and a modem, no matter where they reside, will make state-by-state fundraising regulation a challenging task.

It is plain to see that the wait-and-see approach to dealing with the Internet can no longer be applied. Governments and nonprofit organizations alike need to take a proactive approach and begin working on a dialogue concerning how to turn this regulation challenge into an opportunity that will benefit the regulators as well as the regulated.

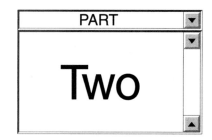
Online Fundraising Fundamentals

Recruiting New Donors Online

Acquiring new donors online is every fundraiser's dream, but so far only a few hundred groups are bringing in significant numbers of new donors over the Internet. A dozen brand-name American nonprofits, many of them dealing with disasters, are each acquiring tens of thousands of new donors and raising $1 million or more every year. Several dozen more (there is no central record-keeper, and many organizations are reluctant to share their results) are finding thousands of new donors and raising hundreds of thousands of dollars a year. In short, while most of the miracle dot-com fundraising solutions have been ineffective, acquiring donors online has proven to be a rising source of revenue, especially for larger organizations that have invested in it.

ACQUIRING NEW DONORS is the holy grail of Internet fundraising, and it's proven to be a difficult quest so far.

The good news is that most organizations that are dedicating staff time and resources to online fundraising are bringing in more and more every year, often doubling the number of new online donors, and revenues, from one year to the next. Thousands of organizations accept online contributions at their sites, many of them via plug-and-play "donate now" buttons operated by service providers. These organizations are finding that the majority of online donors are new donors, and the average online donation is much higher than the average first-time direct mail donation to the same organization. Organizations dealing with crises have been especially successful at acquiring donors online, for obvious reasons.

The bad news is that most organizations don't attract many people (read: prospects) to their Web sites, don't do a very effective job at convincing visitors to give, and haven't invested the staff time or money required to make full use of this new communications channel.

Until nonprofits become more proficient at integrating their online giving opportunities with traditional fundraising efforts, and therefore give donors more options and reasons to give online, the Web environment itself may not be as conducive to giving as other direct marketing methods, such as mail or telemarketing. Giving online usually requires an instant decision, unlike direct mail, which many people put aside to consider later. Heavy Web users tend to be much younger than "heavy" direct mail recipients. The security of transactions is still an issue for some potential donors, perhaps especially older Web users. And, of course, Internet fundraising competes with an increased volume of traditional fundraising: direct mail, telemarketing, major donor events, walk-a-thons, and more.

Despite the problems and the lack of investment so far, major North American nonprofits—as well as their counterparts in Europe, and increasing Latin America and Asia—are forging ahead. They are hiring staff members, investing in e-mail and Web development, and partnering with corporations, e-commerce sites, and others. They are rightfully expecting that the Internet will become an increasingly important source of new donors, as well as a way to cultivate existing online and off-line donors for additional gifts.

There are at least four ways to acquire new donors online:

- Appeals on your Web site (by far the most important and most sustainable)

- Appeals in the messages to your e-mail list or e-newsletter

- Promotions and donated banner ads run on other sites, such as Yahoo or America Online (AOL)

- Independent sites, usually for-profits, such as charity portals (Helping.org, JustGive.org), charity shopping malls (ShopForChange.com, iGive.com), auction sites, or other dot-com fundraising sites (see nonprofitmatrix.com for more sites)

Now I'll review each of those four methods in turn.

Acquiring Donors on Your Web Site

Most visitors to your Web site come because they know or care something about your organization or your mission or they're seeking information. That obviously makes them potentially more open to your fundraising appeals than someone who sees your banner on Yahoo. Effective sites offer fundraising appeals on every page, linking the appeal as much as possible to the content of the page.

If a visitor to World Wildlife Fund's site clicks onto the polar bear page, why not make a fundraising appeal that speaks of WWF's work to preserve polar bear habitat? If the visitor has chosen a page on global warming, why not offer an appeal based on WWF's work on that issue? (Of course, small organizations working on just one issue or program have fewer options.)

Just Like Direct Mail? Many effective Web fundraising techniques are adaptations of direct mail methods. Whereas a direct mail prospect package might contain a four-page letter, a buckslip, a reply card, and a business reply envelope, few people will read long text online (though they might look at several Web pages before responding to an online appeal). As in direct mail, however, an online appeal must make a compelling and urgent case to the prospect, then make it easy to respond. That means short, punchy, evocative, emotional copy and photos (even audio or video), and one click to the donation form.

If Web visitors click on "Donate" or "Support" on one of your pages, take them right to the "reply card" version of the appeal, which might read somewhat as follows:

> Yes, I want to contribute to (or join) your organization to help (achieve your mission). Here is my (tax-deductible) contribution of
>
> ☐ *$35*   ☐ *$100*   ☐ *$500*   ☐ *$1,000*   ☐ *$ other*
>
> [Name, address, e-mail, credit card info]

Test various gift strings, but remember that online donors usually give more than direct mail donors, so consider making the lowest ask at least $35. Keep the form simple—one or two pages at most. Don't ask for information you don't need or won't use, and don't make the user choose among a dozen giving options. Make sure you have an "opt-in" check-box to get donors' permission to send them occasional e-mails. Link to a privacy policy that explains what you do with information the donor leaves.

Who's Been Successful? The poster child for online fundraising has been the American Red Cross, which raised $2.2 million in 2000 from 16,700 donors, with an average gift of $131. In 1999, the year of Kosovo and other high-profile disasters, the Red Cross raised $2.6 million from almost 22,000 donors (average $118). (Keep in mind that 1999 contributions to the Red Cross totaled $817 million, including disaster relief, legacies, grants, United Way, and all other monetary and in-kind contributions.) Catholic Relief Services raised over $1 million in 2000. Other well-known disaster and development agencies, such as World Vision, Mercy Corps, Save the Children, and CARE, also each took in hundreds of thousand of dollars online (and hundreds of millions off-line).

America's Second Harvest, the nation's largest domestic hunger relief organization with a network of 200 food banks and food rescue programs around the United States, was raising about $200,000 a year online, plus some additional revenue from special promotions. The average gift was $105. America's Second Harvest's site averaged 27,000 visitor sessions per month in early 2001. While about 95 percent of online donors were new to Second Harvest in the first years of fundraising, that figure has dropped to 75 percent since the 2000 holiday season. America's Second Harvest's Web site is clearly attracting donors who were not on the lists it uses for direct mail prospecting (or didn't respond to the letters). The fact that more current direct mail donors are giving online may represent increased use of the Internet by America's Second Harvest donors and prospects or suggest that some mail donors prefer to give online or learn more on the Web site before they make gifts.

WWF and the Heifer Project have invested significant resources in online fundraising and have reaped the rewards, each raising over $1 million a year online. In addition to fundraising asks on every page (as it does in the mail), WWF offers a T-shirt as a premium for a gift of $15 or more. The shirt and fulfillment cost might be prohibitive for smaller organizations, but WWF apparently makes it work (as they do in the mail). WWF also offers high-dollar giving clubs, gift donations, and frequent flyer miles on its site.

The Heifer Project is a great example of a compelling case coupled with a creative and easy way for the donor to give online. The project, which provides income- and food-producing farm animals to more than 30,000 families in forty-six countries, solicits donations through an online catalog: Buy a gift of a goat for $120 or a "share of a goat" for $10. It's a very compelling offer. In addition, the site is beautifully executed. In 2000, the Heifer Project raised well over $1 million online, including $192,000 from the Motley Fool's (an investment site) annual end-of-the year "Foolanthropy 2000" online philanthropy drive.

Most smaller organizations raise a lot less than these big-budget national charities. With only a minimal Web presence and virtually no promotion, the National Council of La Raza, the nation's largest Hispanic advocacy organization, raises about $700 per month online, with an average gift of $60 (compared to $30 in prospect mailings). Surfrider Foundation, a national organization working to protect beach habitat, has an active online community (surfers tend to be young guys, who tend to be online) and a full-time Webmaster. While Surfrider doesn't keep detailed statistics on their online fundraising, over 5,300 members have signed up or renewed online. At the minimum $25 gift level, that's $132,500. All told, about 20 percent of members have joined online.

E-Mail Appeals

While the Web gets most of the Internet glory, savvy Internet fundraisers are realizing that e-mail may be the more important element (see

Resource G). E-mail enables organizations to cultivate and resolicit donors in a timely and inexpensive way (and to conduct sequenced e-mail–mail campaigns similar to the traditional mail-phone or phone-mail campaigns).

Most nonprofits have not made aggressive efforts to build their e-mail lists, either from Web visitors ("subscribe to our free e-newsletter") or from existing direct mail, telephone, or event donors. One of our new clients came to us with more than 200,000 active donors, 85,000 page views per month on its Web site, but fewer than four thousand e-mail addresses.

However, some large environmental and other advocacy organizations have built e-mail lists of 200,000 to 400,000. The organizations e-mail these folks to educate them, activate them, and try to convert them into donors. Of course, they could never afford the printing and postage to send a monthly letter to prospects at a cost of thirty to sixty cents apiece; but, for a few cents each, they can send monthly e-mails to prospects. Converting them into donors is not easy, and unfortunately most groups have only started tentative steps in this direction by including appeals in their advocacy e-mails or sending occasional separate appeals to the list.

Typical response rates are under 1 percent, with a $40 average gift. But the numbers can work. For example, assume 100,000 names, 0.3 percent response rate, $40 average gift, $30 per thousand for e-mail messaging. That means revenue of $12,000 at a cost of $3,000. Not bad for prospecting. (Of course, that does not include the cost of obtaining the 100,000 names, though those costs are usually borne by the advocacy department.)

Promotions on Other Sites

Over the last few years, many of the big Internet portals and search engines have donated banner ads (such as public service announcements or PSAs) and other promotions to nonprofits, often related either to disasters or to holidays. For example, Yahoo, Excite, and other leading sites offered banners and home-page links to the Red Cross and others during Hurricane Mitch, the Kosovo emergency, and the earthquakes in El Salvador and India. Yahoo has also sometimes hosted promotions, especially ones fronted by celebrities. eBay and Yahoo Auctions also run auctions benefiting charities, such as Easter Seals and the Elton John AIDS Foundation. Localized Yahoo sites, such as Yahoo Bay Area and Yahoo Seattle, have also run promotions for local charities.

During the heyday of the dot-coms (remember those distant times?), many e-commerce sites offered cause-related marketing campaigns to nonprofits. eBags, an online luggage store, donated a percentage of its sales to various organizations. Webvan, the grocery delivery service, raised $283,000 for America's Second Harvest in the first three months of 2001 from its shoppers and suppliers.

The Motley Fool, an investment site with more than two million registered users, has run a "Foolanthropy" end-of-year fundraising effort for several years. Fool users help choose the charities—groups seen as "entrepreneurial," like Fool investors, are preferred—then users can donate online, make gifts of stock, and so forth. The 2000 campaign raised $772,000 and donated it to five groups: Heifer Project, Lifewater International, Ashoka, America's Second Harvest, and the Grameen Foundation. The Motley Fool itself kicked in more than $25,000. (The Fool was proud that although the Nasdaq stock market declined 39 percent in 2000, Foolanthropy raised about $10,000 more than in the previous year, when the market advanced 85 percent.)

Dozens of nonprofits have run Netcentives promotions, which offered donors ClickRewards frequent flyer miles in exchange for donations. Netcentives sends the offer to at least one million of the five million names on its opt-in marketing list and promotes it at its sites; the charity promotes the effort on its site and in its e-newsletter.

For two years, WWF has partnered with Netcentives to run the "Miles for the Wild" campaign, which offers a rich mileage incentive to donors. The Miles campaign has grossed over $600,000 for WWF, which must pay Netcentives for the miles, typically three to four cents each. The Holiday 2000 campaign raised $172,000, netting $41,000 for WWF.

As in direct mail campaigns, donors who join in exchange for a valuable premium often need another premium to give again. However, WWF and other Netcentives charities typically make money via the ClickRewards acquisition programs. How many of these donors will give again, with or without miles? We don't know, although WWF reportedly received a second gift of around $70,000 from one of the Netcentives donors.

Big Brothers–Big Sisters of San Francisco, a much smaller organization than WWF, netted about $10,000 over six months in a Netcentives program by offering ten thousand miles to $1,000 donors and a hundred miles for $50. Unfortunately, the dot-com downturn caused Netcentives to close its cause-marketing division in early 2001.

Charity Portals, Shopping Malls, Click-to-Donate, Care Bars, and Other Dot-Com Offerings

Starting in 1998, larger nonprofits were besieged by calls from dot-com startups that seemed to promise big money with little effort. Charity portals such as the AOL Time Warner Foundation's Helping.org (one of the few nonprofits), JustGive.org, Charity.ca, and others allowed visitors to search for charities by keyword and zip code (using the GuideStar database, based on the IRS 990 tax filings). Though helping.org has raised about $3 million for charities, most of the other charity portals have closed their doors or changed their business models. Donors don't usually go in search of charities to support; they support organizations they already know and trust, or ones that solicit them directly.

Dozens of online shopping malls, such as Charitymall.com and iGive.com, promised charities that they would receive 5 to 15 percent of the sales price of goods their supporters purchased. Other promoters asked nonprofits to have their Web visitors download applications that would run advertising banners (and messages from the nonprofit) in a special browser window; the nonprofit would get a percentage. Others promised to make easy money by conducting online auctions (see a list of dozens at www.nonprofitmatrix.com).

The Hunger Site, founded by a programmer in 1999, recruited advertising sponsors to donate the cost of a cup of rice to a United Nations (UN) food program every time a visitor clicked on the site. The site was a viral phenomenon, logging over 100 million visitors, who donated 198 million cups of staple foods by early 2001, according to the site. In 2000, the site was taken over by the for-profit GreaterGood, which added other click-to-give sites for AIDS, the rainforest, and other causes. In late 2000, the UN dropped out of the project when GreaterGood was apparently late in making its payments. When GreaterGood failed in mid-2001, the Hunger Site closed.

Although a few organizations made modest money from these dot-coms, most organizations couldn't make them work (or simply didn't have enough online supporters to even make a serious effort). By early 2001, most of these dot-coms had failed, although their Web sites often remained online. The most spectacular failure was Charitableway, started by a former Microsoft executive with $43 million in venture capital. Charitableway began as a charity portal ("find a charity and donate online"), then morphed into a workplace giving vehicle when founder Pete Mountanos realized that charity portals didn't work. Charitableway had contracts with a number of major corporations and United Ways to run their workplace giving system. But profitability was still distant, and Pete was forced to pull the plug.

The problem with the shopping malls (not counting the failure of many of their e-commerce tenants in early 2001) was that most nonprofits don't get a lot of visitors to their sites, so the numbers they can send on to a mall are tiny. And most of those folks visited the mall once, then went directly to Amazon.com or perfume.com the next time, without stopping at the mall to have their purchases credited.

The bottom line is that commercial propositions that depend on high traffic don't work for most nonprofits. What's more, does an organization really want to send Web visitors off to shop somewhere else?

The Future

The collapse of the money-for-nothing dot-coms means nonprofits will get back to basics: acquiring donors by driving traffic to their sites and creating compelling appeals, easy donation systems, and effective acknowledgments and resolicitations. Most large nonprofits are devoting more and more resources to their online acquisition efforts. Although revenues have been relatively low so far, they are doubling every year for most organizations. As it becomes more expensive to acquire (and retain) donors via mail and phone, and as the average age of traditional donors runs into the sixties, the Internet looks better and better. Four years of experimentation ("It seems like everything we do is testing," says one nonprofit Internet manager) have yielded the beginnings of a knowledge base that will benefit every nonprofit raising money online.

Reference URLs

World Wildlife Fund	www.worldwildlife.org (U.S.) www.panda.org (international)
American Red Cross	www.redcross.org
America's Second Harvest	www.secondharvest.org
National Council of La Raza	www.nclr.org
Surfrider Foundation	www.surfrider.org
Heifer Project International	www.heifer.org
The Motley Fool	www.fool.com
Netcentives	www.netcentives.com www.clickrewards.com
Big Brothers–Big Sisters of San Francisco	www.sf-bbbs.org
AOL Time Warner Foundation's Helping.org	www.helping.org
GuideStar charity database	www.guidestar.org

Renewing Donors Online

Although few donors have yet been renewed online, renewing donors online should eventually yield higher response rates and lower overall fundraising costs. Since many donors are just now beginning to consider online giving, conversion to online renewals may take several years. However, now's the time to begin accumulating e-mail addresses of current mail, phone, or event donors and learning how your donors will respond to online appeals.

MOST NONPROFIT ORGANIZATIONS have at least a few donors who have made online gifts and many more who have made gifts by mail, phone, or at events. But most donors have yet to make their first gifts online, and some—especially the older donors who make up the majority of most direct mail files—probably never will. Not everyone has access to e-mail or the Internet (or wishes to transfer money online). Still, as any seasoned fundraiser knows, the low level of fundraising activity online today may have more to do with donors not yet having been *asked* to give online than to lack of interest on their part.

In all fundamental respects, fundraising on the Internet must follow the rules of fundraising long established off-line. Efficient fundraising campaigns and higher-quality donor relations—whether online or off—are possible only when fundraisers precisely target and segment their donors and put in place easy-to-use mechanisms for response. Furthermore, Internet-based fundraising efforts are likely to be successful only when they're well integrated with other, more traditional fundraising methods. (See Chapter Three.) For at least the time being, then, using the Internet to renew donors who have only made off-line gifts will require a combination of Web- and e-mail-based efforts with traditional fundraising methods.

In most circumstances, it's wise to begin by offering donors who have given *off-line* the opportunity to renew their support *online*. For donors who have given online, direct mail can be effective for solicitation; phoning online donors may prove controversial. In general, the more channels of communication you have open to your donors, the stronger your relationships with them are likely to be.

Only One

The online fundraising firm donordigital.com conducted a survey of forty-three national nonprofits with Web sites in late 2000. Thirty-seven of the forty-three offered online giving opportunities. The company made a $25 online credit card gift to each. Only 50 percent sent e-mail thank-yous following receipt of the gift—and only one of them tried to renew the gift online via e-mail! Most of the rest simply added online donors to their direct mail programs, ignoring the fact that they had indicated a willingness, even a preference, to give online!

Donors will only learn about the opportunity to give online if they're aware of it. And their comfort level about contributing online will only rise as the technique becomes more familiar to them. So now, even before the practice is widespread, is a good time to begin introducing this option to donors to prepare for the day in the near future when more robust fundraising and renewal efforts are common online.

Now's the time to begin accumulating information about how your donors respond to online fundraising campaigns. As you conduct traditional campaigns and interact with your donors, encourage them to share their e-mail addresses with you, and start tracking their level of interest in giving online. (See Resource F.)

For instance, in simple surveys on your Web site or in your newsletter or other publications, you can ask donors

- Do you use e-mail? What's your e-mail address?
- Have you ever bought a product or service online?
- Have you ever donated to an organization online? If so, to whom?
- Are you interested in donating to our organization online?
- Would you like to receive e-mail updates from our organization?
- What type of information would you like us to provide online?

Benefits of Renewing Donors Online

There are numerous potential benefits from renewing your donors online. Figure 8.1 highlights two of the biggest ones: increasing response

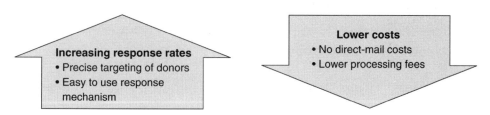

Figure 8.1. Benefits of Renewing Donors Online.

rates (because it's easier online, and an additional solicitation channel) and lowering overall fundraising costs.

Increase Renewal Rates

Different people respond to different types of solicitations. A carefully segmented fundraising campaign almost always increases either the rate of response or the average gift or both, but it's not always cost-effective to create highly segmented and personalized solicitations, because in off-line media the costs may be prohibitive.

In good direct mail programs, targeted gift requests are based on factors such as the size of previous gifts, the recency and frequency of giving, the payment mechanism, and any designation or earmarking of previous gifts. In the future, when organizations are sending their e-mail messages from a database integrating online and off-line donors (with e-mail addresses for most donors), segmenting and targeting via e-mail should be much cheaper than doing so via postal mail.

Easy-to-Use Response Mechanism

Experienced fundraisers know that response rates often rise when it's easy for donors to respond. This is why business reply envelopes with prepaid postage are so often used in direct mail fundraising campaigns. The less work required of the donor, the higher the likelihood of a donation.

In online fundraising, having an easy-to-use response mechanism is even more critical than it is in direct mail. If an e-mail solicitation requires the donor to mail a check or credit card information, the response is likely to be poor. Successful appeals online must not only make a compelling case for giving but also provide a "click-to-give" opportunity for the donor to give online.

Though most online giving today makes use of credit cards, there are several other options that may become popular, including online account debit services (Electronic Funds Transfer, or EFT) that debit donations from the donor's checking account, and direct-transfer services such as check4charity.com or PayPal, which are used by many online auction buyers and sellers.

Quick Start

Here are three examples of easy online fundraising strategies that can help organizations renew donors online.

Use Existing Online Donation Services There is no need to reinvent the wheel by building your own system to accept gifts online. Several online donation acceptance services can assist you in the collection and processing of your online donations. It's simple and easy to link your Web site to services such as charitywave.com, igaveto.com, or Charity-web.net and embed a link in your e-mail solicitations to the appropriate page on your site. Even though gifts may be processed on another site, most donors won't even know that, because it appears that their gifts were made on your own site.

Collect the Donor's Credit Card Information for Manual Processing If you don't yet have a high volume of transactions on your site, or if you're just testing response rates before you invest in a more robust online system, you may want to combine manual processes with a secure server to ensure privacy when you collect donors' credit card information. Then, instead of processing credit card gifts immediately, you can batch them for later, manual entry by using the same system you may already be using for credit card gifts you receive through direct mail or telemarketing. (This option would also allow you to test the effectiveness of online fundraising for your organization before investing in an integrated system.)

Integrate a Real-Time Online Donor Database with a Secure Online Credit Card Verification and Banking Service Whether you set up your own merchant account or use a third party to accept and process online renewal gifts, you can easily integrate the online donation page on your Web site with online credit card verification and banking services, so that gifts are automatically entered and transaction information transferred to your donor database. This level of integration may be too costly at current prices unless your transaction volume is relatively high. However, costs are already coming down and will continue to do so as packaged services are developed and widely marketed. And the ability to offer online renewal with direct access to donors' gift history and demographic information has obvious appeal, because it will enable you to build stronger connections to your online donors.

Lower Fundraising Costs

Off-line, the cost of renewing donors has traditionally been lower than recruiting new ones. This is no less true online. However, the ability afforded by online communications to enable stewardship and intensify dialogue with donors may make online renewals even more successful in the long run. In addition to the possibility that renewal rates will rise through online fundraising campaigns, there is one important, additional benefit: costs will be significantly lower than in direct mail.

The savings are so significant for three principal reasons:

There Are No Direct Mail Costs A direct mail campaign requires postage, printing, and labor. Communicating online eliminates postage and printing and, over the long term, sharply reduces the amount of time and effort needed. Currently, however, fundraisers face a steep learning curve that increases rather than decreases the amount of labor required to launch an online renewal campaign. Proficiency in online fundraising will be a long time coming.

Integrated Back-End Processing Requires Less Labor By integrating a Web-based donor database system with your real-time online credit card processing, you can significantly reduce the labor required compared with the manual processing of donations from your direct mail campaigns. The process can be virtually automatic, seamless, and transparent to your donors.

More Sophisticated Segmentation Will Increase Renewal Rates Renewal rates may increase even more as organizations become more proficient at customizing the online experience, increasing the level of stewardship, and creating a stronger relationship with their supporters.

Five Steps to Successful Online Donor Renewal Campaigns

There are five steps necessary to building a successful online renewal campaign. These five steps are illustrated in Figure 8.2.

Assemble the Lists of Previous Donors The first step in preparing for an online renewal program is to collect lists of current and previous donors in your database management system or fundraising software package.

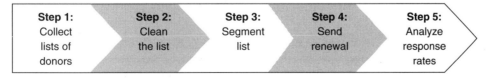

Figure 8.2. Steps Toward Successful Online Renewal.

Your database should include as much detail about prior giving patterns as possible, including average and cumulative donation size; time since last solicitation and time since last donation; age, profession, or other demographic information on the donor; and, of course, whether or not they have e-mail addresses.

Merge and Clean the List Perhaps the most important step in the renewal process, often overlooked, is to "clean" the list. The process for a fundraising campaign includes making sure that the list is current, accurate, has no duplicates, and is not soliciting anyone who has asked not to be solicited. By definition, a clean list will increase the response rate. The U.S. Postal Service's National Change of Address (NCOA) System [www.nationalchangeofaddress.com] and list service bureaus will help clean mailing lists.

While electronically cleaning a list, it's also possible to append demographic information (specific to the individual or household, not the zip code or neighborhood) that will help make every campaign's response rate higher than the last. The types of data that can be purchased and appended to fundraising lists include household income, whether donors own or rent their homes, and what type cars they own. With this additional information, the organization can continually refine and target renewal efforts, resulting in increased response rates. In direct mail, such refinements are beyond the means of most nonprofits; with online communications, they become far more practical. However, many fundraisers feel that such practices violate privacy and pose ethical issues. If you resolve to proceed anyway, Donnelley Marketing [www.donnelleymarketing.com] and InfoUSA [www.infousa.com] can assist you with these efforts.

Some companies are offering ways to append e-mail addresses to current donor files. Currently, the rate of success is much lower than with postal addresses—but "hit rates" should rise over time. There is some controversy about this practice because it precludes the donor "opting in" to receive e-mail, but some fundraisers regard it as fully legitimate when the names involved are those of an organization's prior donors. In any case, using this technique with prospects is not advisable and is not regarded as ethical either by fundraisers or by rank-and-file Netizens: it's called "spamming."

Acxiom [www.acxiom.com] and EContacts [www.econtacts.com] currently offer this service.

Keep in mind that there are only two reasons to feel entirely comfortable using someone's e-mail address. Either (1) they have opted in to the e-mail list you are using (see Resource A), or (2) they have a prior relationship with your organization and you give them the opportunity to opt out of any future e-mail communication.

Segment the List One of the most powerful tools in renewal campaigns is to target donors with personalized messages that reflect their individual giving history or preferences. For example, the list can be segmented by the length of time since the donor's last donation. For someone who has donated recently, the solicitation might include the following phrase: "Thank you for your recent donation." Failure to include this phrase in a renewal campaign for recent donors will most certainly insult the donor. But lapsed donors may smile at such a reference. Instead, for someone who has not donated in over a year, the solicitation might include the following phrase: "We sincerely appreciate your donation last year [or merge in the actual date]. To accomplish our organization's goals, we rely on regular donations from individuals such as you."

In direct mail—for all but a relatively few well-heeled nonprofits—this level of segmentation isn't always practical. It costs too much. Online, however, the costs will drop.

There are many other characteristics by which the donor list can be segmented, such as the issue or event that prompted the last gifts, the frequency of gifts, or the amount of the highest previous gift.

Send the Renewal Online renewal fundraising campaigns can use the Internet via several methods:

- Organizations can send traditional direct mail to the donor and give them the option to donate online as a convenience. Although this method does not save money in direct mail printing and postage, it serves the purpose of making an appropriate ask and inviting donors to use the Internet to make their gifts. This is a good way to introduce donors slowly to online fundraising, while providing the opportunity to collect e-mail addresses for future communication.

- The organization can send e-mail messages to donors inviting them to give online. This method would realize the greatest cost savings.

- The organization can use e-mail and direct mail (and perhaps the telephone as well) in a sequenced approach to the donor, in the same way that traditional fundraising might involve a letter followed by a phone call, or vice-versa (Exhibit 8.1).

Several donor management systems are now integrating e-mail campaign support into their software and ASP offerings. Blackbaud's RE:NetSolutions [www.blackbaud.com] and Chariteam.com offer organizations the opportunity to send HTML or plain-text e-mail messages.

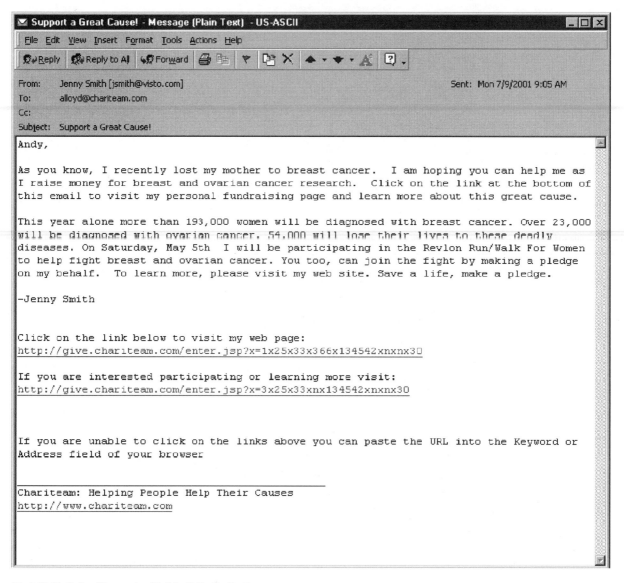

Exhibit 8.1. Sample E-Mail Solicitation.

This integrated system allows organizations to import lists of members and donors from existing databases and compose e-mail messages targeted to specific groups within the list. After the message is sent, the built-in reporting engine allows the organization to track the success of the campaign.

As we went to press, other companies offering these services included

| 123Signup | www.123signup.com |
| 3rdSector | www.3rdsector.net |

Convio	www.convio.com
DonorMax	www.thedatabank.com
eTapestry	www.etapestry.com
Kintera	www.kintera.com
LocalVoice	www.localvoice.com
Social Ecology	www.socialecology.com

In using these services, organizations are encouraged to pay close attention to the company's privacy policy and be certain the ownership of the data is retained by the nonprofit.

It's not necessary to use an integrated system (although it is a good idea); e-mail renewal can be conducted using current database and e-mail systems. As volume grows, a more comprehensive and robust system is advisable.

Analyze Response Rates Finally, as with any fundraising campaign, it is important to analyze response rates. Most of the ASPs and PC-based fundraising packages referred to above provide for analysis of response rate statistics. In addition, organizations can create their own summary reports in simple database or spreadsheet programs. Generally, to analyze the success of a campaign, data should be reviewed for each of the various e-mail segments. Other variables should be considered for analysis, such as geography, time since last donation, and demographics. With this additional information, the organization should begin an effort continually to refine mailings based on what is learned to be successful and what does not meet expectations.

A Final Word

Renewing donors online should become both efficient and effective. However, since many donors are just now beginning to consider online giving, conversion to this highly targeted and cost-efficient medium may take a few more years. Nonetheless, use of the Internet will allow organizations to begin building the base of support and coordinating their online appeals with fundraising efforts conducted through traditional media, and that, eventually, will yield success in online renewals.

E-Mail Campaigns and E-Newsletters

E-mail is inexpensive, easy to track, and very often the preferred mode of communication for some of the people nonprofits are trying to reach: busy professionals with money. E-mail newsletters, in particular, boast a very high rate of return on marketing and cultivation dollars invested. There are four keys to starting and managing a successful e-mail campaign: (1) content, (2) community, (3) relationship building, and (4) giving.

AFTER LISTENING to an hour-long pitch at a recent sales meeting involving three separate vendors and people from several of his own divisions, the executive director leaned back in his chair and huffed: "Isn't this Internet thing just about over?"

I couldn't blame him a lick.

For years, he'd heard the promises of dozens of wired staff members and start-up companies big and small who promised that very soon the Internet would transform the way he conducted his fundraising and development. And yet every year at budget time, he looked at the dollars going out for Internet development and the dollars coming in online, and those promises rang in his ears. His frustration was understandable, and yet the evidence shows that

- Internet use among his donor base is growing rapidly. Nonprofit organizations starting e-mail and e-newsletter efforts as part of their Internet strategy are benefiting from the billions of dollars that have poured into profitless dot-com companies over the last few years by venture capitalists. While many companies have failed and many others have succeeded, they have created in their wake effective tools and efficient strategies borne from many failures and successes.

- Nonprofits can now benefit from the expensive mistakes made by others. Unlike some for-profit companies, nonprofits cannot afford to spend money on experiments in technology. Their investment in the Internet must be cost-effective and have a relatively short path to financial success. After years of trial and error, e-mail campaigns and e-newsletters are ready to offer cost-effective and efficient methods for online fundraising success.

Banner Ads

It's lucky that most nonprofits have missed the hype surrounding banner ads—those ubiquitous blinking rectangles and squares on nearly every Web site.

Banner ads do work, but their effectiveness is limited, especially as the Net-surfing public has learned to ignore them. Nowadays, the accepted *click-through rate*—the percentage of people who see the banner who actually click on it—hovers around 0.5 percent and often below.

The current conventional wisdom holds that Web banner advertising only works as part of a well-integrated campaign, as a small digital reminder of a brand or a buying opportunity.

E-Mail

The utility of e-mail advertising has risen dramatically. And that's wonderful news for nonprofit fundraisers.

E-mail newsletters boast a very high rate of return on marketing and cultivation dollars invested.

A recent Forrester Research [www.forrester.com] study found that e-mail advertising has a high interactivity appeal with the reader and that click-through rates to advertisers' Web sites range from 10 to 22 percent, with a quarter of those who click through actually making a purchase or taking the recommended action.

That means that e-mail readers act on what they read. Sending out direct mail to supporters may cost fifty cents or a dollar each, whereas a targeted e-mail message costs around five cents. (This is not a hard and fast cost standard, but a general range.)

In the for-profit world, e-mail-marketing budgets are growing rapidly. Forrester Research surveyed fifty corporate marketers and found that on average, they planned to triple their e-mail spending in the next three years. The time has come for nonprofit organizations to benefit from this surge in e-mail marketing success. (See Resource F.)

"It's the most measurable marketing vehicle of all time," William Park, the chief executive of marketing firm Digital Impact, told the *New*

York Times ("Marketers Turn to E-mail Experts," August 21, 2000). Response rates are more quickly and accurately measured than in other media. This combination of price and response makes e-mail, particularly e-mail newsletters, very attractive to nonprofits.

Frank Stone, vice president of marketing at the Please Touch Museum in Philadelphia, says "We think electronic communication is an effective and timely way to keep people informed about special events and promotions, and to provide us with valuable feedback."

Four Keys to Success

E-mail campaigns are vital to driving traffic to an organization's Web site, increasing the opportunity for personalized stewardship, and soliciting funds online. There are four keys to starting and managing a successful e-mail campaign. (See Figure 9.1.)

Promote Web Site Content Your organization probably has a lot of written material available in-house: articles, essays, lists, manuals, service guides, annual reports. You may also have either on staff or within

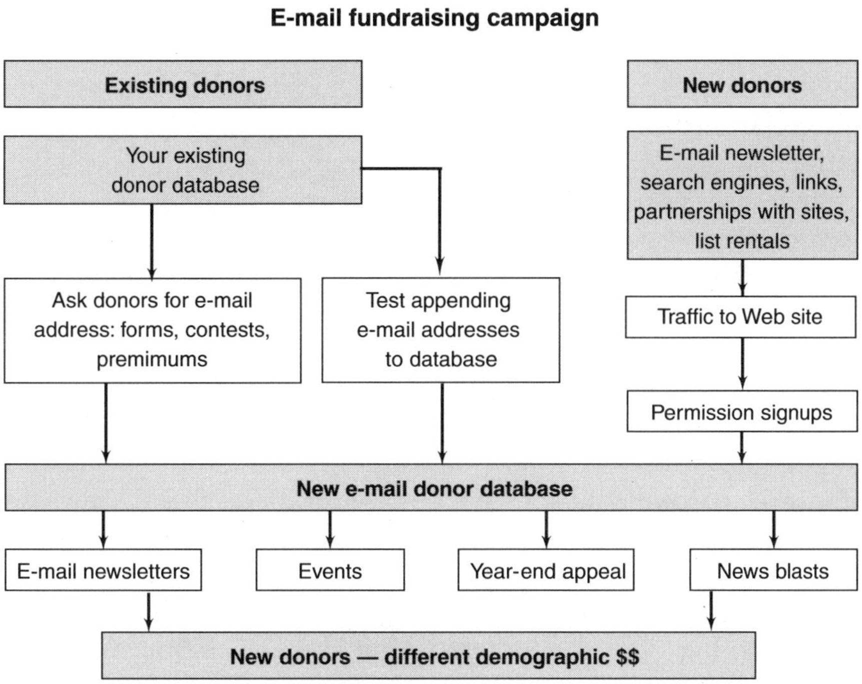

E-mail fundraising campaign

Figure 9.1. Flow of Information in a Successful E-Mail Campaign.

Source: Changingourworld.com.

earshot a number of experts in your field. It's important that you make this information and these connections available through your Web site. But if no one visits the site, no one will read the material. Getting the content out there in front of users in an active manner is an important element of an effective strategy to exploit the potential of online communications.

For example, a health care clinic would have a staff of doctors, health care experts, and professionals as volunteers, and each may have contributed regularly to newsletters, pamphlets, and handouts on various health care issues. It would be easy to leverage that content on, say, a monthly basis by launching a regular e-mail newsletter to the organization's users that feeds them content in a handy, easily digestible format.

Build Community Your interactive toolbox needs to include an effective Web site. But adding a well-written, regular e-mail newsletter to your online communications program will help create a sense of online community far more readily than any stand-alone Web site. E-mail newsletters make a difference and often prompt readers to respond. Most of the time, you won't need statistics about the traffic on your site to see whether your e-mail newsletter is working; the e-mail in-box will tell the tale.

Keep in mind, though, that these new "community members" who respond to your e-newsletter will demand quick response. Be sure you have a plan to answer each and every e-mail the newsletter generates. By answering promptly and competently, you'll let your community of supporters know that you're willing to have two-way relationships with them.

Build Relationships Interaction with those in your online community, over time, will yield results. Repeat communication, over time, will produce the maximum results. Think of your e-mail newsletter as a valuable community service, but also think of it as an inexpensive, highly targeted cultivation program.

Take, for example, the Institute for Nonprofit Management and Southwest Philanthropy at Arizona State University. The Institute sends its e-newsletter weekly to a thousand people around the state. Recently, it polled them on the newsletter's reach and effectiveness and got some interesting results.

Fully 91 percent said that the newsletter made them "much more aware of the Arizona nonprofit community," and 77 percent said they forwarded the newsletter to colleagues.

Promote Giving As any good fundraiser knows, building and enhancing your relationship with your donors means they'll be much more likely to increase their giving. As your organization becomes a trusted information source via your e-newsletter, you'll begin to earn the opportunity to ask for your readers' support.

Changingourworld.com manages Internet campaigns for nonprofit clients. In each campaign we include a direct link to a client's giving page and urge readers to help out.

The Twelfth Annual Radiothon successfully built upon WFAN's prior success using these four key elements and raised more than $127,000 online, a 185 percent increase from the prior year. And the station successfully compiled donor e-mail data for future communications, which will provide stewardship reports and prepare its donors for next year's campaign.

For many nonprofits, any step into the realm of ePhilanthropy is its first step and a sign that its circle of supporters is widening. Nonprofit organizations need to think long-term, just as they would with any other fundraising strategy. You need to discipline yourself to think of the effort as *cultivation first, direct solicitation second.*

Lessons Learned

An e-mail newsletter is just one tool you can use if you're serious about finding new donors online and increasing your pool of warm prospects. The idea behind an e-mail campaign is fairly simple: Use the best technology available and combine it with the expertise of your in-house fundraising and philanthropy professionals or your consultants.

Although e-mail campaigns are relatively new, some important lessons have been learned:

- Draw supporters to an online giving page that allows them to make gifts via credit card or pledges.
- Make sure the technology is secure and robust, but you don't have to worry about all the details if you've set up the system correctly: Gifts will automatically be deposited into your merchant bank account.
- Thank supporters via e-mail.
- Secure permission to send supporters more information in the future and then include them in your donor and prospect database. (See Resource A.)
- Create custom e-mail newsletters with both content and links to giving pages on your Web site.
- Use direct mail to obtain permission to send e-mail in the future. (This is generally known as *opt in.*)

Finding and Using E-Mail Addresses

The techniques I've discussed so far work well if you already have an e-mail list, but what if you don't? What if you have e-mail addresses for only 5 or 10 percent (or fewer) of your donors or members—a condition that's common among nonprofits these days? Since e-mail addresses won't miraculously materialize in your database, and appending won't find many–even if you are willing to try it—you'll need to pursue a conscious course of list-building.

Building Your E-Mail List

Surveys conducted by nonprofits frequently find that 50 percent or more of an organization's donors or members use e-mail every day. But it doesn't necessarily follow that these donors will jump at the first opportunity to supply their e-mail addresses when you simply provide a line for that purpose on a gift coupon or renewal form. Donors typically need to be encouraged to do so. Among the more commonly employed means to attract e-mail addresses from donors are the following:

- Offer a free electronic newsletter at every opportunity—in newsletters, direct mail, at special events, and in the course of telephone appeals

- Feature your "free e-news" prominently on the home page of your Web site

- Offer e-mail "action alerts" or bulletins that provide donors opportunities to act on their beliefs

- Offer online giving options on response forms in your direct mail appeals

- Offer modest prizes (such as a $100 gift certificate for amazon.com) for entries in a "drawing" requiring only an entrant's e-mail address

- Offer discounts on membership dues or attendance at events for donors completing transactions online

When you ask for their e-mail addresses, explain to your donors why you need them: to achieve your mission, to get urgent information in their hands, to save money, to save paper and trees. Advocacy groups can sometimes explain, "With your e-mail address, we can contact you instantly when you need to contact your member of Congress about legislation that would . . ."

Persistence pays. Over time, dogged use of these techniques will build your e-mail list—like drip irrigation, one name at a time.

There's another, more controversial e-mail list-building technique available: the *e-mail append*. In this method, a nonprofit contracts with a vendor to match its existing off-line donor database against other databases, obtaining e-mail addresses in the process. While vendors can often find addresses for half of business customers, they typically get about a 10 percent match rate for individuals with home, not business, addresses. However, many fundraisers question whether this practice is ethical; it is decidedly *not* ethical in the case of names *not* already on an organization's donor database.

Append vendors normally send a message to the donors for whom they find e-mail addresses, inviting donors to "opt out" of receiving any further e-mails. Those who do *not* write back to opt out are added to your e-mail list.

Two companies currently offering this service are

EContacts	www.econtacts.com
Acxiom	www.acxiom.com

Most important, consider your online fundraising strategy as part of your overall development program and integrate them. (See Resource B.) Make sure your message is consistent and that the technology all works—Web, e-mail, and donor acknowledgment alike.

Whether you call them e-campaigns or just online fundraising campaigns, follow the fundraising rules that work off-line: Treat your supporters well, make a convincing case, and recognize them for their contribution.

Building Trust

Ethics are one of the keys to successful long-term resource development. Establish an ethics policy at the outset. If you hope to gain and keep the trust of your online supporters, follow these rules:

Gain Permission Debates over online privacy and spamming—sending unsolicited e-mail—are raging in statehouses across the land. Legislators all over are now writing regulations about the use of information compiled from online users. (See Chapter Six.) The nonprofit world has a huge stake in this policy battle: Charitable organizations that get wide latitude offline—with telephone calls during dinner, mail solicitations, and door-to-door fundraising—are not likely to fare as well online.

By gaining permission over time, you'll be ensuring that only the best, most motivated supporters are in your cultivation database. This will not only help you maximize the fundraising results of e-mail campaigns but also preserve your organization's reputation.

Answer Every E-Mail If you're sending out messages, distributing information, and asking for information, you owe it to your readers to follow up when they respond. The blend of ethical and business reasons for this makes it a no-brainer. Readers want to know that your organization is reachable. A good, two-way flow of e-mail can make that happen.

Let Them Call You Post a contact telephone number on your Web site, especially when you conduct online campaigns. If an ASP or consulting firm is managing your e-mail campaign, post two contacts on every giving page: the outside firm and the key development contact in your organization. Donors considering a gift should have the right to call you.

Be Brief E-mail newsletters that merely send users back to a Web site for the actual information are boring. That's asking readers to do too much. The e-mail itself is a perfectly good medium for publishing the information. When you place most of the content in the main body of an e-newsletter, your readers are more likely to forward it to other people, and thus increase your reach and your response.

Don't Sweat the Technology Unless you have a large in-house information technology (IT) department, it doesn't make sense for you to build the online architecture for your e-mail campaigns. There are several companies that specialize in running e-mail lists, handling subscriptions, unsubscriptions, and bad addresses. Currently, those companies include the following:

MessageMedia	www.messagemedia.com
ClickAction	www.clickaction.com
GetActive Software	www.getactive.com
Sparklist	www.sparklist.com

At press time, the companies that integrate e-mail campaigns and donation processing included

123Signup	www.123signup.com
LocalVoice	www.localvoice.com
3rdSector	www.3rdsector.net
Blackbaud	www.blackbaud.com
Convio	www.convio.com
DonorMax	www.thedatabank.com
eTapestry	www.etapestry.com

If you're running a list of fewer than five hundred people, you may wish to use one of the free Web-based e-mailing programs, such as

Yahoo! Groups	www.groups.yahoo.com
Topica	www.topica.com
FreeLists	www.freelists.org

With a list of more than five hundred names, it makes sense to outsource. Your staff time is best spent on making sure the content is as good as it can be and on responding to e-mail messages from your supporters.

Style Counts Take the extra time to create a simple, straightforward format. Be sure you include all the following elements in your e-newsletter: title, introduction, table of contents, articles, copyright notice.

Stick to that style month after month. Readers react favorably to a predictable format.

Making It Fun

Finally, have fun with your online communications. Don't be afraid to let a little "attitude" sneak into the copy from time to time. After all, the best-paid newspaper writers are columnists; readers identify with the personal approach. Respond to readers, and invite experts to contribute guest pieces. Don't shy away from all controversy, but take pains to portray each side fairly.

E-mail campaigns and e-newsletters will become some of the best cultivation tools you can find. They'll help you increase awareness among your supporters—and, over time, they'll lead to greater fundraising success.

ALETA JEFFRESS | PHIL RICHMOND

Managing Special Events Online

One of the more dramatic ways the Internet can cut costs, save time, and increase the efficiency of nonprofit relationship building is in organizing special events online. Online event management tools enable nonprofits to work smarter and involve more people more easily. With software and services available from a number of application service providers (ASPs)—including everything from sending event invitations via e-mail to reporting the profitability of the event—nonprofits can organize the details of volunteer management, maintain income and expense records, and provide high-quality registration and donor relations service. Online event management can empower everyone involved while increasing both attendance and depth of participation.

SPECIAL EVENTS play a critical role in fundraising for many nonprofit organizations. They may be organized to raise significant net revenue, increase an organization's visibility, provide high-profile volunteer roles for supporters, involve a broader public in the organization's work, or some combination of these purposes. But special events are typically labor-intensive, and there's no getting around that they impose a long list of challenges on a nonprofit organization (or a budgetary burden, when outside event managers are hired).

Golf tournaments, black-tie galas, 5K runs, and charity auctions are only a few examples of the many ways nonprofits use special events to raise money. Managing any one of these events can be a major challenge to the typical understaffed nonprofit.

Attention to Details

Managing any special event requires mastering a myriad of details. Runs, walks, biking events, and jump rope-a-thons are all pledge-based; donors commit to contributing varying amounts of money once someone else meets a certain goal. By contrast, tickets for galas or golf tournaments might be priced at one of several levels and include purchase of a table or of single tickets. Special events are labor-intensive, both in the planning stage and as the event unfolds. Many events require managing an army of volunteers to monitor the course, check in participants, pass out prizes, and run concession booths. Accurately tracking income and controlling expenses can spell the difference between success and failure. Those who give, pledge, or attend events in person need to be added to the organization's prospect list for promotion via direct mail, telephone, or e-mail.

All these details are crucial. After all, your goal in organizing a special event is to provide your donors with a great experience and enhance their relationships with your organization. Because donors have high expectations and prefer you communicate with them on their own schedule, these details are tailor-made for Internet-based tools.

Six Categories of Event Management

Managing any event encompasses a long list of activities. These activities fall into six categories: planning, marketing, coordinating volunteers, registering participants, reporting, and evaluating.

There are numerous application service providers (ASPs) that can help meet the challenges that emerge in most of these six categories. Some of the providers listed in the categories below provide a wide-ranging suite of services that you may need to pay for. Others may offer just the one or two features you need for a particular event, often at a lower cost than the full-service providers. Among the companies offering such services at press-time are the following:

123Signup	www.123signup.com
Acteva	www.acteva.com
Cariteam	www.chariteam.com
C-vents	www.cvents.com
DAXKO	www.daxko.com
Kintera	www.kintera.com
LocalVoice	www.localvoice.com

MaestroSoft   www.maestrosoft.com

seeUthere   www.seeuthere.com

Signup4U   www.signup4u.com

Planning

When planning a special event there are many questions you'll have to answer. These include

- How much money does the organization hope to raise?
- How much staff and volunteer time is available to work on the event?
- What type of event will work best? (Golf tournament? Gala? Spaghetti feed?)
- Is the competition already identified with that kind of event?
- When should the event be held?

As soon as your plans are firm, post all the pertinent details on your Web site. Those details should include

- What is the event?
- Why is the event being held?
- Where will it be held?
- When will the event be held?
- Who is invited?
- Who's the contact person?
- How much are tickets or suggested donation?

After these details are confirmed the organization is ready to start marketing the event.

Marketing

In marketing your special event, the Internet offers new ways for you to reach potential participants. There are many possibilities.

Start with your own Web site. Posting advance notice of the event there can create early interest. And if you request e-mail addresses and promise follow-up information and details about registration, you can later send e-mail notices and bring many supporters back to your site (Exhibit 10.1).

Event vendors or the cosponsors of your event may allow you to set up links on their Web sites. In this way you can reach participants who

Exhibit 10.1. Example of a Web-Based Registration Form.

may not have been directly involved with your organization in the past and so increase traffic at your site even more.

Ask board members and volunteers to e-mail their employees, family, and friends to circulate information about the event. Include a link to the event page on your Web site. For example, a link from your site might offer information on room availability at a hotel the night your gala is to take place. Such a link might include information about a discounted rate at the hotel and take registrants directly to the hotel's Web site to reserve a room. Both you and the hotel will benefit from such an arrangement.

As an event marketing tool, e-mail is extremely attractive, so contact everyone who has "opted in" to your e-mail list. But be sure to provide everyone you contact with the opportunity to "opt out" of future communications. Repeated, unwanted e-mail is not only unethical but could easily damage your organization's reputation. Keep in mind, too, that you can't promote your event online unless you've already collected e-mail addresses of people who might be interested.

In addition to the ASPs cited above, the following online services now offer online invitation and event RSVP services:

Acteva	www.acteva.com
EVite	www.evite.com
InviteDepot	www.invitedepot.com
PleaseRSVP	www.pleasersvp.com
seeUthere	express.seeuthere.com
Sendomatic	www.sendomatic.com/fundraising.html

Coordinating Volunteers

Sophisticated event management systems allow event coordinators to create task lists, not only for themselves but for many other people (staff or volunteers) as well. By reviewing reports posted in an online database, a coordinator can then track progress made by each volunteer or staff member, set follow-up dates, and report on completed tasks. At the same time, volunteers, staff members, or vendors involved in the event might access the same database (or portions of it) to view their current responsibilities and update their records when they complete their tasks.

Your event coordinator can use e-mail to notify volunteers of the tasks they've been assigned, send notices of upcoming meetings, remind volunteers of imminent deadlines, send appreciation for completed tasks, and offer counsel as needed. Notices can be sent either automatically to all volunteers or individually to a few.

Through an online message board, anyone involved with the event might post questions or answers or place "memos" or notices regarding the event overall.

If the event involves people at different locations, the event coordinator can schedule virtual meetings. Online collaboration tools allow staff and volunteers to share applications and presentations via the Internet that incorporate real-time video conferencing or voice conferencing.

Among the online services now offering help with volunteer coordination and communication are the following:

AOL Groups	http://groups.aol.com
BlueStep	www.bluestep.net
DoTheGood	http://dothegood.com
internet4associations	www.internet4associations.com
Yahoo! Groups	http://groups.yahoo.com

Registering Participants

Web-based special event registration provides a new measure of ease for event attendees. In addition to eliminating paper forms, Internet registration can facilitate collaboration among registrants by making it easier for attendees to invite family and friends to take part in the event.

For event planners, online registration offers an easy way to solicit, collect, and view registrations; a convenient means to communicate with registrants; a way to coordinate registrants; and the ability to move data to donor databases and accounting packages. These four advantages will save event organizers a tremendous amount of work and time.

One major factor in determining whether an event will succeed or not is how the organization manages data. There are several packages and services available to track event information, collect credit card information, and provide up-to-the-minute reporting. (Many of these services are listed earlier in this chapter. For an updated list, go to [www.nonprofitmatrix.com].)

When considering how information should be managed, the organization should ask the following questions:

- How are event and participant data transferred from the Web site to the donor database?

- What are the fees associated with accepting online registration payments?

- Does the software or service allow for electronic funds transfer (EFT) from the participant's to the organization's bank account?

- Can the participants review their individual information, make changes, or be recognized online when registering for subsequent events?

- Can participants review their fundraising (pledge) progress if the event is a walk, run, and so forth?

- Can the registration page be customized? By whom—the provider or the organization itself?

- Is reporting done online or must information be downloaded? Is the information real-time or updated in a batch fashion?

The efficiency and economies of processing registration fees online are one of the biggest advantages of online event registration. (Collecting funds online also eliminates worry about when attendees might pay.) But not everyone is comfortable transacting business or making gifts online. As you begin offering online registration, continue to keep alternative options available, such as by allowing registration by telephone or by downloading and printing a form to be mailed.

Online registration programs can help prepare nametags and seating assignments. Since registrants themselves fill out the form online, they can ensure that their names are correctly spelled and their preferences properly stated. Such details can help make the event a big success.

As each supporter registers online, the software package can create a unique log-in ID and password that will allow the participant to return to the event, via the Web site, and make changes to her or his preferences, mailing address, e-mail address, or the number attending the event. This cuts down on staff time in tracking down last-minute changes.

Reporting

With coordinators updating event information, participants and attendees registering, and options changing, one major advantage of online special event management is that all this information is collected in one place and is instantly accessible online.

Reports can now be generated in real time, including monies coming in and monies being spent (such as payments to vendors). Online and traditional software packages may also track expected expenses and compare it to the event budget; this information can then be exported to an accounting package. Reports for the number of registrants, who has paid and who hasn't, and who is going to volunteer can all be accessed twenty-four hours a day, seven days a week. There is no need to go back to the office to generate this report; anywhere you have Internet access you can get the information you need (Exhibit 10.2).

Choose a software or service provider very carefully. Make sure you obtain a contract that follows recognized ethical principles (see Resource A).

Training services, previously limited to costly on-site training, may now be handled via the Internet as well. This training can be done with Internet access for the product and a phone connection for the audio portion. Make sure you know whether training is provided with your initial purchase or contract or whether there is an additional charge.

The time to go "live" will depend both on the vendor and on how complex your event may be. Plan ahead. The more time you want to allow potential participants to register, the further ahead you'll need to organize your online services.

Evaluating

The final step in planning a special event is evaluation. A participant survey form should be e-mailed out within a week of the event. There are several online survey tools available. These now include

iNetSurvey	www.inetsurvey.com
Sparklit	www.sparklit.com
Quask	www.quask.com
Votations	www.votations.com
Zoomerang	www.zoomerang.com

As soon after the event as possible, the planning committee should gather to critique the event and prepare a written summary of their findings. If the evaluation is favorable, and the organization decides to hold the event again, then the report, along with copies of the advertising, the invitations, and any other information that will be useful for next year's

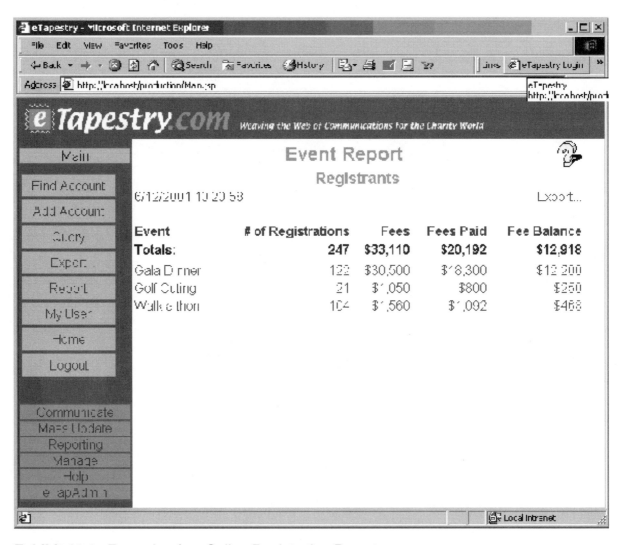

Exhibit 10.2. Example of an Online Registration Report.

planning committee, needs to be carefully and securely filed in a place where next year's event committee or coordinator can easily find it. If next year's event organizers learn from this year's, then the same number of people working the same amount of time will raise more and more money every year.

Specialty Events

In addition to basic event management, there are several online services that provide specialized event modules catering to almost any type of event an organization may want to offer.

Auctions

Many vendors handle both silent and live auctions. They may also offer an accounting module to help track income and expenses. Many of them produce invitations, thank-you letters, forms, and catalogs. Current examples of companies that offer such services include

BenefitEvents	www.benefitevents.com
eBay Auctions	pages.ebay.com/charity
MaestroSoft	www.maestrosoft.com
MissionFish	www.missionfish.com
WebCharity	www.Webcharity.com

Golf Outings

These systems enable participants to register online. Sponsorship information can be assigned for logos, promotional messages, and signage. Printed material for scorecards, golf carts, tees, and so forth can be generated from within the program. And tee times, player status, scoring, and post-tournament accounting can be accomplished in real time. Vendors now offering these services include the following:

Kintera	www.kintera.com
MaestroSoft	www.maestrosoft.com

Banquets and Galas

An ASP can provide you with a database for guest registration, RSVPs, table assignments, and seating arrangements. Registrations are real-time and instantly shown in status reports up to the day of the event. These programs also generate printed items such as invitations, name badges, place cards, menus, and awards. Many systems include utilities for budgeting and the capability to generate contracts for vendors. Current examples include

Convio	www.convio.com
Kintera	www.kintera.com
LocalVoice	www.localvoice.com
MaestroSoft	www.maestrosoft.com
seeUthere	http://express.seeuthere.com

Conclusion

Online event management tools enable nonprofits to work smarter and involve more people more easily than ever before. Plans can be made, meetings can be held, marketing can be done, and money can be raised starting from a single Web site. But the crucial point is this: Web sites afford nonprofits the ability to build stronger relationships with everyone involved in a special event in ways that are important to all of them individually. The donor can give, the volunteer can participate, and the nonprofit can manage. The organization's fundraising base becomes even more solid. And everyone wins.

Donor-Advised Funds Online

Donor-advised funds (DAFs) are changing the landscape of philan-thropic giving. Although DAFs aren't yet widely recognized by most people, they're gaining popularity among financial service companies, lawyers, accountants, estate planners, and nonprofit organizations because they provide a more efficient and strategic way to give. The primary method of DAF promotion and management is via the Inter-net. Organizations have successfully integrated both educational infor-mation and online DAF management to meet the growing interest on the part of donors in actively managing their charitable funds.

TRUE STORY: In the summer of 1998 I explained donor-advised funds to a friend. I explained that few people have heard of them but soon everyone will. Later that year, my friend tried to open a donor-advised fund (DAF) account but was amazed to find that no one—not his bro-ker, his lawyer, or his accountant—knew anything about them. After hunting around, he finally found a solution and made a donation to fund the account.

A year later, I spoke to him again and he said, "You know, I've already made three grants, and I haven't touched any principal yet. Even better, my kids have gotten involved. My six year-old is 'sub-advising' a grant to the zoo, and he loves it."

My friend went on to find that the best benefit of a DAF was that it completely changed the way he thought about giving. Instead of scram-bling to write checks before the end of the year, he has begun to think strategically about his giving: considering the long term, planning ways to make a bigger impact, and involving his family.

He has become a philanthropist.

What Is a Donor-Advised Fund?

A donor-advised fund is a charitable asset account that an individuals (or families) establish with a nonprofit organization and from which they can issue grants to other public charities. The DAF is owned and controlled by the nonprofit organization that offers it, and donors may only "advise" on the disposition of, not officially grant, assets they've donated.

The Internet is the primary method to market and manage DAFs. Successful organizations are integrating both educational opportunities and online management tools into their Web sites to meet the growing interest on the part of donors in actively managing their charitable support.

Donors can advise on the investment strategy for their DAF accounts, based on the choices offered. Typically, there are at least three:

- The *income* strategy generates income with little or no capital gains.
- The *growth and income* strategy is typically a fifty-fifty split between equities and cash and generates both income and capital gains.
- The *growth* strategy is typically an eighty-twenty split between equities and cash and generates mostly capital gains, with modest income.

Donors receive tax deductions only for their donations, not for growth (if any) in the value of their DAFs.

Donor-Advised Funds Versus Private Foundations

Donor-advised funds have been referred to as the "poor man's foundation," but today, many donors view DAFs as superior to private foundations. Table 11.1 summarizes the differences between the two from the perspective of the *individual donor.*

How Does a Donor-Advised Fund Work?

In order to run a donor-advised fund, the nonprofit offering the DAF must provide proof of the following:

- A 501(c)(3) legal structure.
- Registration to accept contributions in all fifty states, or in fewer states if that's the DAF's mission.
- DAF status recognized by the IRS. Such status starts as provisional, which is lifted after five years of compliant operations.

Table 11.1. Differences Between Donor-Advised Funds and Private Foundations.

	Donor-Advised Fund	Private Foundation
Start-up costs	None	Several thousand dollars (often more)
Federal annual excise tax	None	Up to 2%
Annual tax reporting	None (1)	State and Federal required
Annual required distribution	None (2)	5% of total assets
Anonymous giving possible	Yes	No
Annual expenses	Low	Substantial to High
Record keeping responsibility	None (DAFs Board responsible)	Full responsibility
Level of IRS regulation	Low	High
Tax deduction for Cash	50% of AGI (3)	30% of AGI (3)
Tax deduction for publicly traded securities	30% of AGI (3)	20% of AGI (3)
Tax deduction for restricted stock and real estate	T30% of AGI (3)	20% of AGI (3)
Donation of property other than securities (real estate, art, etc.)	Not usually (some Funds allow)	Yes, within IRS guidelines
Can issue grants to qualified public charities	Yes	Yes
Family involvement: multiple and successor advisors	Yes	Yes
Family employment	No	Yes, within IRS guidelines
Personal liability	None (DAFs Board is liable)	Yes, as well as the Foundation's Board
Typical minimum amount required to open	$10,000 to $50,000	$500,000 to $2 million
Can it be named?	Yes (4)	Yes

1 The tax reporting is handled by the nonprofit that offers the DAF, not the donor.

2 Some nonprofits that offer DAFs are required to distribute 5 percent of their assets annually; some are not.

3 Adjusted Gross Income.

4 For instance, "The Jan & Chris Lee Family Fund."

- Fiduciary oversight for all DAF activities, including responsibility for the investment vehicles chosen to house the DAF's assets.

- Gift transfer and liquidation policies, procedures, and operations. Most often the donations are in the form of appreciated stock and mutual fund shares.

- Grant administration. Timely verification, review, and release of grants to qualified public charities.
- Tax filing. Annual IRS form 990 filing and audit management.
- Philanthropic guidance offered to donors when they make grant requests. The amount of guidance offered is determined by the nonprofit that offers the DAF and differs widely from one nonprofit to another.

Costs of Running a Donor-Advised Fund

As you can see in Table 10.1, running a DAF is no simple matter. Once in existence, a DAF incurs a number of fees in order to operate. Typically, as economies of scale are achieved, the relative costs decline.

Asset Management Fee The DAF pays an asset management fee to the money management firm that manages the DAF's investments. Typically, the fee ranges from 1 to 2 percent per year. For instance, a $10,000 DAF account would typically pay between $100 and $200 per year in money management fees. The fee is deducted directly from the DAF's assets rather than being a new charge to, or donation from, the donor.

Charitable Management Fee The nonprofit offering the DAF is paid a fee for the services it provides to run the DAF. Typically this fee is 1 percent per year. The fee is deducted directly from the assets under management in the DAF, just as is the asset management fee.

Additional Fees Some nonprofits charge additional fees for issuing grants beyond a set limit. Typically, the donor will be able to recommend five or ten grants at no cost, but for grants beyond that limit the DAF account is charged a processing fee. The fee varies from nonprofit to nonprofit, but is typically a few dollars per grant. The fee is deducted directly from the DAF's assets.

What Are the Benefits of Offering a DAF?

There are two main benefits to offering a DAF to your members and constituents: (1) it's a source of new funds for you, and (2) it opens up affinity marketing opportunities.

Source of Funds As already mentioned, one source of funds for the sponsoring nonprofit is the charitable management fee. This fee can be substantial, based on the amount under management.

A second, and potentially more lucrative, source of funds is to require that a certain percentage of the donor's giving go to the organization that offers the DAF. Such requirements are written into the DAF contract.

Here are two good examples of offers made by nonprofit organizations that accept DAFs:

- The Harvard Donor-Advised Fund: "You, your spouse, and in some cases, adult children may request at any time that a portion of up to 50 percent of the income and principal of your fund be distributed by Harvard to other charitable organizations. Harvard benefits from the balance of the income and principal of your fund" (quoted from the planned giving section of Harvard's Web site).

- World Vision's Donor-Advised Funds: "As with all of its Donor Advised Fund donors, World Vision asks its Advisor-Managed DAF donors to contribute a minimum of 10 percent of their fund's principal and income to one or more of its humanitarian projects" (quoted from the World Vision Financial Advisors Network Web site; see Exhibit 11.1).

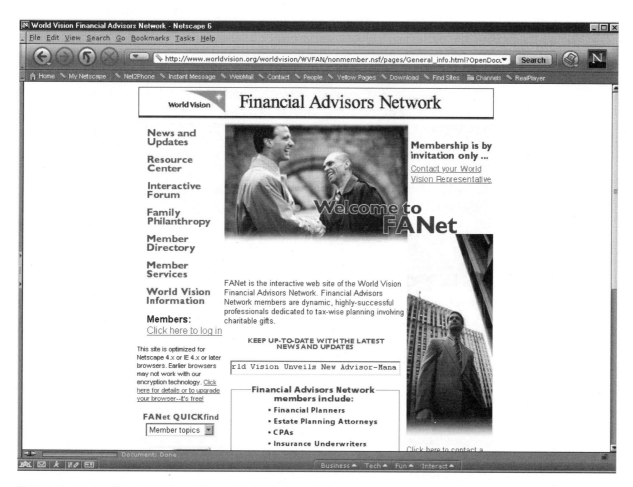

Exhibit 11.1. World Vision Financial Advisors Network.

In these two examples, the amount going to the nonprofit offering the DAF is 50 percent in one case and 10 percent in the other. Other DAFs have different requirements.

Marketing Opportunities Offering a DAF can also be a powerful affinity-marketing vehicle. For instance, when benefactors open a donor-advised fund with Harvard or World Vision, they are demonstrating a high level of interest in the organization. In turn, the organization is given a special opportunity to communicate with the donors about its program and mission. A DAF is a great way to cement the relationship between your organization and your most dedicated benefactors.

Should You Offer a Donor-Advised Fund?

If you are a large organization, with fifty major donors or more, then offering a donor-advised fund is definitely worth considering. If you're a smaller organization, then a DAF is probably too time-consuming and expensive to create and administer *today*.

In any case, you should only offer a DAF if you have enough major donors who view your organization as their most important nonprofit commitment.

Web Site Integration

To implement and operate a DAF is not a trivial matter, but it can become an important tool for your fundraising success and worth all the trouble.

Don't consider offering a DAF until you have established a reliable and involving Web site that attracts repeat visits. You can then offer the DAF and administer it over the Internet as a practical benefit to donors.

Unless your organization is very large, it rarely makes sense to build the online architecture necessary to administer a DAF online. A convenient way to implement a DAF quickly is to contract with a service provider to handle the "back-office" administration and provide the interface for your Web Site. This will free resources and time for your staff to manage the promotions and donor relations for the DAF. Even if you contract with a third party provider, you'll still be fully responsible for the fiscal aspects of the DAF.

The following are examples of companies that currently provide DAF services:

Renaissance	www.reninc.com
The American Gift Fund	www.giftfund.org
The U.S. Charitable Gift Trust	www.charitablegiftfund.org
The National Philanthropic Trust	www.nptrust.org
GivingCapital	www.givingcapital.com

There are some rules, caveats, and fears involved.

Rules

- Get the legal parts right. You will have legal responsibility for the creation of the DAF, its administration, and tax reporting.

- The charity must develop the expertise to accept and process donations of appreciated stock and mutual fund shares *efficiently*, because these shares will be the most common donations to your DAF.

- Launch the DAF only after you've built the necessary infrastructure into your Web site and your staff has been trained on how to help donors use the site to learn about and establish DAFs.

Caveats

- Follow the leaders. Stay informed on best practices for marketing and managing DAFs.

- Talk to your donors. Find out their level of interest, but don't expect your donors to ask for the service. They'll expect that leadership to come from you.

- Be prepared to educate. Today, the DAF is a new concept to virtually all donors regardless of their wealth, age, or giving history. You should be prepared to educate your donors about the DAF, just as you do with other planned giving options.

Fears and Rebuttals

- Funds might go to others instead of you. By definition, any donor may "advise" your fund to issue grants to other organizations. This is one of the key *benefits* you're offering donors.

- Giving may be delayed. Donors with DAFs generally begin to think more long-term, which means their level of giving increases, but distributions are not always immediate. You can set policies for your DAF that give you more control; for instance, requiring that the donor make at least one gift to your organization every three years.

The Donor-Advised Fund Opportunity

As we've already seen, a DAF can be seen as a better option than a private foundation in almost every respect. Most major donors will also be interested in DAFs once they understand what they are and how to open one. A study by Russ Alan Prince found, "Every donor included in the study expressed at least moderate interest in learning more about foundations as a charitable giving strategy" (*Seven Faces of Philanthropy*, 1994, p. 166).

So, what does the DAF opportunity entail?

Tax Planning Advantages A DAF has so many major advantages over a private foundation that inevitably more people will open them.

Strategic Giving Versus Episodic Giving Once people have established DAFs they tend to think more strategically about their giving; they consider long-term consequences and their philanthropic priorities rather than just pulling out their checkbooks when asked. Once you begin thinking strategically, you tend to give more and expect higher impact from your giving.

More People Will Become Major Donors DAFs lower the threshold necessary for donors to make major gifts by means of a vehicle that offers long-term appreciation and successor advising.

Today Today, DAFs are mainly marketed to the wealthy by community foundations and nonprofits related to financial services firms. A few large nonprofits have created their own DAFs, and more will soon. Donors are slowly becoming more aware of DAFs. In many cases they are hearing about DAFs from their financial planners, tax advisors, and brokers.

The Future Over the next few years, media coverage and the marketing efforts of financial services companies will make DAFs widely known. Account minimums should dramatically fall from their level today ($10,000 to $50,000) to between $1,000 and $5,000. If current trends continue, most major donors will have DAF accounts, and many will have more than one. It's possible that smaller nonprofits will form consortiums to spread the cost more widely and allow them to offer DAFs, too.

Resources

Web Sites Several good Web sites provide helpful information for both nonprofits and donors regarding DAFs:

Philadelphia Foundation [www.philafound.org] is a community foundation, founded in 1918, that offers a variety of funds to its donors, including a donor-advised fund. The site provides good information and examples.

World Vision [www.wvfan.org] offers several donor-advised funds and is one of the innovators in their use. The Web site describes its program and serves as a good example.

Harvard [www.haa.harvard.edu/html/contin03.html], like World Vision, is an early adopter of the donor-advised fund and provides good information on its site about its program.

The Planned Giving Design Center [www.pgdc.net] is one of the largest Web sites dedicated to planned giving and a good starting point for information.

Planned Giving Today [www.pgtoday.com] is a newsletter and Web site that offers practical information and resources to the planned giving community.

Nonprofit Charitable Orgs [www.nonprofit.about.com] is an excellent information source about all aspects of running a nonprofit organization, planned giving, online donations, and more.

Search Terms For the latest information, search the Web by using a search engine site. I recommend Dogpile.com, because with it you can search Google, Yahoo, Excite, Lycos, and many more engines, all at once. Here are a few terms to try:

Donor-advised fund (or donor advised)

Planned giving

Community foundation

MARTIN SCHNEIDERMAN

CHAPTER

12

Online Strategies for Foundations and Grantseekers

A growing number of grantmakers are now using the Web to disseminate information about their foundations and solicit grant applications online. The Web can streamline the application process and improve the efficiency and accuracy of data collection. Grantseekers are also turning to the Internet to conduct prospect research and identify potential sources of funding. Online applications are easier to complete and are making it possible for grantmakers to speed the decision-making process.

NOWADAYS, an increasing number of foundations are connected to the Internet and have Web sites that disseminate information about their programs and proposal guidelines. Most of these sites are simple *brochureware*—that is, online versions of their printed materials.

Many foundations are providing downloadable versions of their paper-based grant application forms in word processing format or PDF (Adobe Acrobat Portable Document Format). This has the advantage of making it easier for grantseekers to get printed copies of the most current version of the application form—an especially big help for those applying from overseas, as well as for domestic applicants. But completing these forms is rarely better than using the paper version.

Forward-thinking foundations have started to implement grants management systems that enable grantseekers to complete a Web-based form and submit their proposals online. As of the writing of this chapter, many of the major providers of commercially developed grants management software and services offer this capability (see www.cof.org/foundationnews/0700/technology.html). Whereas some vendors offer fully integrated solutions, others are just stand-alone Web forms with no links to a core grants management system.

Some funders and commercial service providers have designed systems that promote information-sharing and collaboration by inviting nonprofits to use a common online grant application form. Once completed, applications are accessed and reviewed via the Web by multiple funders who can then provide either individual or joint support. This approach is especially useful for community foundations and other grantmaking organizations with a geographic or subject area focus.

Solicitation for Proposals via the Web

Web-based proposals and integrated online systems are still relatively new, and the pioneers in the field have taken different approaches. Figure 12.1 illustrates how a well-conceived and fully automated online system works.

Online systems have many advantages over traditional paper-based application forms. They can collect information from multiple sources and store the current and all historical information in single a database. A seamless link between the online application form and the grants management system enables the automation of many repetitive labor-intensive tasks. Program staff, reviewers, and board members can be

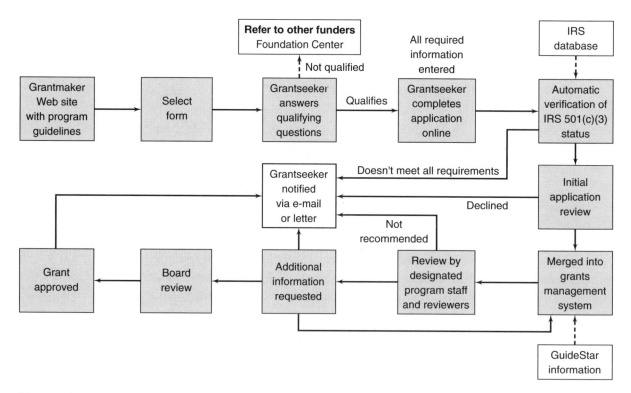

Figure 12.1. The Online Grant Application Process.

provided with secure system access from anywhere at anytime—each with different view and approval rights appropriate to their needs. As a result, the workflow is streamlined and grantmakers have more time to focus on relationship building and making informed decisions.

The best systems start by requiring the grantseeker to review the program guidelines and to then complete a series of qualifying questions. Only those who meet all the requirements should be encouraged or permitted to proceed. If well implemented, this requirement can reduce the time spent writing and reviewing ineligible applications—a major advantage, since many foundations report that over 70 percent of the paper-based applications that they receive don't meet the basic eligibility requirements.

Grantmakers need to collect basic organizational, program, and contact information for all new requests. This is accomplished effectively through the use of a Web form that ensures the completeness of information. Applicants should then be invited to attach and send supplemental files that provide expanded descriptions of their organization's impact and details of the proposed project.

Online systems can be automatically linked to the IRS and Revenue Canada's databases of nonprofit organizations to verify the organization's current status. It's even possible to design dynamic links to GuideStar's online database of over 700,000 nonprofit organizations to gather detailed published information about the nonprofit's mission, programs, financial data, and leaders.

Let's take a closer look at the key capabilities, limitations, and future of these systems from the funder's and the applicant's perspectives. The findings presented in this chapter are the result of feedback compiled in 2000 from over 300 U.S. and Canadian grantseekers and grantmakers.

The Digital Divide

In order to use these online systems, applicants must have Internet access and a minimum level of technological proficiency. But do they?

The Chronicle of Philanthropy reports that many charities are struggling to make effective use of technology (S. Greene, "Astride the Digital Divide," *The Chronicle of Philanthropy*, January ´11, 2001 http://philanthropy.com/free/articles/v13/i06/06000101.htm), even though at the rate that nonprofits are getting online, it won't be long before almost all will have Internet access. In July 2000 Gifts In Kind International conducted a survey of 2,094 U.S. and Canadian nonprofits. They learned that 89 percent of these organizations had Internet access, 87 percent had external e-mail, and 66 percent had their own Web site.

Although access is becoming less of an issue, many nonprofits lack the technological capacities to take full advantage of these powerful new tools. In 2000 the Pew Partnership for Civic Change reported, "Most nonprofit leaders view the new technologies as invaluable tools for their organizations, though with regard to the Internet most of them do not use it very often, except for e-mail" (J. Dugery, C. Hamner, "Coming of Age in the Information Age," University of Richmond, 2000 [www.pew-partnership.org/pubs/coming_of_age/printable.html]).

In February 2000 a poll of the leaders of the fifty-five largest corporate giving programs showed that there was widespread understanding of the issues related to the digital divide. All these companies were committed to accepting proposals and communicating with nonprofits both online and via traditional means to enable the largest possible number of organizations and individuals to express their needs and share their good ideas.

The Search for Grants Online

One of the best places to go online for information and to search for funding sources is the Foundation Center Web site at [www.fdncenter.org]. This site receives an average of over 14,000 user sessions per day. The Center hosts the Directory Online at [www.fconline.fdncenter.org/]. For a monthly fee an organization can obtain unlimited access to the center's searchable database of the largest 10,000 foundations in the United States. The researcher can query by field of interest, type of support, and geographic focus. There are also options to search the 20,000 largest and mid-sized foundations, plus a database of 160,000 grants.

Some community foundations and regional associations host searchable databases of grant information, too.

Benefits for Grantmakers

Some grantmaking organizations can benefit from online applications more than others. Grantmakers who have implemented Web-based applications have identified the following primary benefits. Web-based applications

- Streamline the process and substantially improve efficiency and accuracy of data acquisition and storage

- Enable higher throughput and lower cost of data entry—a particular benefit to funders who receive a high volume of proposals or have seasonal peaks

- Make it possible for staff at remote locations to participate in the review and approval process

- Provide for ease of creating, disseminating, and updating applications forms for different programs (for example, domestic and international)

- Screen out most ineligible proposals via Q&A or branching screens and automatic verification of tax-exempt eligibility

- Provide optional password protection that can restrict access to only solicited proposals

- Capture all required information with file attachments during the application process

- Allow quicker decision making and applicant notification via e-mail

- Provide the grantseeker with selective access to the system to review past funding support and to update the organization's mission statement and contact information

Grantmakers' Concerns

Although the advantages for some funders may be substantial, others are more cautious about using technology in this way. The most common concern that I've heard expressed by grantmakers is that online systems may insulate them from grantseekers. Another worry is that use of online systems will disadvantage applicants with limited Internet proficiency or access.

DaimlerChrysler Fund Vice President Lynn Feldhouse points out that "Philanthropy is based on relationships and we must be careful not to turn the application process into an on-line business transaction. The potential of using the Web is exciting and we're all still learning how to make the best use of this new technology."

Some are worried that they'll receive a flood of new online applications in addition to the ones that they're already processing. But there is little evidence of this happening.

Cost and security are also major concerns that are being addressed by most of the commercial software developers and service providers.

Benefits for Grantseekers

Grantseekers are generally positive about the online grant application process and recognize that the greatest benefits are for the funder. Those that have used the Web to identify a funder and then submitted applications online identify the following benefits to this approach. Online grant applications offer

- Quick and easy access to funders' up-to-date program guidelines and application forms

- No guessing about what information the funder wants and in what format

- Predetermination of eligibility prior to proposal development
- Program-specific applications
- Availability of online help
- An equalizing effect for proposals—especially for smaller organizations
- Referrals and links to other funding organizations and useful references
- A speedy submission process, especially when all prior organizational background information is preentered
- Fast acknowledgement of proposal receipt—a particular benefit for nonprofits in remote locations of the world
- Much faster overall response time

Grantseekers' Concerns

Despite the benefits, a significant number of nonprofit staff that have used first-generation online grant application forms have expressed some reservations. Grantmakers and system developers should listen carefully and address these concerns in their next-generation systems. Funders should invite anonymous feedback about these systems and use this as the basis to make improvements. Here are a few representative comments:

From a Community College grant writer: "In general, I have found that when forms are on the Web, they are in Adobe PDF format, which does not give applicants the ease of filling them out on screen. This is an area where the grantmakers who use forms are not current with the technology or the reality that the toughest part of this job these days seems to be finding a typewriter and someone to fill out paper forms."

From a New England early childhood educator: "I wish that there was a way to print out the whole application in advance so that I could have prepared my response off-line."

From a Western state grantseeker: "By all means give me well thought out guidelines, but I prefer not to be limited to a rigid form or format."

From a consulting grant writer: "It's stifling not to be able to submit supplemental materials as file attachments and to be denied the opportunity to convey our message."

From a Canadian community foundation program officer: "Some large established nonprofits don't like it because it levels the playing field and disadvantages them."

Fourteen Practical Tips for Applying for a Grant Online

Here are some steps to take and things to keep in mind before going online to apply for a grant:

- Upgrade to the latest release version of your browser software, it's free. (If you use Microsoft Explorer, go to [www.microsoft.com/windows/IE]. If you use Netscape, go to [home.netscape.com/download].)

- Download and install a free copy of Adobe Acrobat Reader from [www.adobe.com/products/acrobat/readstep.html].

- Use a PC with a reliable Internet connection.

- Use the Foundation Center's Directory Online at [www.fconline.fdncenter.org/] to identify potential funders.

- Register your organization with GuideStar at [www.guidestar.org/], and be sure to keep your information up-to-date.

- Review grantmaker guidelines very carefully to ensure eligibility. Find out what the organization does and does not fund. If you're not eligible, don't waste your time.

- Determine which application method is best for you, online (if offered) or the traditional off-line method.

- Print out the online application form in advance and prepare all responses off-line. Then log in to the form again to complete it. Cut and paste sections of text that have already been spell checked.

- Follow the directions carefully and answer all questions completely. Get help if you need it.

- Use only simple text. Most online applications won't recognize any formatted text (such as bold, italics, symbols, graphical bullets, scientific notation) or embedded graphics such as logos, pictures, or charts.

- Prepare background and supplemental materials for submission in electronic formats if they can be submitted. It's best to do this using Microsoft Word or Rich Text Format (RTF), which are both supported by all popular word processors. Excel is the most popular spreadsheet format. The Adobe Acrobat PDF file format is well suited for complex documents that contain graphics.

- Scan all attachments for viruses via the latest software and virus signatures before attaching and sending them. Try [www.mcafee.com] or [www.symantec.com].

- Print and save a copy of the completed application and all attachments.

- Provide feedback to funders about your experience using their online systems. Make specific suggestions about how they can be improved. Be constructive and do this separately from your application.

Lessons for Grantmakers: Tips for Successful Grantmaking Online

Grantmakers can learn a lot from the early adopters. Here are some tips for designers of second-generation systems.

- Go beyond brochureware (that is, don't just reproduce already printed materials), make your site more interactive, keep online program guidelines up-to-date, and be clear about what you do and don't fund (Exhibit 12.1).

- Guide grantseekers to other funding sources and resources that can help them.

- Promote and encourage online submissions (Exhibit 12.2) but continue to provide traditional application routes to ensure equal opportunity for all grantseekers.

- Design online applications that work with older versions of browser software. Use a minimum of Java or JavaScript to minimize problems and ensure reliability.

- Implement Q&A or branching screens that prequalify grantseekers. (See http://foundation.verizon.com/06018.html)

- Create separate forms for different programs and make them easy to find and use. (See www.arts.state.va.us/guidelines.htm)

- If you're using downloadable applications, create them by using Adobe Acrobat's forms feature. This permits applicants easily to complete the application by using Adobe's free Acrobat Reader and then return it to you. Check out [www.adobe.com/products/acrobat] for more information.

- Provide detailed online help with clear examples. (See www.wshf.org/apply/online)

- Make it easy for the grantseeker to print a sample online application so that they can prepare all required materials in advance. Make it easy for grantseeker to print and save a copy of the completed application, too.

- Design systems that save an application after each section is completed so that the grantseeker can return and complete the form in stages. This will also prevent everything from being lost in the event of a connection failure.

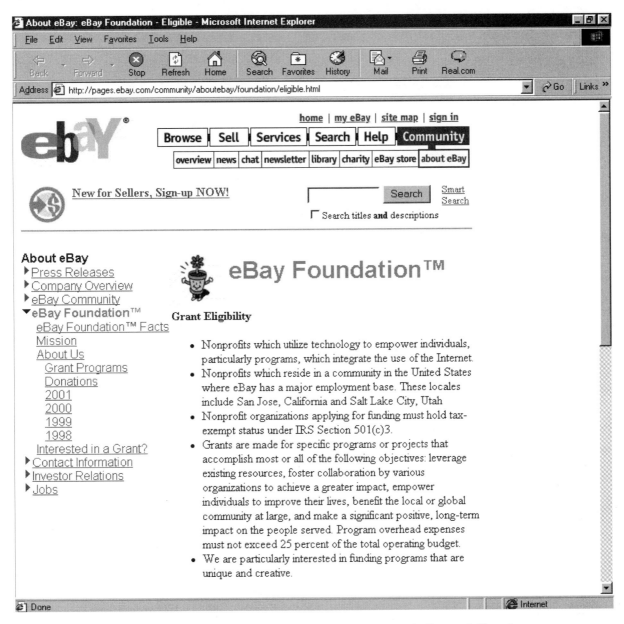

Exhibit 12.1. Example of a Grantmaker Making Clear What It Doesn't Fund.

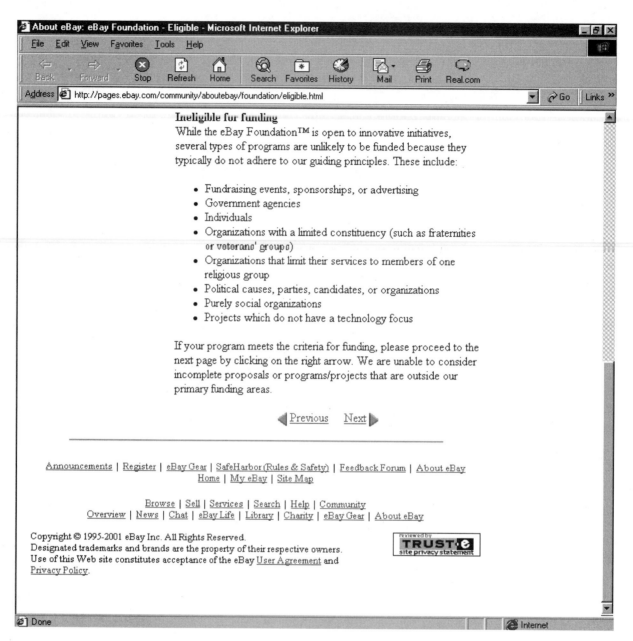

Exhibit 12.1. Continued.

- Start by asking the grantseeker to complete required sections of the application form. Then provide a means for them to attach files that contain expanded and supplemental materials. Be sure to check all attachments for viruses.

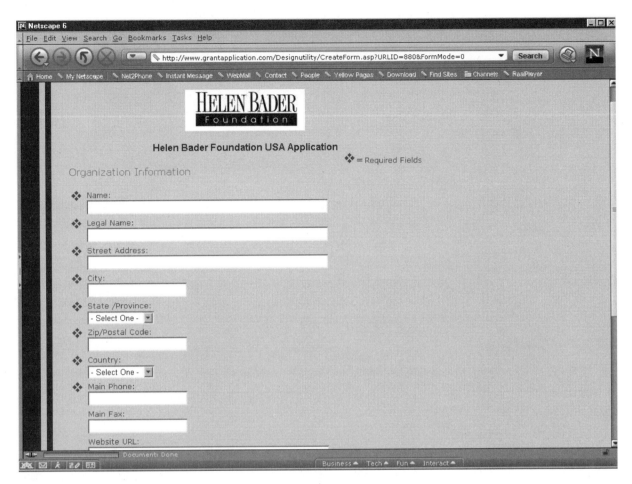

Exhibit 12.2. Example of an Online Grant Application.

- Configure systems to import data into your grants management system accurately without creating duplicate organizations.
- Ensure that you have all the necessary expertise to implement the system and provide ongoing support.

Acknowledgments

Assistance in developing this chapter was provided by MicroEdge, Inc. [www.microedge.com], a provider of software and services for the philanthropic community.

| LEE HOFFMAN | TED HART |

Using the Internet for Planned Giving

The details of planned giving can seem complicated to both donors and nonprofits. For legacy donors who do not choose simple bequests, learning what other options exist is the first step toward matching their charitable intentions with their estate plans. For nonprofit organizations, the biggest challenge is to identify those who may support their missions with legacy gifts and provide them with the details they need to choose the right planned giving vehicles. The Internet can help both donors and nonprofits meet their goals efficiently and, often, less threateningly.

USING THE INTERNET to promote and enhance planned giving efforts has the potential to level the playing field between large and small organizations by allowing more nonprofits to provide detailed information regarding tax-wise giving to more of their donors. And current demographic trends make a powerful argument for fundraisers to look very closely into these new online planning giving tools.

According to the online research firm MediaMetrix, older Internet users now constitute the fastest growing demographic group in the U.S. Internet market. One fifth of U.S. Internet users are aged forty-five to sixty-four, and the proportion is growing. A MediaMetrix study shows that users in this older age group access the Internet more often, stay online for longer periods, and visit more Web sites than younger users. If your organization fails to provide planned giving information to this growing population, you risk becoming "invisible" to your primary target audience for planned giving prospects.

A survey conducted by NFO Research for the National Committee on Planned Giving found that 11 percent of Americans say they have already earmarked money for charities in their wills or have committed to another type of planned gift. The survey found that another 25 percent of Americans is considering making such charitable bequests or gifts (Debra E. Blum, "More Americans Making Bequests and Other Planned Gifts, Study Finds," *Chronicle of Philanthropy*, 2000). This strongly suggests that your organization needs to connect with a much larger segment of its donor base and provide donors with detailed planned giving information. You can't do this economically via direct mail, personal contact, telephone, or other traditional means of communication. But you can use these traditional channels to direct donors and prospects to your Web site and its planned giving content.

According to the Internet measurement company NetValue, the Web users who are sixty-five and older are only 4.6 percent of the online population in the United States, but they surf the Web more than younger people. Seniors surfed the Web for an average of 14.7 days per month, exceeding any other age group. During this time, the average senior Internet user visited more than seventy-four unique domains, viewed more than five hundred pages, and clicked on an average of 1.8 banners. Even though 4.6 percent is a relatively small proportion of the population of older Americans, those other numbers about seniors' online behavior are big enough to thwart the popular belief that older donors are not online. And by the time your organization has built and worked the bugs out of its online planned giving pages, even more prospective legacy donors will be online.

Why Provide Planned Giving Content on Your Web Site?

In his book *Mega Gifts* (Precept Press, 1998), major gifts expert Jerold Panas identifies twenty-two key reasons people make million-dollar gifts to charity. Following are Panas's top ten, presented in order of importance. When developing the planned giving content on your organization's Web site, be sure to target as many of these hot buttons as possible:

1. Belief in the mission of the institution
2. Community responsibility and civic pride
3. Fiscal stability of the organization
4. Regard for staff leadership
5. Respect for the institution locally
6. Regard for volunteer leadership
7. Serve on the Board of Trustees, a major committee, or other official body of the institution
8. Respect for the institution in a wider circle—region, nation, state

9. Has a history of being involved in the institution

10. Leverage or influence of the solicitor

Of the twenty-two motivators, tax considerations rank twenty-first on Panas's list in order of importance to those making gifts of $1 million or more. So if mega-donors rank tax considerations so low, why should you even place planned giving on your Web site? If it is on the Web site, where should it go in the grand scheme of things?

Although tax considerations are not the chief reason donors make gifts, they do play an important role in many individual cases. Planned gifts allow donors to match their estate plans to their charitable interests. After all, three of the greatest financial fears in the minds of most potential donors, two of which involve tax considerations, are

- Will I have sufficient assets to permit me to live in the style I desire for the rest of my life?

- What will happen to my loved ones when I'm gone?

- Will the things I stand for, the causes I believe in, continue when I am gone?

Planned gifts and the benefits they provide donors and their heirs are a way to answer these questions and make giving more affordable. As nonprofits are able to show donors *why* they should give, planned giving vehicles show them *how*.

Show Donors Why They Should Support Your Organization

As Panas points out, the number one reason that donors support an organization is belief in its mission. That mission needs to be highlighted at every opportunity. Yet making the case for support can be as complex as the individual relationships a nonprofit builds with its donors, and the mission can be spotlighted in ways many and varied. For example, in developing your Web site, you could use any or all of the following methods to build support for your mission among prospective donors:

Include a Message from the President Your Web site should feature a personal message from your CEO. This message provides an opportunity to cite tangible examples of how philanthropy has helped the organization accomplish its mission, including an example of how a planned gift has made a powerful impact. Naturally, the CEO's message should include a link to the planned giving section of your Web site for more information.

Describe Programs and Services In many organizations, a certain program or service has been endowed or in some other way made possible through a major gift. If this is the case in your organization, and if the gift was some sort of a planned gift, share that fact with your Web site visitors and provide a link to the appropriate area of the site for more information on that form of giving.

Provide Contacts Directories are an important part of any Web site. Make it simple for visitors to find the contact information of staff persons and advisors responsible for your planned giving program.

Present a Calendar of Events Be certain to include any planned giving seminars you offer when you update your online calendar of events. You might also highlight other events (such as an open house or an issue briefing for donors, for example) as ways for prospective planned giving donors to meet with staff and learn more about planned giving off-line.

Disseminate Information via E-Mail Newsletters Whenever it's appropriate, use your e-mail newsletter or online donor bulletin as a way to disseminate information about planned giving seminars or changes in the tax code or to celebrate a recent planned gift. Include a link to your planned giving pages, of course.

Share Stories Provide your donors with samples of how others have helped your organization while helping themselves and their heirs through planned giving.

Show Donors How They Can Support Your Mission

Make your online information about planned giving exciting and easy to understand. Legalese impresses no one, not even attorneys. And be certain to consider planned giving from the donors' perspective, providing information helpful to them in attaining *their* goals as well as those of the organization.

Planned giving options should be described as answers to financial and philanthropic concerns and problems donors might be facing. Remember, tax considerations are twenty-first out of twenty-two major gift motivators in Panas's list.

See Table 13.1 for a guide to planned giving techniques viewed as possible solutions to financial problems.

Feel free to reproduce Table 13.1 on your Web site (so long as you attribute it to the authors of this chapter and this book). If you do, however, or if you prepare something similar on your own, be sure to include links to the technical and legal descriptions of these planned

Table 13.1. Options and Benefits for Planned Gifts.

Donor Goal:	The Donor Can:	Benefits to Donor Are:
Avoid tax on capital gains	Contribute long-term appreciated stock or other securities	A charitable deduction plus no capital gains tax
Share a collection or other personal item	Donate tangible personal property related to an exempt function	A charitable deduction based on the full fair market value
Make a revocable gift during their lifetime	Name charity as the beneficiary of assets in living trust	Full control of the trust terms for donor lifetime
Defer a gift until after donor lifetime	Put a bequest in donor will (give cash, specific property, or a share of the residue)	Donations are fully exempt from federal estate tax
Make a large gift with little cost to donor	Contribute a life insurance policy donor no longer needs	Current and possibly future income tax deductions
Avoid the twofold taxation on IRA or other employee benefit plans	Name charity as the beneficiary of the remainder of the assets after donor's lifetime	It lets donor leave family other assets that carry less tax liability
Avoid capital gains tax on the sale of a home or other real estate	Donate the property to charity, or sell it to charity at a bargain price	An income tax reduction plus reduction or elimination of capital gains tax
Give donor's personal residence or farm, but retain life use	Create a charitable gift of future interest, called a retained life estate	It gives the donor tax advantages plus use of the property
Create a hedge against inflation over the long term	Create a charitable remainder unitrust	It pays donor a variable income for life and gives donor tax benefits
Secure a fixed life income while avoiding market risks	Create a charitable remainder annuity trust	It gives donor tax benefits and often boosts donor's rate of return
Receive guaranteed fixed income that is partially tax-free	Create a charitable gift annuity	Current and future savings on income taxes, plus stable income
Reduce gift and estate taxes on assets donor passes to children or grandchildren	Create a charitable lead trust that pays income to charity for a specific term of years	It has the estate tax benefits of a gift, but donor's family keeps the property

giving instruments, so any donor who chooses one solution from the chart will be able to cite the appropriate language when speaking with legal, financial, or tax advisors. Be certain, too, to include the technical and legal description of each planned giving vehicle in your Web site's search engine; this inclusion will allow those who might be searching for some specific term or approach they may have heard of or read about elsewhere to jump quickly to those details.

How to Optimize Planned Giving on Your Web Site

Once you've established a planned giving component on your Web site, there are a variety of ways you can optimize its potential to work for your organization.

Keep Your Web Site Current with Help from Commercial Content Providers

Although putting planned giving information on a Web site is relatively easy for most nonprofits, the tasks of keeping the site updated and legally accurate and providing interactive and informative tools are more difficult, and they can be costly. You may find it more cost-effect to purchase commercially available Internet-ready tools to keep your Web site updated and accurate. Commercial providers of complete contents for planned giving Web sites include

FutureFocus	www.futurefocus.com
Stelter	www.stelter.com
VirtualGiving	www.virtualgiving.com

Tools offered by ASPs to perform planned giving calculation on nonprofit Web sites include

Crescendo Interactive	www.crescendosoft.com
FutureFocus	www.futurefocus.net
GiftCalcs	www.pgcalc.com/giftcalcs
PhilanthroCalc	www.ptec.com

Also, AssetStream [www.assetstream.com] offers a planned giving support system for online contributions of stock to nonprofit organizations.

Reach Donors by Increasing Traffic at Your Web Site

Once your organization has created the planned giving section of its Web site, invite donors and prospects to visit it. Most board members and staff members hesitate to discuss planned giving with donors and prospects for fear they'll be asked questions they can't answer. The Web site provides a valuable tool in reaching out to these donors by providing self-explanatory planned giving pages, thereby expanding the organization's reach and potentially its planned giving support. Here are some strategies for maximizing your marketing coverage:

Online Marketing Strategies

- Use all of your organization's printed materials—letters, articles, newsletters, brochures—to draw attention to the planned giving pages on your Web site.

- Include the site's URL (Web address) on staff members' business cards.

- Contact local accountants, attorneys, financial planners, and other advisors to the wealthy to announce the creation of the site and invite them to direct their clients to it. Ask them to feature a link to your site on their own Web sites.

- Conduct presentations on planned giving for community groups and refer them to your Web site for additional information.

- Enhance your site with updated pictures, stories, and content as traffic builds.

- Keep donors and prospects abreast of federal and state laws regarding planned giving.

Keep Abreast of Current Regulations

Make sure your organization is properly registered in all states requiring registration if you're seeking donors there. You'll find information on states that accept and do not accept the Unified Registration Statement at [www.nonprofits.org/library/gov/urs]. (See also Chapter Six.)

Many nonprofits choose to offer charitable gift annuities, which require additional federal and state registration. Federal Law (Public Law 104–62) requires charities to supply a Gift Annuity Disclosure Statement to all annuitants, and to all prospective donors prior to their making their first annuity gift. This is separate from state-mandated disclosure language required in gift annuity agreements of twenty-four states. Information about state and federal regulations on gift annuities is available at [www.pgresources.com/sumreg.html#anchor1] and [www.acga-Web.org].

The American Council on Gift Annuities annually issues suggested guidelines on payment rates on gift annuities. The most recent information is currently available at [www.acga-Web.org].

The following Internet resources can help you stay up-to-date on changes in the law and help identify professionals who can assist you and your donors in establishing trusts and other planned giving vehicles:

> The American College of Trust and Estate Counsel
> www.actec.org
>
> GiftLaw
> www.giftlaw.com

The Planned Giving Design Center, LLC
www.pgdc.net

Planned Giving Resources
www.pgresources.com

Law & Estate Planning Sites on the Internet
www.ca-probate.com/links.htm

Connect with Planned Giving Professionals Online

The Internet provides a convenient way to exchange information with people who share an interest in planned giving. The following listservs offer free subscriptions. Each provides a connection with colleagues working in planned giving.

CDN-GIFTPL-L is an online forum for discussion of planned giving in Canada. To subscribe, send an e-mail message to [listproc@list-serv.mcmaster.ca] that states in the body of the message "subscribe cdn-giftpl-l Your Name." Leave the subject blank, and do not include e-mail addresses in the body of the message.

Gift-PL—An is an online forum for discussion of planned giving in the United States that is maintained by the National Committee on Planned Giving. To subscribe, send an e-mail message to [listserv@list-serv.iupui.edu] that states in the body of the message "subscribe gift-pl Your Name." Leave the subject blank, and do not include e-mail addresses in the body of the message.

The Charity Channel offers three planned giving discussion forums:

United States
www.charitychannel.com/forums/GIFTPLAN.htm

Canada
www.charitychannel.com/forums/GIFTPLAN-CANADA.htm

United Kingdom
www.charitychannel.com/forums/GIFTPLAN-UK.htm

In addition, the following associations offer opportunities to learn from colleagues and join in advocacy for laws and regulations that encourage planned giving:

Canadian Association of Gift Planners
www.cagp-acpdp.org

European Association for Planned Giving
www.plannedgiving.co.uk

National Committee on Planned Giving
www.ncpg.org

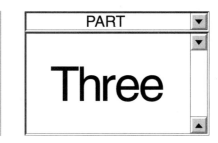

PART

Three

Technology and Your Organization

JIM McGEE | TED HART

Electronic Prospect Research

Prospect research has long been the cornerstone of major gift fundraising. Until recently, only the very largest institutions could afford prospect research. Although many data have been available for some time, mining that data had proven to be costly, time-consuming, and very difficult. "Smart searching" and data-mining have now made prospect research available and affordable to any office with Internet access.

ACCORDING TO *GIVING USA 2000,* of the $190 billion donated to nonprofits in 1999, individuals gave $159 billion, or nearly 84 percent. Individual donors dominate not just the bottom of the donor pyramid, with modest gifts of $50 or less, but also the top. Seven-figure gifts from individuals are increasingly common, and the pressure to secure those gifts has risen to a fever pitch at many large nonprofit institutions. Smaller organizations compete intensely for major gifts of $1,000, $10,000, or more.

Almost all those major gifts come from face-to-face meetings with donors—meetings to which fundraisers typically go armed with detailed information about donors' previous giving history, their wealth, their capacity to give, and their interests. That information comes from prospect research.

In the Beginning

Before the active use of the Internet, prospect researchers haunted the halls of libraries and dug through periodicals, *Who's Who* directories, foundation publications, newspaper articles, annual reports, and public records of every type and description. Prospect research was a long, tedious process that required a trained and patient soul willing to plow through all available sources and uncover those nuggets that are the core of a good research report. The drawbacks of this style of research were many: cost, lack of timeliness of the data, and the inability to research more than a handful of prospects.

As competition for donated dollars grew more intense, the need to identify the likeliest donors from within large files of prospects, donors, alumni, members, and former patients became increasingly acute. Even small nonprofits felt the need to secure ever larger numbers of major gifts, year after year. Then the first wave of research tools using electronic data gathering, designed for the nonprofit world, began to appear in the 1980s.

Demographic Overlays and Computer Profiling

Marts & Lundy introduced the first Electronic Prospect Research program specifically tailored to the nonprofit community. Under this program, an institution would send its file to Marts & Lundy, which would append to the records a group of demographic data elements, including age, marital status, income, and home value. The source of this data was (and still is) the large household files maintained by the data providers to the direct marketing industry. In many cases the data were derived primarily from census statistics and aggregated at the neighborhood level, so they applied generalizations to individual donor records—generalizations that may well have been untrue about any given individual.

Once these data were appended to a file, each record was rated with a "propensity to give" score via computer models and the donor's known giving history at the institution. The computer models, the data elements captured, and the level of sophistication have evolved over the years. However, the technique and methodology remain largely the same.

Some of the key providers of these services are

> Marts & Lundy
> www.martsandlundy.com
>
> Thomson Financial Wealth Identification
> www.wealthid.com/pmat.htm
>
> Grenzebach Glier & Associates
> www.grenzebachglier.com
>
> Econometrics
> www.econ-online.com
>
> Community Counseling Service
> www.ccsfundraising.com/services4.html

This information has proven to be very valuable for many institutions and has been used effectively in a variety of fundraising campaigns across the country. However, while profiling has its advantages, it's just the first step toward identifying "a needle in the haystack." Those matching to the wealth profile, in many cases, need to be researched further to verify the accuracy of the information.

Tools for Identifying Top Prospects

In the late 1980s and into the 1990s, the first versions of online prospect-research services involving individual prospects began to emerge. These new services sought to provide in-depth data about small numbers of very wealthy prospects. In the process, they helped pioneer the integration of the Internet into fundraising for many nonprofit institutions.

Through these new services, it's now possible to match your prospect database against databases of wealthy philanthropists. Rather than simply profiling a database for trends or demographic expectations to find prospects, these services place an emphasis on matching your prospects against known persons with private wealth, entrepreneurs, private company owners, high-income professionals, and corporate and foundation executives. This information can often be searched online and results provided on demand without delay.

Some of the key providers of these services are

Target America
www.tgtam.com

Knowledge Base Marketing
www.knowledgebasemarketing.com

PROspect Research Online
www.iwave.com

P!N
www.prospectinfo.com

WealthEngine
www.wealthengine.com

Research Databases

Two services that were designed to search information databases and automate a lot of the manual review of books and periodicals have emerged as very powerful tools for developing full-text profiles on top prospects. These services require a trained user and tend to be expensive, but they capture many of the data available in online databases. They are widely accepted as very effective tools if you have the staff resources and the budget to use them fully.

Lexis/Nexis [www.lexis-nexis.com] taps into hundreds of databases. This is a great source for articles, annual reports, business financials, and biographical data. Dialog [www.dialog.com] competes with Lexis/Nexis. It, too, searches online databases. Both services are designed to produce large amounts of data online, but they're set up to review one name at a time and are time-consuming.

APRA: Ethical Prospect Research

The Association of Professional Researchers for Advancement (APRA) [www.aprahome.org] has developed an extensive curriculum to train its members on the effective and ethical use of the Internet in prospect research. APRA has also developed a code of ethics for prospect research. (See Resource E.) Although these ethical principles were developed for all forms of prospect research, they're particularly relevant for information obtained via the Web. Whether or not you are a member of APRA, understanding what constitutes ethical behavior when dealing with confidential or sensitive information obtained via the Internet is important.

In addition to respecting ethical research practices, nonprofit organizations must pay close attention to the management and use of information gathered on their Web sites. Establishing a comprehensive privacy policy is an important first step toward protecting sensitive and confidential information.

Some Internet resources regarding online privacy issues include

Online Privacy Alliance
www.privacyalliance.org

Electronic Frontier Foundation
www.eff.org/privacy.html

Electronic Privacy Information Center
www.epic.org

Europe's Privacy Policy Generator
http://cs3-hq.oecd.org/scripts/pwv3/pwhome.htm

Search Engines

Here are five steps to embarking upon prospect research to identify top prospective donors for your organization:

- Identify what sources, subjects, key words, and other pieces of information you have. Include prior giving to your organization. Develop a search strategy before going online.

- Select at least two search engines, and use them as long as you feel they're providing you with useful and reliable information. Two of the best are Google [www.google.com] and Northern Light [www.northernlight.com].

- Combine what you have learned from your favorite search engine with information found in specialized databases and resources, such as online news sources, corporate records, and professional directories.

- Pull all the information you have found into a comprehensive report, noting identified wealth and total assets where possible.

- Although there are several commonly used methods for establishing the ability to give, often all income and assets are not available to the researcher. One of the following formulas should be helpful in identifying a target gift level:

  $20 \times$ level of consistent annual giving = giving ability (over five-year period)

  10 percent of annual income = giving ability (over five years)

  5 percent of total known assets (real estate + stock holdings + annual income for five years) = giving ability (five years)

Learn from Others, Share with Others

A terrific feature of the Internet is the ability to connect with people who share your interest in prospect research. There are two free listservs you may subscribe to. Each allows you to stay in touch with colleagues engaged in prospect research, learn from them, and share your experiences.

One of these is PRSPCT-L. It features discussion of prospect research issues, developments, sources, and techniques. To subscribe, send an e-mail to [listserv@bucknell.edu]. In the message, type [subscribe prspct-l <your real name>]. To post a message send it to [prspct-l@bucknell.edu].

The other free listserv is Charity Channel GiftProspecting, which focuses on all aspects of prospect research, including techniques, privacy, legal aspects, and ethics. You may log on at [www.charitychannel.com/forums/GiftProspecting.htm].

Internet Research

The Internet is a treasure trove of raw data. Some of it is extremely valuable, and much of it is simply a waste of space. The challenge for prospect researchers is to wade through all this and extract the information needed to support fundraising while wasting minimal time and effort in the process.

There are approximately 550 billion Web pages on the Internet. The goal of search engines is to "crawl" or comb electronically through that information, building easy-to-use indexes of the unique information they find. Internet users can then view anything the search engine has found by picking and choosing much like skimming a book's table of contents. Although search engines help Web surfers find information, no single search engine hits more than 16 percent of Internet sites. Using key-name search logic, search engines go out onto the Net and bring back site addresses that, based on the title of the page, appear to meet the criteria entered by a user.

Here are three keys to understanding search engines. First, each engine has its own search criteria. By changing from one search engine to the next, you'll find they yield dramatically different results for the same search parameters. Second, to learn whether the information is useful, relevant, or accurate, the researcher must then open up each page. Third, search engines do not summarize the data, provide it in useful format, or allow for any form of automated updating.

Search engines worth trying include

AOL.com	www.aol.com
AltaVista	www.altavista.com
Ask Jeeves	www.ask.com
C4 TotalSearch	www.c4.com
Dogpile	www.dogpile.com
Excite.com	www.excite.com
Google	www.google.com
HotBot	www.hotbot.com
LookSmart	www.looksmart.com
Lycos	www.lycos.com
MetaCrawler	www.metacrawler.com
MSN	search.msn.com
Northern Light	www.northernlight.com
Webcrawler	www.Webcrawler.com
Yahoo!	www.yahoo.com

There are many ways to search the Web for prospect information. The first step is to know where to go. Several of the best prospect research offices and individuals have developed sites that pull together a broad array of links that will help you find the right resource to identify useful information about your best prospects and donors.

Fortunately, information sharing within the prospect research community has allowed us to compile a list of top sites that have proven to be most appropriate for fundraising. The following constitute a representative sample of sites that have proven valuable to the fundraising community. They're best grouped in two categories: nonprofit sites, and commercial and government sites. Together, they represent a small part of what's out there.

Nonprofit Sites

Internet Prospector [www.internet-prospector.org] is the very best customized nonprofit site for doing manual prospect research over the Net. The site is set up as a roadmap to resources that have direct bearing on gathering information on prospects. Staffed by a national network of volunteers, this nonprofit site provides a unique service that "mines" the Internet to report on resources of use to prospect researchers. Internet Prospector provides links to a wide range of resources: Web sites, databases, search engines and meta-indices, news sources, specialized directories, people locators, reports, and articles.

If you are interested in Internet-based prospect research, we recommend subscribing to the free monthly Internet Prospector e-newsletter [www.internet-prospector.org/subscrib.html].

The biggest advantage of this site is that it takes some of the guesswork out of where to go for information. It does not automate the searching in any way, but it's a very good starting point for manual searching (Exhibit 14.1).

NETSource@USC [www.usc.edu/dept/source] is a Web site maintained by the University of Southern California Development Research Department. This site provides many links to online databases, some free and some subscription. NETSource links to corporate, foundation, and individual research; articles written by University staff; tools; lists; and more.

The Princeton University Development Links [www.princeton.edu/one/research/netlinks.html] site features a categorized list of Internet links the Princeton Development Office maintains as sites its staff members have found most useful in their work. Unlike some sites of this kind, Development Links provides links to all aspects of development work, including a number of international sites, not just prospect research.

Northwestern University Development Research [http://pubWeb.acns.nwu.edu/~cap440/bookmark.html] provides one of the most comprehensive lists of search engines, access to newspapers and news outlets, and business research links available on a University-based site.

Foundation Center [http://fdncenter.org] provides the most comprehensive information on foundations, the grants they make, and their board members. It also offers copies of foundation IRS 990 Forms.

Exhibit 14.1. Home Page for Internet Prospector.

Commercial and Government Sites

Although the nonprofit sites listed above will help you find sites likely to be of most value in your research, some commercial sites are also worth particular mention due to the accuracy of their information and relevance to prospect research.

EDGAR (Electronic Data Gathering, Analysis, and Retrieval system) [www.sec.gov/edgarhp.html] is the site through which the Securities and Exchange Commission requires all public companies (except foreign companies and companies with less than $10 million in assets and 500 shareholders) to file registration statements, periodic reports, and other forms electronically. Anyone can access and download this information free of charge. The database includes annual reports on Form 10-K or 10-KSB, including information on officer compensation and assets of corporations.

Hoovers Online [www.hoovers.com] is an outstanding site that offers information on nearly 10,000 companies and their key executives.

Merger & Acquisition Marketplace [www.mergernetwork.com/default.html] lists thousands of businesses for sale with sales from under $1 million to more than $500 million.

David Lamb's Prospect Research Page [www.lambresearch.com] contains comprehensive links and more about the sites he uses and recommends to others. Mr. Lamb is a consultant and the former director of prospect research at the University of Washington and Santa Clara University.

Osworth Consulting [new-Web.com/consulting/free.html] offers links to free sites that aid in identifying information about individuals, including information on adoption, genealogy, and professional licensing.

The U.S. Census Bureau [www.census.gov] offers demographic information collected by the federal government and provides links to other federal statistical agencies.

Looking for Someone?

The following online databases will help you find individual and business addresses, phone numbers, directions, and e-mail addresses:

Switchboard (telephone and address)
www.switchboard.com

WhoWhere(e-mail addresses)
www.whowhere.lycos.com/Email

InfoSpace (reverse telephone look-up)
www.infospace.com

International Phone Directories (white and yellow pages)
www.infobel.com/world/

Research Reports

Several new services are attempting to simplify and automate Internet-based prospect research by building full-text profiles of prospects from information from online database searches.

The pioneer in full text profiles has been P!N [www.prospectinfo.com]. P!N has developed a program that taps into online databases, not necessarily HTML pages, and builds a prospect research profile. The sources that the company uses have information on both individuals and companies, including financial information. This service has been designed for fundraising and provides formatted research reports, in which data are organized into readable form.

Target America [www.tgtam.com] introduced its Sherlock program about a year and a half ago. Sherlock uses a combination of Webcrawlers and search engines to develop automated research profiles. This program allows someone with little background in research (or just in a hurry) to develop in-depth text profiles on top prospects. Sherlock reports summarize the data and provide Web links to full-text pages it has found. It offers the added benefit of automatically refreshing reports whenever the user designates.

Everyone Can Do Research

The Internet has leveled the playing field, so that charities of all sizes can now uncover rich data resources and build profiles of top prospects. The traditional, labor-intensive, costly research conducted by highly skilled researchers is being augmented with high-speed, automated research programs that sweep the Internet and online database resources, building research profiles at prices within the reach of small nonprofit institutions. As valuable as these tools are today, their reliability and usefulness will continue to grow with time.

It's no longer necessary for organizations to cultivate their major donor prospects without the benefit of knowing their capacity to give. The Internet has made it possible for all nonprofit organizations to benefit from the kind of information that until just recently was available only to the largest organizations fortunate enough to employ professional researchers.

| JOHN PARKE | TED HART |

Recruiting, Retaining, and Organizing Volunteers Online

Recruiting, retaining, and organizing volunteers can be done effectively by leveraging the power of technology to make it convenient for people to get involved. As nonprofit organizations continue to embrace technology to reach volunteers, the real rewards of collaboration, communication, and community will be realized. However, "the rules still apply." Good online volunteer management still requires building strong relationships with your volunteers.

IN TODAY'S TIME-STARVED WORLD, nonprofit organizations realize how important it is to focus on the recruitment, retention, and efficient organization of volunteers. In the past it might have possible for organizations to recruit volunteers by means of traditional networking. Today, potential volunteers are harder to locate, more difficult to schedule, and even tougher to retain. Mobilizing either large or small groups of people to spend time on volunteer efforts requires a new approach to volunteer management. As nonprofits seek to recruit new volunteers and retain those who are already engaged, nonprofit leaders must ask some fundamental questions: What messages should we convey to capture the attention of potential volunteers? How do we attract volunteers to our causes? How can we make it easy to get involved? How do we keep volunteers engaged and active?

Nonprofit leaders who realize the importance of using technology to remain competitive in a fast-moving world have begun to take advantage of opportunities online (Table 15.1).

Table 15.1. Volunteer Management Then and Now.

Then	Now
Most nonprofits did not feel they needed a Web presence.	The same organizations realize the Web is their twenty-four-hour, seven-day-a-week face to the community and a way to inform the public and attract new volunteers.
Nonprofits were unsophisticated and afraid of technology providers.	Nonprofits are much more sophisticated; many successfully turn to the Internet to attract and retain new supporters and volunteers.
Organizational leadership was afraid to make important technology decisions due to cost and political risk factors.	Internet applications are much more flexible and offer greater shelf-life than traditional software solutions that are outdated virtually from the day of arrival.

Selecting Technology Partners

Innovative leaders today are realizing how important it is to use the Internet strategically to enhance volunteer management. It is no longer possible for most nonprofit organizations to develop technology solutions in-house in a cost-effective way. Instead, most nonprofits are wise to select technology partners and integrate solutions that have already been developed by others, usually in the private sector. Most technology partners serving charities today have staffs that come from the nonprofit world and understand the issues charities face, including financial limitations and volunteer constraints.

Recruiting Volunteers Online

There are many opportunities to recruit volunteers online. Generally, it's not necessary to recruit online on your own. For most nonprofits, it's advisable to partner with one or more well-established online services. You can learn a great deal from the growing expertise of many online service providers in recruiting volunteers on the Internet.

Enlisting volunteers online is effective, fast, and easy, and it doesn't entail any additional costs. It's an excellent way to reach nontraditional volunteers, including populations that might be underrepresented in an organization's volunteer ranks (seniors, ethnic minorities, people with disabilities).

To find a local volunteer center that will help you with technical assistance, resource sharing, and training and consultation, contact the

Points of Light Foundation's Volunteer Center National Network [www.volunteerconnections.org].

If you're interested in posting volunteer opportunities online, there are several services that will accommodate your needs. On the Internet you'll find a vast network, including sites to help you locate volunteers, track them, and assist you in managing them. One of the largest is ServeNet, which powers General Colin Powell's America's Promise and other volunteer Web sites [www.servenet.org].

At press time, other Web sites promoting volunteer opportunities in the United States, United Kingdom, and Canada included the following:

Action Without Borders	www.idealist.org
Amigos de las Americas	www.amigoslink.org
Catholic Network of Volunteer Service	www.cnvs.org
Charity Village, Canada	www.charityvillage.com
City Cares, U.S., U.K.	www.citycares.org
Do Something	www.dosomething.org
Make A Difference Day	www.usaweekend.com/diffday
ServeNet	www.servenet.org
Volunteer Canada	www.volunteer.ca
Volunteer Match	www.volunteermatch.org

Organizing Volunteers Online

As the Web has changed our daily lives, it has also shaped the way volunteers interact. There are many ways to use the Internet to increase coordination, education, collaboration, and communication with and among volunteers. One emerging trend is virtual volunteering. Volunteers are equipped with tools that enable them to communicate in new ways, allowing both large and small groups of volunteers mobilized around a common cause to engage in a variety of volunteer-centered activities.

For instance, volunteers can *coordinate* their efforts by managing projects online via new Web-enabled tools, and volunteer leaders can coordinate multiple teams of people performing various tasks in remote locations. Volunteers can also *educate* each other by sharing cause-related information, along with links to relevant sites and timely articles to keep informed on current trends. Finally, volunteers can *collaborate* by sharing best practices and *communicate* more efficiently by using chat rooms, surveys, and discussion groups.

The Internet offers a great way to support volunteers, particularly those that work away from an agency's direct supervision. For example, e-mail is an easy and free way to communicate with volunteers quickly and provide them opportunities to communicate easily with nonprofit staff members. An online discussion group for your volunteers is an ideal tool to help them collaborate, share what they have learned, and increase their teamwork. Sometimes it's easier to ask a question of a peer. Regular e-mail updates on important organizational news and volunteer activities can help retain volunteers. Volunteer manuals, guidelines, statistics, and other information that volunteers may find helpful to their service can all be posted online, making them available anytime. Online calendars can help volunteers remember important assignments and deadlines.

Currently, there are several free online services that can help you with some or all of these tasks:

MediaLot	medialot.brandera.com/medialot/Medialot
Yahoo! Groups	http://groups.yahoo.com
AOL Groups	http://groups.aol.com

In addition, for an extensive list of free and fee-based services, refer to [www.thinkofit.com/webconf/hostsites.htm].

Some for-profit online services can also help your organization manage groups of volunteers, whether they are board members, teams of volunteers providing mentoring programs to children, or other people engaged in any activity requiring them to coordinate actions and share information. These for-profit companies package many strategies into one convenient service for the nonprofit to manage and the volunteer to access. For example, Team™ [www.bluestep.net] is a program that provides each volunteer with a Web page that can coordinate files, calendars, team training, and chats (Exhibit 15.1).

Other virtual service providers include the following:

WEGO	www.wego.com
Convio	www.convio.com
internet4associations	www.internet4associations.com

Retaining Volunteers Online

The key benefits of online collaboration tools are improved coordination and teamwork among volunteers, more effective communications, and improved efficiency in project management. In turn, all these results contribute to improved volunteer retention. But the online collaboration tools do not take the place of in-person meetings. Rather, they increase retention by sustaining communications between meetings.

Exhibit 15.1. Online Volunteer Management.

The Virtual Volunteering Project, an online resource provided by the LBJ School of Public Affairs, University of Texas at Austin [www.serviceleader.org/vv], states that "virtual volunteering means volunteer tasks [are] completed, in whole or in part, via the Internet and a home or work computer." Virtual volunteering combines technology with good old-fashioned volunteer recruitment efforts, so organizations can expand their reach by attracting volunteers from new areas and increasing volunteers' level of participation.

Success factors for virtual volunteer management include

- Commitment from all levels of the organization to online volunteer management. This means devoting time and resources to keeping the online volunteer efforts current and vital.

- Use of virtual service providers to enable volunteers to become involved over the Web anytime, anywhere (home, office, airport, and so forth). Services such as e-mail, chatrooms, and discussion boards can be cost-effective as well as easy to use.

- Use of online tools to manage assignments and perform tasks quickly and easily.

- Recognition programs that are the same as or similar to those used to keep on-site volunteers engaged and motivated. This is important for retention; online volunteers need to feel their efforts are appreciated, just as do other volunteers.

Summary: Volunteers Working Online

Not only can you recruit and manage volunteers online, but you may also be able to put them to work at any one of several jobs online. Volunteers with expertise and well-developed skills can provide technical assistance in the following online activities (adapted from the Virtual Volunteering Project with permission):

- Online research for legislative issues, grants, useful Web sites, and databases
- Advocacy efforts
- Language translation
- Production of publications
- Wed site content and design
- Database management

Clearly, the key benefit of managing volunteers online is the ability to cross geographic and other boundaries to attract, retain, and engage volunteers more efficiently. Other benefits include reaching people through nontraditional means (as opposed to telephone, advertising and mail), saving time, money, and natural resources.

Volunteers can now gather information quickly and exchange ideas using online tools. By using the Internet to extend an organization's resources, agencies can reach out to people with disabilities or other limitations—people who have the skills necessary to volunteer but may be physically unable to participate. For many of these people, volunteering online is the best (or only) way to get involved. This is also true for young people—who tend to be more technology-friendly than their parents. This new breed of volunteers already understands how the Internet works and is receptive to using the Internet as a means of interacting with an organization.

According to a recent report issued by the Pew Partnership for Civic Change [www.pew-partnership.org], 41 percent of those interviewed said they wanted to get involved in their communities but didn't know how or whom to call. Many nonprofit organizations have lacked the resources to reach out and find volunteers, while many potential volunteers have not known how to get involved. The Internet can help provide solutions to both these problems.

Mario Morino, founder of the Morino Institute in Washington, D.C., stated at the October 2000 Networks for People Conference, United States Department of Commerce, "It's easy to install technology, but it's difficult to change what people do in order to apply and benefit from technology." As nonprofits begin to manage volunteers online, they will need to recognize the fundamental changes taking place in volunteer management. Nonprofit organizations need to allocate resources and develop processes that will support these new ways of recruiting, retaining, and organizing volunteers.

Online or off-line there are simple rules that still apply to volunteer management. As you begin looking at various ways to use the Web to add convenience and efficiency to volunteer management, keep in mind these six rules for successful volunteer relationships developed by CompuMentor [www.compumentor.org]:

Six Rules for Successful Volunteer Relationships

1. Prepare. The first step in the process of creating successful volunteer relationship is to identify realistic ways that volunteers can help your organization. Most successful volunteer projects are short-term and nonurgent. In other words, don't ask for too much. Keep in mind that most people volunteer because it feels good; the best volunteer projects offer opportunities to make significant contributions to an important cause and for meeting new people and having fun. Provide something substantive for volunteers to do. Don't bore them to death!

2. Have a plan. When you have identified volunteer projects, write a description. The "job description" should include the specific project objectives, available resources (such as budget and supplies), needed skills, and time commitment. Taking the time to clarify the scope of work will ensure that you don't forget important parts of the job, and will help volunteers know what they should expect and when they have succeeded in completing the task.

3. Provide a staff contact. Identify a staff person who will be responsible for all communication with a volunteer. This makes communicating with your organization easier for the volunteer. The staff contact should be available to meet with the volunteer when convenient, which may mean having the flexibility to work occasional evenings and weekends. This person should respond to e-mail requests and help manage the online relationship with the volunteer.

4. Provide orientation for volunteers. Your first meeting with volunteers can be very valuable. Before talking about the problems they can fix or the work you want done, introduce them to your mission, staff people, and facility. Many people volunteer because they are interested in helping the community and interacting with new people. Show the volunteers how their work will directly contribute to your mission. Then discuss

the volunteer project and make sure that you both have the same expectations for the project's outcome. Consider having a written "letter of agreement" that outlines the expectations and responsibilities of both the organization and the volunteers. Make sure volunteers understand the essential information regarding the project: budget, timeline, and who's involved.

5. Communicate, communicate, communicate. The staff liaison should communicate with volunteers regularly to talk about their progress and any problems or changes to the plan. This is also a great way to let volunteers know you value their time and energy.

6. Remember the Golden Rule: Thank the volunteer! Thank your volunteer with a card, letter, meal, or any other way you feel is appropriate. Don't wait until the project is over. Thank every volunteer at every opportunity.

ALISON LI

Raising Money Online for Multilevel Organizations

Moving fundraising onto the Internet can raise complications for multilevel nonprofits. An organization's established arrangements for soliciting and allocating funds among its many divisions, regions, or chapters might be challenged by the prospect of raising money via the Web and e-mail, since these methods reach beyond the geographical boundaries that were built into door-to-door solicitation, direct mail, or telephone campaigning. However, the key to good online fundraising remains the same as it is for off-line fundraising: focusing on what your donor wants. Moreover, online fundraising offers new possibilities for greater efficiencies and for tapping the strengths of each division of a multilevel organization.

THE MULTIPLE SCLEROSIS (MS) Society of Canada undertook a lengthy consultation process to launch a renovated national Web site. A Web task force consisting of representatives from every region was actively involved in the months-long development of the new site through regular telephone conferences. The results included the following:

- The revised national site provided a Web presence for each of the society's 140-plus chapters and seven divisions in either French or English.

- Each chapter was able to select a technical solution appropriate to its needs and experiences.

- Those with fewer technical resources could opt to use a chapter Web site "wizard" designed for the MS Society, which allowed chapter personnel to update the content and look of their Web sites via a simple and accessible web interface.

- Chapters with greater Web experience could choose to maintain more complicated sites with a more flexible Web-authoring software application via File Transfer Protocol (FTP). They were provided with a basic template and a bank of images. Those with existing Web sites could also opt to have their sites be linked to the national site through a frameset.

- Great effort was taken during the consultation period to ensure that differing needs and abilities were accommodated. The "Give Now" link from each of these chapter and division Web sites takes visitors to a central online donation facility that provides secure credit-card transactions and electronic tax-receipting, a functionality that added great value to all of the sites.

As you might imagine, however, this success story was not just long in the making but also involved skillful management that could confront a number of challenges along the way.

The Challenges

The clear utility and seeming ubiquity of Web sites, combined with the ease with which they can be produced, can often lead to a complicated situation for a multilevel organization. Even a small local unit of an organization, with few resources but just a single eager and technically minded volunteer or staff person, might by now have been able to mount and operate an active Web site for several years.

Even a simple Web site can contain a solicitation for donations. At the most basic level, this solicitation might consist of a request that donors contact the organization by telephone or e-mail. It might be a donation form that can be printed off and mailed or faxed.

With a few more technical resources, an organization might have a secure online donation form by using a Secure Sockets Layer (SSL), a universal protocol for encrypted communication developed by Netscape, or the services of an application service provider.

Local and regional levels of an organization might have carried out a variety of fundraising activities simultaneously, and without competing or interfering with one another. Local groups would have carried out door-to-door solicitations, direct mail, and telephone campaigns within their own clearly defined geographical areas.

A multilevel organization will very likely have developed clear regulations concerning how money collected by particular local or regional groups is to be treated and whether it is retained in that region, submitted to a higher level of the organization, or shared according to some formula. Once these groups take their activities onto the Internet the traditional boundaries in which they have worked dissolve.

A multilevel international organization might find that some of its divisions have already made the move into soliciting donations online. The sophistication of Web-related activities will often vary considerably from division to division in a nonprofit organization, since it depends not only on the technical and human resources available at the local level but also, less tangibly, on a certain sense of vision and comfort with technology in its leadership.

In a smaller office, one or two enthusiastic, technically savvy individuals might be responsible for driving these efforts; the results can be quite distinct, even idiosyncratic. There may be very little coordination of their efforts with other divisions in the organization in terms of policy and branding.

This situation can be made even more complicated by the rise of hundreds of commercial enterprises serving the online needs of the nonprofit sector. The list includes for-profit (or nonprofit) providers such as charity giving portals, click-to-donate sites, affinity shopping malls, and charity auctions. (See Chapters Nineteen and Twenty-four in this volume.) Many of these vendors have strong marketing programs and are vigorous in approaching new prospects. A multilevel organization might find that some of its local and regional members have already signed up with some of these services, especially since many of them are provided without any direct charge to the nonprofit.

Coordination of Online Efforts

If the central body of the nonprofit attempts to coordinate the online activities of the organization as a whole, it may encounter some resistance from its local units who've already invested much energy and many resources in their own Web ventures. At the same time online fundraising can be an opportunity to bring together an organization, rationalize the way it administers donations, and build its relationship with donors.

The higher levels of the organization are likely to be better able to provide technical solutions to soliciting and administering online donations. By making technical solutions such as a secure online donation function, centralized Web site and e-mail hosting, or a centralized donor database and donor management system available to its member groups, a central body can provide leadership and facilitate local fundraising activities while also bringing some coordination to their efforts.

Each organization has its own culture and rules for dealing with circumstances like this but I would suggest that any coordination effort include the following:

Extensive Consultation to Gain from the Experience and Skills of the Member Units A multilevel organization should be able to determine the best practices among its divisions, gain a sense of what works and what doesn't, and learn the sorts of human and technical resources that are available within the organization.

Respect for the Existing Efforts That Have Been Made and Honor for What Each Level of an Organization Might Do Best Although it might prove more efficient to have a central body be responsible for the provision and administration of an online donation function, it is important that in rationalizing and centralizing the donation process you not neglect the human side of fundraising. The 1999 Mellman Group survey of socially engaged Internet users found that the majority of respondents felt that it was appropriate that there be future contact from a group to which they had made an online donation ("Socially Engaged Internet Users: Prospects for Online Philanthropy and Activism," September 1999, a study conducted by the Mellman Group for Craver Matthews Smith and Company, CMS Interactive, [www.craveronline.com/documents/cmsi_report.pdf]). It is interesting that they felt both online and off-line contact were appropriate. An organization might be inspired to follow the example of the Ontario Red Cross, which has its local volunteers hand-deliver receipts to the door of donors who make gifts over a certain dollar amount. Here, technology can be used centrally to bring about efficiencies in the donation process, but the existing strong network of volunteers can be engaged to keep the human element of fundraising in focus.

A Range of Solutions That Will Suit Various Levels of Experience, Technical Skill, and Comfort with the Web and Allow for Flexibility A multilevel organization might provide the technical solution for receiving online donations but allow member groups to customize the function or interface to suit local programs. More sophisticated divisions might be provided with a larger set of tools, perhaps to allow member groups to run e-mail solicitation campaigns or online management and registration for special events.

The range and diversity of charitable Web sites can create a confusing situation for a prospective donor. It is very important that a multilevel organization develop clear policies and guidelines to direct its online presence. General policies should include

- A privacy policy indicating to visitors how their personal information is handled.

- A security statement explaining to them how their donation information is kept secure.

- Branding guidelines with Web-appropriate specifications of logo and colors.

- A linking policy to indicate to which Web sites (commercial enterprises, other nonprofits) it is appropriate to link and how the Web sites of different levels of the organization should be linked to one another.

- Guidelines concerning the types of information that are appropriate to each level of the organization. For example, the national-level organization of a health charity might be responsible for information about research and health issues, whereas regional-office Web sites would provide information about services and local-office Web sites could provide information about local events and volunteer recognition.

It is also important to consider how supporters will locate a non-profit's Web site. What domain names will each level of the organization use, and how will these domain names be marketed? When visitors search for the organization by name on a major search engine like Yahoo, which entries will appear? Will it be clear to the supporter how the Web sites of the different divisions of the organization relate to each other? Are there also Web sites that have been created for specific special events or campaigns, and are they clearly linked to the parent organization? If supporters arrive at the Web site of one division, will they be able to find their way to the Web site of the central body or that of another region? If not, prospective donors might be confused about where and how they are to make a contribution. The nonprofit might appear disjointed and disorganized.

In dealing with online fundraising activities, an organization will want to consider these policy issues in particular:

- If different levels of the organization solicit online donations via their Web sites, how should the donations be collected and distributed, how should the donor information be collected and shared, and how should future contact with the donor be managed?

- What sorts of sponsorships can be accepted and how they should be acknowledged? For example, is a sponsor's logo displayed? Where? Should a banner ad be included? A hyper-text link?

- What relationships with giving portals, click-to-donate sites, and affinity shopping Web sites should be fostered?

What Do Your Donors Want?

Organizations sometimes make the mistake of organizing their Web sites according to their internal organizational structure rather than thinking from the perspective of those who will be coming to the site. For example, some mistakenly set up the main navigation categories according to their departmental structure—Fundraising, Programs, Communications, Volunteering, and so forth—rather than presenting visitors with the choices they are more likely to be looking for. Examples include Donate Now, Our Services, What's New?, and Become a Volunteer.

Similarly, donors probably will not want to be embroiled in the intricate internal debates about how a multilevel organization's donations are distributed. They should, however, be given real options that empower and engage them in relation to your organization.

There are a number of different approaches that a multilevel organization might want to take in presenting meaningful options to their donors. Two approaches stand out.

In the first, donors indicate which branch of the organization corresponds to their places of residence. For example, see the Salvation Army's international secure server facility at [https://secure.salvationarmy.org]. (See Exhibit 16.1.) Many of the member countries have their own Web sites, but they can all link to this central online donation facility by using a uniform "Online Donation" icon that is placed prominently on their Web sites. Once visitors have clicked through to this secure site, they are met with a screen that asks them to select their country of residence from a pull-down list of over two hundred countries or regions.

This approach provides a great deal of efficiency and consistency of experience to your donors. It can enable smaller divisions to accept gifts on a secure server when otherwise they might not be able to offer their donors this option.

The top level of an organization like this might choose to administer the funds collected from such a form in a couple of different ways. The donations could be funneled directly from the online donation facility into separate merchant accounts for the designated division. Alternately, the money could be retained by the top-level organization for distribution according to another formula, but the donor contact information could be forwarded immediately to the office closest to the donor's home so that nearby staff could begin to look after the donor following the initial contact.

Donors may not necessarily wish the money to go to the office in their own region. For example, an international environmental organization might find that some donors want to have their gifts go to a region where a particular project is taking place. A donor to a health services charity might want to make a memorial gift to the office in the

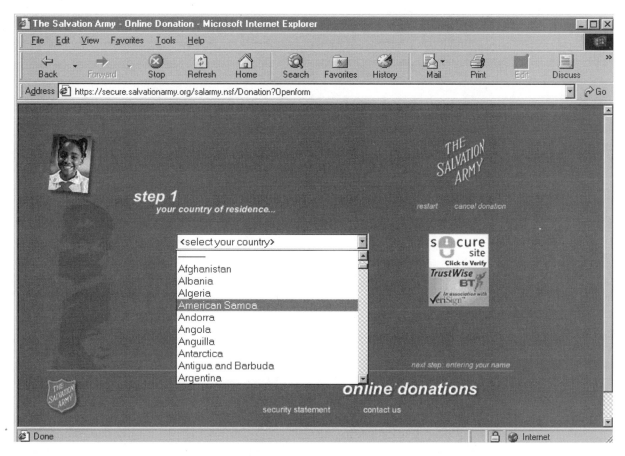

Exhibit 16.1. The Salvation Army International Online Donation Facility.

area in which the person to whom they are paying tribute lived and received services. Would the nonprofit want to provide this option?

In the second approach to offering choices to donors, a multilevel organization might want to present donors with choices not explicitly tied to its internal geographical boundaries. A national health charity might, for example, offer its donors the choice of making a gift either toward "Research" or toward "Services." In the organization's own terms however, it might be understood that a research donation is directed toward the national body while a gift for services is distributed among the regional and local levels of the organization.

Giving supporters greater control over their interaction with the nonprofit can also enrich the donor relationship. At a basic level, this might consist of allowing donors to submit change-of-contact information via a Web site form, which reduces the chance of clerical error that might be introduced in data entry from a form that is mailed in. Donors might be empowered to choose how and how often they want to be contacted by the organization—for example by e-mail rather than mail—or by newsletters, e-newsletters, or emergency bulletins.

Beyond the Online Donation Form

The value of the Internet as a fundraising tool goes far beyond the donation form that is presented to the public. For example, fundraising staff and volunteers from different levels of the organization might benefit from a private Web site where they can exchange information and ideas with each other. This can bring together a wealth of practical wisdom and cultivate a sense of community.

The Crohn's and Colitis Foundation of Canada developed a password-protected "Volunteer Leaders Area." Volunteer leaders from across the country are able participate in a "Tips and Clips" bulletin-board where they can discuss fundraising events that they had successfully run in their own local chapters and provide feedback and support to each other. The area also contains manuals and other resources that volunteers can download.

There are also exciting opportunities for multilevel organizations in managing fundraising events online. The Canadian Breast Cancer Foundation used a sophisticated event registration application to provide online registration for its Canadian Imperial Bank of Commerce Run for the Cure. In such a system, staff and volunteers from different levels of an organization can be provided with the tools and information appropriate to their needs.

Individual runners could spread the word about the event through *viral marketing* by soliciting pledges from their friends by e-mail. They could log in to check how many pledges had been made; they might receive e-mail reminders about the progress of their pledge sheets or about event details. Team captains could find out how many runners had signed up for their team and how much had been pledged. Local organizers could receive lists of registrants, teams, and donation amounts; they might try to galvanize captains by arranging competitions between different teams. Regional directors could have an overview of the all the runs occurring in their region, while the national office could have access to the full spectrum of tools and information.

A multilevel organization has a great deal to gain by moving its fundraising activities online, but it must take care to keep the donor's needs at the forefront. Moreover, consultation, flexibility, and a respect for different skills and approaches will mean that a nonprofit can tap the strengths of staff and volunteers at all levels of its organization.

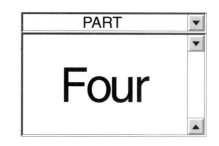

PART

Four

Tapping into Outside Resources

Managing Donor Data Online

Fundraising software systems have evolved from basic card files and paper-based systems to sophisticated behemoths of integrated software with complex design and extensive scope. Prior to the explosion of the Internet—and, more important, the World Wide Web—such systems provided a great deal of functionality but often at a high price: depend- ence on vendors for maintenance and upgrades; requirements for highly trained and highly paid in-house staff; and usually a substantial investment as well. Today's emerging Application Service Provider (ASP) model—similar to the service bureau arrangements of a couple of decades back—offers nonprofits more direct control over data, lower cost, less demanding requirements for training, and the ability to pro- vide access to donor data as widely as policy permits.

TIMES ARE CHANGING fast in the staid old business of donor datafile management. For example:

• Blackburn College doesn't have to worry any more about being embarrassed because volunteers who are helping with the college's $8.5 million capital campaign unknowingly and repeatedly ask the same alumni for contributions. The small, liberal arts college, based in Car- linville, Illinois, is in the process of replacing its old DOS-based database system, originally developed to track student records, with a Web-based donor management and communications system that gives Blackburn College real-time information on its donors. Updates to the college's archaic DOS-based system could take more than a day, and designing and creating reports was a real problem.

• Board members of Atlanta-based Literacy Action, Inc., were ready to spend more than $20,000 on a proprietary donor management software system over a two-year period even though the purchase would mean that the nonprofit's development director would have to maintain the software and the independent server that the program needed. After examining the alternatives, the board opted instead for two years of service, training, and other features for a Web-based donor database and communications management system at a cost of about $5,000. The deal-breaker? That in-house staff would have had to maintain the in-house software, whereas the Web-based system was maintained by an application service provider.

• Staff members at the Prostate Cancer Research and Education Foundation no longer have to negotiate custody of a donor database laptop to access the foundation's database, as they did before the foundation's adoption of a Web-based donor management system. Now, any staff member with clearance can access the system over a home Internet connection to enter notes on a conversation with a major donor while another staffer in the nonprofit's office enters donation information and the foundation's chairman checks out the donor list from his medical office. Training on this system—provided by the application service provider—was conducted for five foundation staff members while they were in three locations. All five could hear each other, as well as the instructor, as each was manipulating a separate training database.

The road to this new reality was long and winding. Fundraising software systems evolved from basic card files and paper-based systems to sophisticated behemoths of integrated software with complex design and extensive scope. Virtually all such systems in the late 1990s were Windows-based, client server-based, or both. Prior to the explosion of the Internet—and, more important, the World Wide Web—such systems provided a great deal of functionality, but often with a price.

The technology world continues to march forward. However, due to the Internet, this march actually takes us full circle in several ways. The Application Service Provider (ASP) model—similar to the service bureau arrangements of a couple of decades back—offers some very special and beneficial twists. Many of the new functions go far beyond what has normally been found in fundraising systems. I'll elaborate on those later in this chapter. Meanwhile, let's explore some of the reasons for the explosive growth of this new ASP concept and its added communications functionality.

Fundraising software systems were created to handle the record-keeping duties associated with fundraising activities. The responsibility for using and maintaining these systems was, more times than not, relegated to support staff members only. Over time, various add-on modules for items such as executive reporting, prospect research, planned giving, and membership moved some usage onto other staff members' desks. This may or may not have included executive management.

However, rarely, if ever, did such systems include as users of certain important groups such as board members, volunteers, donors, affiliated agencies, attorneys, financial advisors, prospective donors, or other related individuals.

Unintended Consequences

The increased sophistication in fundraising database systems has led to significant and perhaps unintended consequences:

- The raw size and complexity of such sophisticated systems are daunting. These systems encompass hundreds of thousands if not millions of lines of code. This complexity requires an equally large and powerful hardware and operating-system environment, often requiring hundreds of megabytes of storage; multiple, high-level processors; and maximum memory—not only at the core server but also for every workstation. Storage, memory, and processor requirements for the software system itself as well as the operating system frequently means that a nonprofit must invest in the very latest in hardware to operate at anywhere near an efficient rate.

- The appropriate budget and staff need to be in place before the organization even starts implementing such a system. Hence, a charity must truly plan far ahead—and invest heavily—to make use of such in-house database management systems and software.

- The high cost of such systems has other, direct implications. In practice, the number of individuals allowed to interact with the system is often limited due to budget constraints. Also, when costs escalate (as they do all too often), other areas of the organization are typically affected, since the extra money has to come from somewhere.

- The maintenance of these large and sophisticated systems requires a lot of help from the organization's information system (IT) department. This assistance may include system administrators, database administrators, local area networks (LAN) or wide area networks (WAN) specialists, report-writing specialists, and communication specialists—or some combination of these often highly paid people.

- Less obvious consequences of maintaining these large-scale in-house database management systems involve implementation services and training. Implementation services include system administration functions and data conversions; the larger and more sophisticated the system, the more complex each of these services will be. In fact, it isn't uncommon for the implementation and training costs to be equal to or greater than the initial software cost—and require six months to a year to put in place. If you're tempted to disregard the cost and delay in converting to such a system, consider that an entire industry of implementation and training consultants has been created—and it's thriving.

These factors have prevented the majority of nonprofit organizations from adopting such sophisticated in-house systems and have led to the birth of online ASPs, which seek to address virtually all of these disadvantages.

Open Access

Take just one factor, for example: access to data. Traditionally, direct access to the donor database was limited to one or a few individuals in the IT or development department. But typically there are lots of people who could benefit from access to such systems. With online ASP-based databases, it's now possible to permit everyone involved with the charity to access appropriate portions of a nonprofit's donor file—access that will encourage them to communicate, learn, become more intimately involved, donate more time, raise more funds, and become a true partner in the charity's family. These individuals and groups may include any or all of the following:

Senior management	Middle management
Entry-level staff	Field staff
Board members	Committee chairman
Committee members	Volunteers
Major donors	Annual fund donors
First-time donors	Affiliated agencies
Financial advisors	Special event attendees
Press	Retired staff
Potential donors	

What an Online ASP Can Do

Online ASP-based donor-data systems are built on two premises: (1) that nonprofits can access their donor data more directly and more flexibly online than from a self-contained in-house system, and (2) that having data online will allow them to integrate that data into their Web sites and other Web-based functions.

The online ASP model can transform the fundraising system, as it is known today, into a total communication system—one that can involve every one of the organization's stakeholders (constituents, partners, program recipients) anywhere in the world.

The vast, global pipeline of the Internet makes all this possible. Not since the telephone has a single invention advanced person-to-person communications so simply and cost-effectively. Due to the emergence of the World Wide Web—within the Internet—millions upon millions of people are using the same user interface every day of the year. This, in turn, has allowed a complete set of rules governing online commerce to evolve.

Web-based fundraising systems thus allow nonprofit organizations to sidestep or completely eliminate most if not all of the five unintended consequences of dedicated in-house database management systems. Use of an ASP-based donor database provides fundraisers with the following advantages:

• Donor data can be managed effectively with any standard browser running on any Web-capable device—even legacy equipment such as 486s, slower Pentiums, and network computers. I cannot emphasize enough the importance of being able to use legacy equipment. Numerous surveys have revealed that the number of truly high-speed, state-of-the-art computer systems in the nonprofit world is extremely limited. And a recent study conducted in July 2000 of 2,094 nonprofit groups in the United States and Canada and reported in *The Chronicle of Philanthropy* showed that fewer than 25 percent of all nonprofits have either a part-time or full-time information-systems staff person. The ASP model allows the need for such staff to be drastically reduced. Ironically, that same study verified that 89 percent of the nonprofits had Internet access.

• For most nonprofits, the adoption of an ASP-based system requires no special planning or preparation. In fact, many of the online ASP-based donor management systems do not require any capital investment. These systems themselves and ongoing support are leased or rented on a monthly, quarterly, or annual basis.

• With proper safeguards, virtually everyone related to a nonprofit or its work can be given access to the data online. No extensive training is necessary.

• The need for highly trained and highly paid IT personnel to become involved in making use of an online donor database system is reduced. Staffing costs can thus be considerably lower. Even the mundane but ever-so-important tasks of daily back-ups and weekly restores are outsourced to the provider.

• The need for training and the time required in implementing a system are reduced, since so many of the tasks are handled by the ASP. In fact, most training, like the application itself, is conducted online. And help is available at the click of a mouse. This makes it possible for the 75 to 80 percent of charities who have not yet implemented formal fundraising database systems to do so.

Equally important, by adding the appropriate password(s) or other form of authentication, any nonprofit staff or board member, any donor, or any program beneficiary can become a high-level user with secure access to whatever information in the database is pertinent to them. Data security, which is always a legitimate concern of nonprofit executives and trustees, is assured.

Constituent Self-Service

Virtually every other industry has proven that people love to find and use information on their own. Companies such as Federal Express, Southwest Airlines, Citicorp, Fidelity Investments, and numerous others have taken such Web-based systems and customer communication to levels of usage even beyond their own optimistic estimates.

In the book *Webonomics* (New York: Bantam Doubleday Dell, 1998), Evan Schwartz eloquently states: "Self-service is becoming mandatory in many industries—as consumers demand increased comfort, control, and convenience. Open twenty-four hours per day, seven days per week, the Web is well suited to be the point of customer contact . . . a way to reduce costs, increase efficiency and boost customer loyalty . . . within one, easy to use user interface."

The use of an online donor database can facilitate the new models of self-service stated above in the nonprofit world. Linking the database directly to the charity's Web site and to other partner Web sites allows functions such as prospect registration; event registration; online giving; volunteer sign-up; online pledging; meeting collaboration and planning; online stock transactions; planned giving; dissemination of e-mail, direct mail, and newsletters; prospect research; shopping; voting; auctions; and just plain old communications. (See Figure 17.1; Exhibit 17.1.)

These new capabilities allow the online donor database to become a marvelous tool for any nonprofit. However, it's important to keep in mind that no database can eliminate the need for timely and accurate recording and crediting of gifts and pledges as well as careful, observant campaign management. (See Figure 17.2; Exhibit 17.2.)

A note of caution (which applies to the adoption of any new donor database management system): It will take work—and require both time and money—to ensure that an online donor data system interfaces properly with a nonprofit's accounting and other legacy systems.

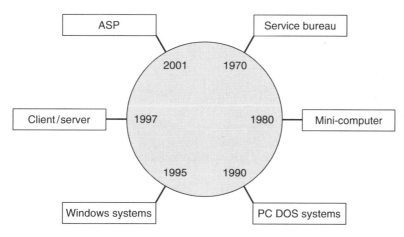

Figure 17.1. Have We Come Full Circle?

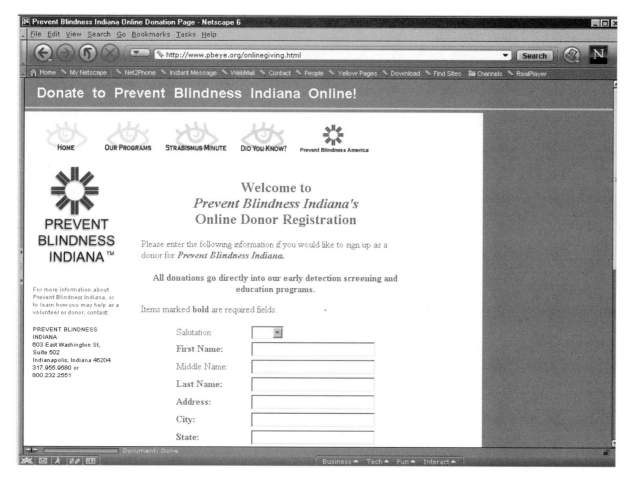

Exhibit 17.1. Donate Online.

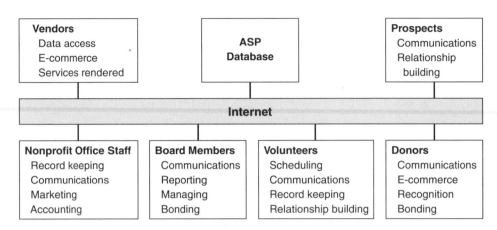

Figure 17.2. ASP-Based Donor Management System.

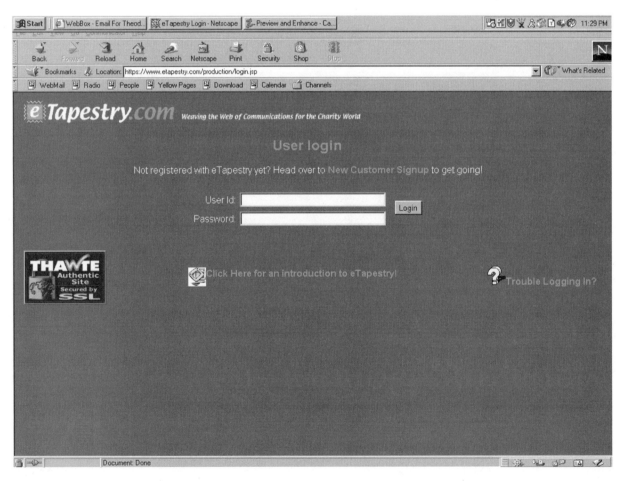

Exhibit 17.2. ASP User Login.

A Few Safety Measures

Since online donor-data systems rest so much responsibility in the hands of the ASP, it's important to exercise extra care in a few areas:

- Be sure that the security provided by the system provider and any related partners are up to industry standards, with stringent encryption of all data transmitted according to SSL standards.

- The safety and confidentiality of all data elements must be fully accounted for. A complete privacy statement should be part of any agreement.

- It's vital that your data be handled with utmost caution and protected daily. Verified back-ups and restores should be fully outlined. (In some cases, you will even be able to back up your records locally.)

- Make sure that the provisions for the conversion of your data and training of your staff are outlined in detail and fully agreed upon in advance. Since you can switch from one ASP to another with relative ease, take care to secure a full explanation of what's involved in returning your data, including both costs and procedures.

SHAUN SULLIVAN

ePhilanthropy and Donor Management Systems

Just as word processing software provides rich facilities to build and format complex documents, a donor management application offers a wealth of services that permit fundraising professionals to store and extract meaningful data about their constituents. These services encompass five functions: data entry, query, reporting, export, and import. In less than one decade of rapid evolution, donor-database management systems have already gone through three distinct phases: the static stage, the early adopter stage, and the integration stage. With the new tools spawned by years of rapid change in all aspects of online communications, nonprofits now have within their reach the ability to harness the full power of the Internet for philanthropic purposes.

MOST (IF NOT ALL) donor management systems perform at least five basic functions. At the most fundamental level, each component is inextricably linked to the underlying database, providing services that allow efficient access to the data. (See Table 18.1.)

The Donor Management System: Your Most Valuable Resource

As attractive as the Web is, it's clear that traditional fundraising methods are not going away. An online presence can certainly be a great complement to your organization's fundraising efforts, but it won't replace the need for you to cultivate donors and "market" to your constituents via direct mail and other traditional fundraising efforts. (See Chapter Three.)

165

Table 18.1. The Core Functions of Data Management Systems.

Categories	Usage
Data entry	Services that allow the user to enter and update data.
Query	Services that extract meaningful data from the system (e.g., "Give me all the constituents who gave last year but not this year").
Reporting	Services that extract and tabulate information from the system, yielding useful, understandable results. Many donor management systems have pre-built (or "canned") reports designed to meet the majority of a nonprofit's reporting needs.
Export	Services that allow for the transfer of information from the donor management system to other applications. For example, information can be "exported" to a word processing program for a mail merge or to an accounting program for statistical analysis.
Import	The natural complement to export services, import services make it possible to move data from external systems into the donor management database. Often the export and import functions are tightly coupled. For example, the nonprofit can export constituent information in a readable format to a third party that provides services such as address correction or prospect rating. After the data have been "scrubbed," import provides the ability to bring it back into the system, with updated information attached.

The common denominator of all these efforts—and the most valuable resource—is the data in your donor file. Accurate, clean data on your constituents make it possible for you to pursue a wide range of both online and off-line fundraising opportunities. Easy access to accurate donor and prospect information is essential to improved donor relations and increased fundraising capacity.

With increasing frequency, nonprofits that have client server–based, donor-database systems are asking how they can harness the benefits *and* the power of the Internet without abandoning the off-line database management systems they worked so hard (and paid so much) to build. As you look at how you can tap the vast resources of the Internet to strengthen your fundraising program without having to reengineer your entire donor management system, it's helpful to reflect on the history both of donor databases and of the Internet.

When the Internet explosion began in the 1990s, it became clear that for an organization to establish a strong Web presence—one that provided real benefits both to its external constituency and its staff—it had to bring in the experts. Creating a compelling design, maintaining the Web site, publishing content, establishing security, and creating all the other important characteristics of a good Internet presence involved foreign terms such as HTML, FTP, SSL, HTTP, Perl, CGI, and far too many others. In these early days, the up-front investment that was involved often outweighed any tangible benefit. Generally, e-commerce, e-marketing, and other Internet-centric initiatives were thought to have more direct application in the for-profit realm than for nonprofit organizations.

Fortunately, many donor management system providers, productivity software vendors, and Internet startups saw the need for a simplified, less expensive route to the Internet. The services these firms provided and the speed at which Internet publishing and hosting services matured made it possible to build Web sites by using data management tools as simple as a word processor. Hosting services sprang up overnight, many of them extremely inexpensive or even free. These services offered to host nonprofit Web sites remotely without a large investment either in hardware or in programming.

All these forces converged to enable many nonprofits to reach what might be called the *static stage*, at which a nonprofit has staked its claim on the Web, maybe even securing a domain name such as "www.mycharityname.org" but not beginning to mine the potential of online communications. A static Web site usually serves a nonprofit organization as a passive communication vehicle, a way to make publicly available news about its mission and goals, e-mail and contact links, and various other tidbits of information.

The static stage was a great achievement for its time. But since it amounted to little more than posting a brochure online, this approach became stale very quickly. Donors rarely found such Web sites inviting.

The Drive for More Dynamic Content and Integration

As the demand grew for a more dynamic Web presence, it became obvious to many in the nonprofit sector that they could greatly benefit by putting the valuable data they maintained in their donor management systems to work on the Web. Web sites and e-mail served as great starting points for communicating with existing donors and prospecting for new ones.

At this time, some savvy users began to leverage all this power. They had the data, a means to use it in their donor management systems, a Web site, and e-mail capability. It was time to bridge these elements into a cohesive and efficient fundraising tool.

Take, for example, the West Point Association of Graduates (AOG). AOG's Tom Mulyca, LTC(R), was an early adopter of the Internet. Long before most nonprofits were dipping their toes into the online waters, Col. Mulyca was using West Point's donor management database to build e-mail campaigns and Web-based graduate services. Mulyca states, "At West Point we have a strong association with class. If a class member passes away, I want to notify classmates quickly and effectively."

Because Col. Mulyca was already tracking all this information in detail in the AOG's donor database, he decided to try e-mail as a new way to communicate with graduates. Using query and export tools provided by his donor management software, together with homegrown programming, Col. Mulyca built an automated e-mail system capable of notifying graduates of information in a timely fashion. "I included links in the e-mail to drive graduates back to our Web site as well as links so they could pass on information that they had. The result is we have very up-to-date, accurate records," says Mulyca.

As is good practice, Col. Mulyca included a link at the bottom of the e-mail allowing the graduate to unsubscribe from the mailings. This is often referred to as an *opt-out* capability. "We only had three graduates unsubscribe!" says Mulyca. (See Resource A.)

Col. Mulyca has expanded West Point's offering to include the ability for graduates to log onto the Web site and update their contact information, which is verified and imported into the donor management system. "My philosophy is that we should provide good, quality content on a regular basis. If the content is good, the graduates realize its value and the benefits they get in staying up-to-date with AOG," says Mulyca.

"For example, we were building a business resource directory recently, so we extracted information from the donor database on each person and e-mailed it out for updates and corrections. We sent out 8,000 e-mails, and within ten days we had a 33 percent electronic response rate! This program alone saved AOG close to $4,000 in mailing costs."

It is clear that without a good donor management system and database serving as a foundation, Col. Mulyca would not have been able to build such an impressive arsenal of services. His ideas embody what could be called the *early adopter stage* of Internet development. This second stage (after the static stage) involved making creative use of the tools provided by donor management systems. Col. Mulyca is a prime example of an early adopter with the vision and technical expertise required to open up new possibilities online. Of course, not every nonprofit had (or has) a Col. Mulyca. Integration of donor management systems and the Internet was still out of reach for most nonprofits.

Donor Management Systems Mature: The Integration Stage

Many donor management system vendors responded to the obvious challenge of moving from the early adopter stage to what might be called the *integration stage*.

Two options emerged: application service providers (ASP), which manage the entire process online (see Chapter Seventeen), and integrated donor management services, which bridge the Web with traditional client server-based donor management software systems. The major database software vendors focused on building into existing donor management systems first-class tools for Web publishing, donation capture, and e-marketing. Today nonprofits can reap the benefits of these early efforts.

Take online donations, for example. Initially, the idea of accepting secure online donations at a nonprofit's Web site was thought to be reserved for "Web gurus." Building a secure online e-commerce site meant constructing a robust, secure site with a database storage solution, dynamic content-generation tools, and credit card processing. That meant custom development, almost always performed by outside consultants—and almost always expensive.

In response, many software vendors introduced products that allowed a traditional donor management system to publish donation capture pages and other dynamic Web content directly from a nonprofit's database to the Web. Typically, the page was hosted on a secure server managed by the vendor, providing a bridge between the Web and the client server-based database.

Most services started by offering "Donate Now!" links to clients' Web sites. The vendors' own, professionally maintained Web servers handled all the details of encrypted, secure data transmission and credit card transaction. Their clients were then able to download transaction data directly into their existing donor management systems as part of a seamless integration strategy. With such services available, the difficulties of building customized, secure e-commerce sites quickly lessened.

Creating a secure online donation capability is a vital first step in building your organization's Web development strategy. However, even the best, most efficient donation site is of little value if your constituency doesn't visit your Web site. E-mail can help you maximize traffic on your site. Through e-mail, Col. Mulyca was able to gather important, current information as well as to drive traffic to his Web site, all while reducing costs by using his donor management system not only as a data source but also as a publishing tool. Integrating these tools is the easiest, quickest route to using the Internet successfully.

Many donor management software vendors are providing these tools today. Companies that can help you build integrated donor management systems bridging the Web and traditional client server-based software programs include the following:

3rdSector	www.3rdsector.net
Blackbaud	www.blackbaud.com
Convio	www.convio.com
eTapestry	www.etapestry.com
FundGem	www.capricorninc.com
Kintera	www.kintera.com

Blackbaud's Raiser's Edge 7, for example, provides a set of tools collectively referred to as RE:NetSolutions. RE:NetSolutions is a software module that allows users to build Web pages, accept online donations, send targeted e-mail appeals (and measure the results), offer online registration for events, and publish online directories.

For example, offering online registration for events typically requires running users through a simple software "wizard" that allows them to select existing special events from the database. As users sign up online, the information they enter is downloaded automatically into the database, which is hosted on the vendor's server. Donation pages are built in a similar fashion, and as constituents donate online, their credit card transactions are securely processed, and gift and constituent records are automatically created or linked in the donor management software. This combination of seamless data integration, simplicity, and power is a compelling offering for the donor developing an online presence.

RE:NetSolutions serves as an example of bridging ePhilanthropy techniques and traditional donor management systems. Users need not be HTML-savvy: the tool handles the implementation and presentation details, and Web servers hosted by the vendor handle the transaction processing.

The Future of Web Integration: Seamless Donor Management

The Internet is playing a key role in helping build the momentum toward easing the data integration process. Nonprofits may be using disparate Internet-based services, each collecting data and ultimately transferring the data back to the organization, many times in vastly different formats. Obviously, the data are much less valuable if they are housed in a number of different systems. Ideally, data should be centrally managed.

How can you get all these data into your primary system? For the most part, data are transferred in electronic format and manipulated so that they can be transferred into a donor management system. Today, the typical solution involves using import and export tools to move data from one system to another. Most donor management and third-party applications provide flexible tools to ease the process.

This process, while acceptable, needs to be refined. While the ideal situation may be one centrally located donor management database system, the reality is that there's a need for multiple systems to work together.

Enter OPX, a common XML language for transferring data online. In mid-2000, a number of software and Internet industry leaders recognized the importance and scope of the data integration problem. To this aim, the Open Philanthropy Exchange (OPX) Consortium was formed. Though integration is now within reach for most organizations, as the complexity of fundraising online increases with success, creating an even more efficient way to transfer information reliably becomes even more important.

Open Philanthropy Exchange is a specification for data transfer between institutions involved in the nonprofit sector. The purpose of the OPX standard is to help philanthropic institutions communicate in a common language. Through seamless transmission of data, OPX removes technical barriers and allows data to flow seamlessly from one organization to another.

OPX is based on XML (Extensible Markup Language), an emerging technology that has captivated the software community. XML is a standard language used to structure and describe data so a broad range of applications can understand it. Additional information and current status on OPX can be found at [www.opxinfo.net].

A Call to Action: Define Your Internet Strategy Today

If you already have a traditional client server-based donor management system, you are probably armed with the tools you need to extend your fundraising efforts online. With the new tools spawned by years of rapid change in all aspects of online communications, nonprofits now have within their reach the ability to harness the full power of the Internet for philanthropic purposes.

GEORGE IRISH   KEN WEBER

CHAPTER

19

Faster, Cheaper, Better: Internet Outsourcing to Boost Your Online Presence

Outsourcing Web site services is a viable option for an increasing number of nonprofits that want to improve their presence on the Internet without incurring the costs and delays of developing new applications in-house. For many small and medium-sized nonprofits, this option opens the door to using tools they would otherwise be unable to build on their own. Nonprofits should keep in mind, however, that the marketplace for outsourced services is very competitive, and many ASPs are expected to fail in the coming years. Decision makers should proceed carefully when they make decisions about which services they may acquire from an ASP, and make sure contingency plans are always in place.

FORTUNATELY, a new form of commercial supplier has appeared in the nonprofit marketplace—application service providers, or ASPs— that offer plug-in Web services that can help organizations easily expand their Web sites and add sophisticated new features. By using an ASP-provided solution, a nonprofit organization can avoid the big investment necessary to build its own Web tools and start using the new features right away.

Nonprofits can also expect to get better-developed products than they could build on their own. ASPs are continuously testing, refining, and improving their services, so from the nonprofit's point of view, any outsourced services are automatically kept up-to-date, with data properly stored and backed up.

The potential benefits of Internet outsourcing can be summed up as *faster, cheaper, better*. Of course, there are also many challenges associated with outsourcing, some of which we'll discuss below.

How Does It Work?

Application service providers are much like any other supplier that your organization employs, except that the services they provide are primarily accessed and managed via the Internet. Some ASP services take the form of special Web pages that are added to your organization's Web site: an online donation page, for example. These pages are usually customized to match the look and feel of your Web site, so that visitors to your site may not even be aware that they are accessing an outside service. Other ASPs provide purely back-end services that have no public presence on your site. These are primarily office administration and management tools for donor data and campaign management and for special events ticketing.

ASPs may be split into two groups according to the variety and scale of services they offer to nonprofits: all-in-one services, and single service specialists.

All-in-One Services

The largest service providers offer comprehensive, one-stop shopping, whereby nonprofits can select from a variety of functions they wish to employ. These all-in-one services attempt to cover many or all of the outsourcing needs of a nonprofit from online donations to e-mail campaigning, special event ticketing, and donor data management. Benefits include the following:

- One supplier to deal with instead of many
- Access to a larger pool of resources
- Consistency in design
- Better integration of components

Among the potential drawbacks are two: the ASP may be good at many things but not great at any one thing; you may become reliant on a single point of service (and thus risk potential failure).

Single Service Specialists

The do-it-yourself approach to Internet outsourcing is to seek out and contract a different provider for each service. Single service specialists abound on the Internet, especially in providing opportunities for affinity shopping and online donation processing to nonprofits. These companies can vary widely in size, from full-size corporate giants to garage setups run by a single individual. The benefits of these services include these:

- You keep your options open
- Smaller companies with less overhead may be cheaper
- A small-company focus on one aspect of Web development may mean greater outcomes in each area

Potential drawbacks include access to fewer resources, the difficulty of integrating the services provided, and the higher administrative costs you sustain to coordinate a number of vendors.

Types of Outsourced Services

There are now dozens of well-financed firms that have invested in developing robust Web-based tools for nonprofits. The services they offer fall into several categories, as explained in more detail below. An up-to-date listing of ASP services and providers can be found on the NonprofitMatrix Web site [www.nonprofitmatrix.com]. (However, this Web site lists *all* providers; it does not rate them or tell you which are likely to survive.)

Donor and Member Management

Many nonprofits use sophisticated database software to manage their records of donations and supporters. The cost of setting up and maintaining these systems, and of periodic upgrades, can be quite high, especially for smaller organizations. A better solution for some organizations may be to use a Web-based management solution that's offered on a subscription basis via the Web. All the donor and membership management can take place via a regular Web browser.

A number of the leading online donation ASPs have added donor analysis and management tools that can perform many of the functions of sophisticated donor management software programs such as Blackbaud's Raiser's Edge. Examples of companies offering Web-based donor and member management include eTapestry.com, Donormax.com, and Changingourworld.com.

E-Mail Campaigning

E-mail membership and supporter lists are becoming an important asset for nonprofit organizations. E-mail solicitation and marketing are new tools for development offices to use to build their organizations' support bases, and for communication departments to use in their outreach, education, and advocacy strategies. A number of new services have appeared in the dot-com world that make it easy for organizations to create and manage sophisticated e-mail campaigns linked to fundraising, advocacy, or community-building. Through the end of 2000, e-mail campaigning and other CRM (Customer Relationship Management) tools were most often available as stand-alone services. Recently, however, these tools are beginning to be bundled with end-to-end or *all-in-one* services. Look for these tools to become a staple of nonprofits' Web presences. At the same time, be aware that there are significant issues of data integration with these Web-based tools; very few of them have yet to integrate successfully with traditional back-end fundraising applications.

At this writing, examples of companies offering tools for e-mail campaigns included getactive.com (Exhibit 19.1), LocalVoice.com, and SocialEcology.com.

Events Management

Online events management services offer tools to assist organizations in organizing and accounting real-life events of many shapes and sizes. There are two primary services that online events management can provide: organizing the event (including specialized task lists and scheduling, and links to suppliers), and executing the event (handling online registration and payment, tracking memberships, printing name tags). Services are provided either on the basis of an annual license fee or in proportion to the number of event registrants and the fees they pay.

For most nonprofits, events are complicated affairs. Many management tools for online events are useful because they can capture and process basic information related to events. However, consider carefully to what extent your events management outsourcing partner can successfully customize your version of their software to accommodate group registrations, member discounts, and other special considerations, for example. Contemporary examples of companies offering events management services include DAXKO, Acteva, 4charity.com, and MaestroSoft.com.

Online Donations

Since the early days of the Internet, nonprofit organizations have considered online fundraising to be a kind of El Dorado, and they have been waiting for someone to announce its unraveling. Nowadays there are many organizations actively raising funds online, and everyone else, it seems, is talking about the Internet and how to make it work for them. The technical details of setting up your own secure e-commerce server can be daunting, and many organizations have gone the much easier route of "leasing" a secure donation page from a third-party vendor (ASP).

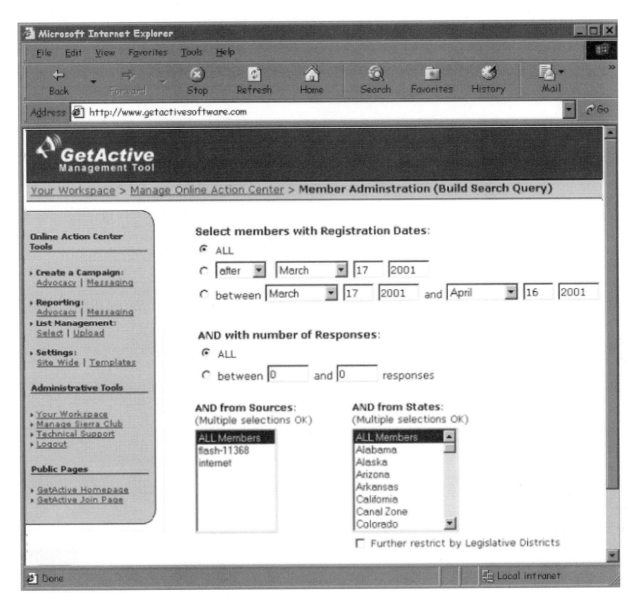

Exhibit 19.1. Sample E-Mail List Management Screen.

The first online donation ASP services offered secure Web pages where donors could record donation information, including credit card details, which would be passed along to the nonprofit organization for processing as a regular donation. With the rise of e-commerce over the past couple of years, most of the online donation ASPs have extended their services to include processing of the credit card information, so that the nonprofit just receives a regular bundle of money deposited to their merchant account, without all of the processing overhead (which is included in the fee or in the percentage cut that's taken by the ASP).

The latest trend in online donation ASPs has been to add donor analysis and management tools that can perform many of the functions of sophisticated donor management software programs such as Raiser's Edge. Examples of online donation ASPs include Entango (Exhibit 19.2), CharitEx, and JustGive.org.

Planned Giving Tools

Although planned giving has not yet received much attention from the online nonprofit community, this is likely to change. By the time you read this book, you may find a wholly new planned giving picture online.

So far, most of the focus has been on harvesting immediate donations through credit card transactions, or on signing up supporters for monthly giving plans. However, the Internet is an excellent medium for planned giving information, especially given the popularity of personal finance management Web sites, which assist individuals in analyzing

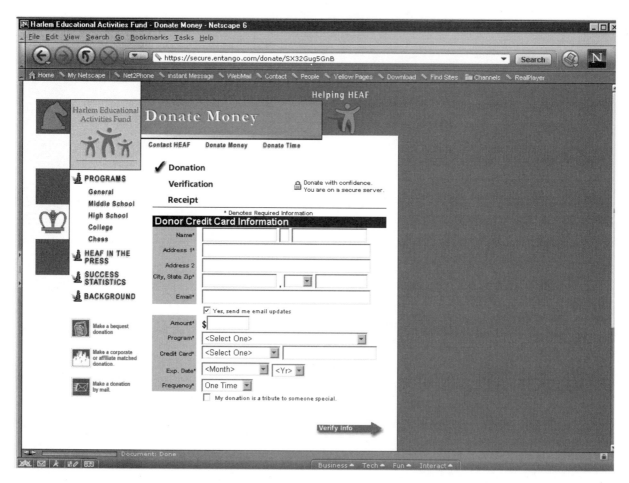

Exhibit 19.2. Sample Outsourced Online Donation Service.

and modifying their long-term investment portfolios. Some Web-based planned giving tools are already available, including tax calculators and other applications. (See Chapter Thirteen for more information on planned giving online, including a listing of useful ASPs.)

Some Keys to Outsourcing

As you consider the prospects of outsourcing Web-based services for your organization, keep the following considerations in mind:

1. Have a clear idea of what you want before seeking outside help. First explore the many options highlighted in this book, and choose a place to start.

2. Choose the right partners for the right reasons. *Note:* the right reasons do not necessarily include the lowest price, pro bono services, relationships between vendors and board members, or pretty graphic design. Essentially, the right reasons boil down to who you believe can help you solve your problem(s) with viable solutions and a sustainable approach.

3. Plan to spend time working closely and proactively with vendors. Vendors generally respond very well to organizations that put forth a sustained effort to help themselves. Help them achieve the best possible outcome for you.

4. Frequent and open communication, both with vendors and internally—especially on technology projects—will help ensure success. It will also go a long way toward integration with current operations and staff.

5. Set clear expectations for both the project and the outcomes of whatever is created.

6. Co-manage the budget tightly, but do not overdo it. Nonprofits are notorious for penny-pinching under the guise of "controlling costs for donors, members, etc." Avoid having to take this position with sound project planning and budgeting and effective co-management along the way.

7. Plan to get educated and stay open to new ideas. You are outsourcing because you do not have the expertise or personnel in-house. Allow your outsourcing partner to demonstrate its expertise.

What Are Typical Outsourcing Costs?

Outsourcing can cost next to nothing, or it can cost hundreds of thousands of dollars. From a fundraising standpoint, expect to make allocations—or have them covered or bundled by an application service provider—in the following areas:

- Strategy and planning
- Technical development
- Creative and design services
- Software and licensing; for example, content management, CRM, database
- Transaction processing and fulfillment
- Integration or coordination with other media; for example, tele-marketing
- Online fundraising program management, including marketing
- Hosting and support

For the most part, outsourcing costs can be predicted by the direct, positive relationship between the size (and budget) of an organization and its outsourcing needs. In terms of basic online fundraising, effective Web sites can be created for as little as a few thousand dollars, as has been demonstrated by some of the smaller organizations nominated each year for the Association of Fundraising Professionals Commerce One Outstanding Achievement in Internet Fundraising Award. However, if you expect your Web presence to handle information dissemination, public or media relations, donor development, advocacy, and other functions—all of which will enhance your fundraising effectiveness—then the costs of your Web site will increase substantially. The bottom line is that you should make investments in outsourcing that correspond well with your expected ROI (return on investment). Whatever you invest should be geared toward increasing your ability to create and sustain meaningful—and profitable—relationships online.

Also, a nonprofit that's looking at outside vendors to add new services to its Web site should consider carefully how likely it is that its chosen supplier will stay in business. Dot-com companies fail for a number of reasons, but a leading cause of failure is an unsound business plan: not enough revenue to cover startup and operating costs. Keep this mind when choosing a vendor: the cheapest solution is not necessarily the best solution. If your supplier is not making enough money to stay in business, you will eventually have to face the added expense and effort of relocating.

Planning Your Web Presence (Strategic Planning)

Even the most straightforward Web presence needs to be planned carefully. What does this have to do with outsourcing? Everything. Here's why:

- Proper strategic planning enables you to select appropriate vendors, based on the specific needs of your Web presence or project.

- If you have clearly defined the strategic objectives for your Web presence or project before engaging a third party or parties, your organization will be in the best possible position to make the most of outside help once it arrives. Having your vendors focused from the outset on specific tasks and outcomes will ensure that your precious resources are directed toward maximum impact.

- Strategic planning also helps avoid one of the most common pitfalls of going online: leading with technology. Decisions about what you want the Web site to accomplish and what functions and features it should have should precede most, if not all, decisions about what hardware, software, or other technology will be used.

- Strategic planning for Web projects helps control costs, including the cost of vendors. One of the awesome challenges of the Web is that you can use it to accomplish so many things. Setting priorities first will help ensure that your organization is not paralyzed by trying to solve everything at once—a common reason for failure, even among otherwise highly functioning organizations.

- Strategic planning helps you establish an approach to staffing, including which staff will interact with vendors during a project.

- Strategic planning forces organizations to set goals and establish clear measures for a Web presence's success. As with traditional fundraising, this is critical to determining whether or not your investment in a particular Web program is paying off. Clear parameters for success will also spur you to make adjustments along the way, adjustments that could mean the difference between success and something less.

For information on Web hosting (Internet Service Providers, or ISPs), please see Resource C, "Web Hosting." Also see Resource D, "Tips for Creating Effective Vendor Contracts."

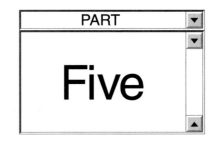
Beyond the Basics

CHAPTER

20

Web Site Content: Keep Them Coming Back

Nonprofit Web sites are competing with thousands of others for the attention of people surfing the Internet. If your organization wants to dip into this pool and fish for financial support, you first need to pay attention to the infrastructure, the very basics, of your Web site. In this chapter, you'll learn why one organization found the most advanced technology isn't right for their visitors; you'll find pointers and ideas for special features that will help people want to bookmark your site even if they may not be ready to donate on their first click-through; and you'll understand why it is important for you to consider all revenue brought into your organization through your Web site.

CONGRATULATIONS! Your Web site is up and running, and you believe that your organization is now firmly entrenched in the twenty-first century. You're excited to learn that you've had "hits," and you've gotten a few donations. You've listed your Web site on numerous search engines; you're satisfied that the key words will help you connect with people you want to attract. You've even subscribed to a Web statistics tracking service, and reports indicate that visitors and donations to your Web site continue to go up and up.

But then, for some unexplained reason, the numbers level off. Even worse, they start to go down. You can't imagine what's wrong. The Web site is still as informative, compelling, and beautiful as the first day you launched it, but visitors and donations are dropping off. As you sit back and view the statistics, you realize that you've run head-on into one of the biggest challenges to providing a Web site: competing for the attention of a somewhat fickle audience surfing the World Wide Web.

Through this experience, you're learning a lesson that's far from obvious to most people—that launching a Web site is only the beginning of a very involved process. Your Web site is competing with millions of other sites for attention. It is your responsibility not only to capture your visitors' attention on the first visit, but also to give them a reason to return. And you know little about your first-time visitor, with the exception of understanding that they selected your Web site and could potentially provide greatly needed support to help your organization flourish.

Getting Back to Basics

To ensure that visitors return to your site again and again, you must answer some fundamental questions: Why do you want to invest in a Web site? What is its purpose?

"Everybody else is building Web sites" isn't a good enough answer to these questions. Your Web site is an open door to your organization. When visitors enter your site, you have a minute, perhaps less, to capture their attention. Your site needs to be designed to make the best possible use of that minute. Here are six sets of questions to ask before you set out to build a dynamic Web site:

- What do you want your site to accomplish? Do you want merely to inform your constituents and the public at large? Are you serious about soliciting donations? Or do you have some other strategic goal in mind for the site?

- Have you spent enough time on the Internet visiting other Web sites, especially those for other nonprofits engaged in similar work? Do you know what you like on those sites and what you don't like?

- Have you asked staff, board members, volunteers, or others to critique your Web pages before you launch? Is the site easy to navigate? Are the features you've chosen compelling?

- Have you built in a way to ask for donations—and made it easy to give? Is there a "donate now" button on the home page? Do you have to click on "giving" to find the correct page? (Remember that most first-time visitors won't go many layers into a Web site to look for information.)

- Have you planned your Web site as a business, with thoughtful goals, a budget, and realistic revenue projections?

- Are you taking into account all the staff time that will be required to maintain the site and respond promptly to the inquiries it will generate?

Keep in mind that there is no magical path to a strong Web site—and certainly no plan that will bring you to a realized profit. If you research what's happening online, you'll find that even the best online business models are not "cash cows." Most have no solid hope of profit even after years of work, millions of dollars spent, and the best expert advice.

Keep Your Web Site Simple But Interesting

There are dangers when you use cutting-edge technology. Christopher Botosan with the Union Rescue Mission (Los Angeles) [www.urm.org], has conducted research on what works well or not so well on the Mission's site.

For example, he found that users and donors tend not to have the latest and most sophisticated computers and browsers. As an experiment, he constructed the site to identify visitors who had no plug-ins for contemporary software such as Flash and Shockwave (which are used to create the animated features you see on many opening pages). These plug-ins require visitors to download and install the software before they can see the special effects. Mr. Botosan diverted these visitors to a Web page that required them to download Flash to see an animated feature or, if they chose, simply to continue to the site without seeing the animation. Most visitors (83 percent) not only chose not to receive the plug-in, but almost without exception they left without visiting the site. It's also highly likely that those potential donors will not return to that Web site.

If your organization wants a Flash-like animated effect, consider keeping it simple by using an introduction that's actually made to run in a standard browser without the use of a downloaded plug-in.

Incorporate Components That Appeal to Potential Donors on a Web Site

Several years of online experience have demonstrated that certain features attract donors and prospects and keep them returning from time to time. These features include the following:

News and Information At the American Red Cross [www.redcross.org], visitors can find daily news updates providing them with vital updates on Red Cross activities. At the John F. Kennedy Center for the Performing Arts [www.kennedy-center.org], visitors find a wealth of information (Exhibit 20.1). Each of these sites is an excellent example of homepages that provide the visitor with timely information and clearly marked and useful internal Web site links.

Involvement Devices Many sites are designed to arouse strong emotions in visitors as their number one priority. Visitors may feel sad or compassionate about an issue or about the people affected by it—or

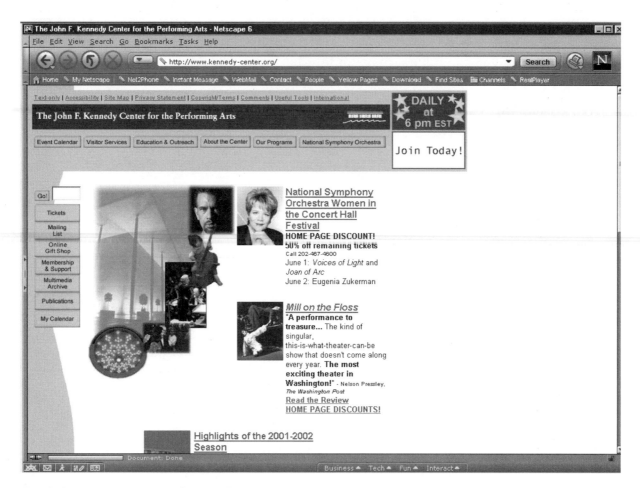

Exhibit 20.1. Kennedy Center Provides Timely Information.

they may feel joyful about having given a gift to the organization. Some think emotions are one of the motivational keys to giving. However, Mr. Botosan of the Union Rescue Mission reports that donors' comments directed to the Mission center mostly on wanting to do something to help once donors see the size of a problem. People like to feel they make a difference. To reinforce the connection between a gift and its effect on homeless people and to take advantage of a widespread desire to play online by trying out new features on the Web, the Union Rescue Mission [www.urm.com/newlook/new2.htm] encourages giving with its "homeless counter" and "donation calculator" (Exhibit 20.2).

Educational, Advocacy, and Volunteer Opportunities Remember, as compelling and informative as your Web site may be, first-time visitors may be interested in your work but not ready to take out their credit cards or checkbooks. Long before online giving, most nonprofit leaders understood that donors need to be cultivated and nurtured. That need

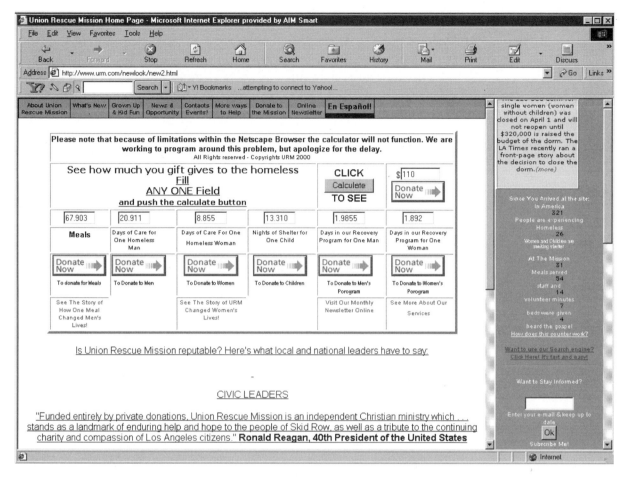

Exhibit 20.2. Innovative Approach to Engaging Donors Online.

hasn't changed with online giving. The longer people are involved with your organization, the greater the likelihood they will become donors. Remember to use your Web site for posting educational, advocacy, and volunteer opportunities. For example, The Nature Conservancy of North Carolina [www.tnc.org/northcarolina] offers general information, a quiz, and an easy connection for volunteers and donors on its Web site.

Make Your Web Site "Sticky"

"Sticky" sites encourage visitors to return over and over. On a sticky site, content changes often, giving visitors the impression that there is always going to be something new and interesting on the site. But visitors come back not just because there's new content but also because it's interesting to the eye. That can't be stressed enough. New content isn't enough.

Will your site interest someone looking at your Web site for the first time? For the tenth time? How will it affect them? What will it make them do or feel? Is it a call to action—one that they'll respond to? You need to be able to answer each of these questions with a definitive yes!

A good example of stickiness can be found during the year-end holiday season at the Union Rescue Mission Twelve Days of Homelessness site [www.urm.com/12daysofhomelessness]. Each day for the twelve days before Christmas, Mission staff would add new content on a different facet of homelessness. When visitors came to the site, they were encouraged to sign up for e-mail reminders that would give them a brief and compelling overview of why they should visit the site. The regular visitors to the site received precursor e-mails telling them about the Twelve Days of Homelessness and other events on the site each day.

A Web site with magnetic qualities makes visitors want to invite others to visit. An example of this can again be found on the Union Rescue Mission Web site, which uses a "chain-reaction" feature. If visitors give gifts or submit names to the e-mail list, they are brought to a page called Chain Reaction [www.urm.com/newlook/chain2.html]. If visitors show interest in the cause, the reasoning goes, it's worth the effort to encourage them to let others know about the site and the work of the Mission. In this case, visitors have the option of composing their own messages or selecting from a preset list of messages.

Not only does this chain-reaction feature involve donors, it also links to others, in hopes that they, too, will visit the site. The Mission notifies the original donors whether their friends do or don't visit, thus giving this feature "friendraising" as well as fundraising value.

Hosting Web Site Events

Some organizations have used their sites to make conferences or special presenters available to more people. The Union Rescue Mission took that one step further with a Web site event focused on Thanksgiving. A live video Webcast showed Mission staff and volunteers feeding the homeless on skid row. News coverage of that event was extensive, with stories in forty-one newspapers around the country, significant TV coverage of the Web broadcast itself, and over 140,000 viewers to the Webcast who tuned into the site on Thanksgiving and the few days after the holiday.

This is just one example of how the Mission uses features on the site to attract media coverage, which in turn helps drive more traffic to the site. To cite another example, one Thanksgiving the Mission promoted the sale of a "Digital Turkey" on the site [www.urm.com/thanksgiving/turkey.htm] (Exhibit 20.3). Many media representatives found it interesting and humorous enough to feature the story.

Looking at Revenue: It May Not Be as Low as It Seems

Keep in mind that there are different types of Web site revenue.

Direct Revenues This is the easiest to account for, since it comes directly from your Web site. People can use their credit cards on the secure server (or, in a few cases, mail a check along with a form they've printed from the site). It's pretty straightforward.

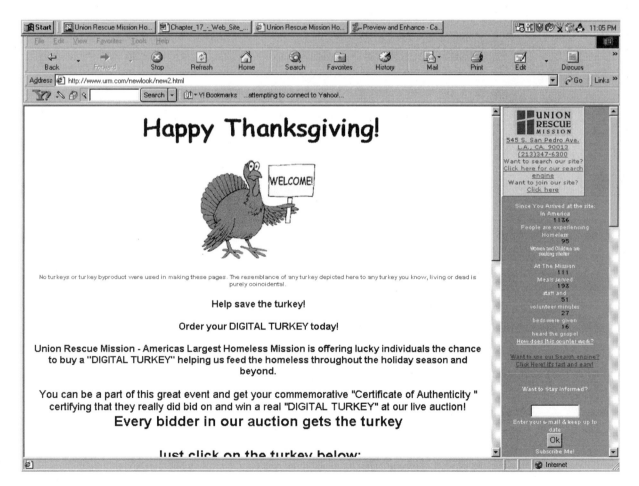

Exhibit 20.3. The Union Rescue Mission "Digital Turkey" Sale.

Ancillary Revenue Ancillary revenue includes donations, often not financial, that benefit your organization. For example, the Union Rescue Mission Web site includes a quick and easy form for potential donors of automobiles to complete. Currently the Union Rescue Mission is taking in an average of fifteen cars a month, which yield ancillary revenue of more than $90,000 a year. Without the Web site to provide that giving opportunity, it's likely those cars would go to some other organization. If your Web site offers similar noncash-giving options, your chief financial officer and development officer can take the resulting revenue into account when evaluating the return on your Internet investment.

| SHIRLEY SEXTON | STEVE LOVE |

Dos and Don'ts of Web Design

The design and architecture of your Web site create the experience users have with your organization and establish their perceptions of your brand, for better or worse. The guidelines in this chapter will help you avoid the pitfalls and mistakes of those that have come before you, so you can build a site that truly characterizes your organization's mission and helps you fulfill it.

IN A SPLIT SECOND, new visitors to your Web site will form a lasting impression of your organization—an impression based on the design, the "look and feel," of the first page they encounter. They'll also immediately begin assessing the information they can find on your site, how that information is structured, and how easy or difficult it will be to find what they're looking for—all elements that constitute the "architecture" of the site.

Together, the design and architecture of your Web site create the *experience* that users have with your organization. They establish their perception of your brand, for better or worse.

As senior creative strategists at a firm that has created Web sites for more than 150 nonprofit clients, we've done almost everything. And as avid watchers of the independent sector's presence online during the past five years, we've seen all the rest. With the following guidelines, we hope to help you avoid the pitfalls and mistakes made by those who come before you, so you can build a site that truly characterizes your organization's mission and helps you fulfill it.

Do Trust Professional Designers and Their Expertise

Don't ask your nephew, who is a high school freshman, to do the job instead.

Repeat after us, "Just because my intern has Photoshop on her computer, does not mean I have an in-house Web design staff." The Web is littered with thousands of sites of organizations that do not understand this fundamental fact. You've seen them yourself, sites that visually scream, "Our organization is held together by a rubber band and a shoestring!" Would you be willing to give a large donation to that organization? Would you feel confident that the money would be spent well?

The problem is that too many people think they have design skills. As a consumer, you've been trained to think so. You're given a myriad of design choices for your home, your wardrobe, your car, and so forth. The difference—and this is critical—is that those decisions are for you. It's a whole different ballgame to be able to make design choices that will resonate with others. Decisions that not only persuade and enable visitors to make a donation, but also make them feel good about it afterward to engender donor loyalty. For that, you need a professional.

One large, internationally known nonprofit had a vice president who hated purple. Just hated it, without explanation. He would not approve any designs for anything representing the organization that was predominantly purple. So for years, until this man retired, purple was absent from everything produced by this organization, even though one of its primary audiences is *children,* and purple is a very popular color with kids. (Think Tinky Winky and Barney.)

A designer worth her salt is not designing for you. She is designing for your *audience.* That's her true client. She won't ask you about your likes and dislikes. Instead, she'll ask you what market research you've done on your audiences. Experienced and skilled designers are trained in the psychological aspects of persuasion and the behavioral aspects of interface design. Their job is to use graphics, layout, and design to elicit the desired response from your site visitors. Let them do their job.

Do Choose a Design Firm with a Proven Track Record of Relevant Experience

Don't select an interactive design firm based on its print work or its designers' personal styles.

Selecting the right interactive design firm is difficult. The selection process can be awkward for both the potential firm and your organization. Those of us representing an agency are veterans of "the dance," but for many organizations this is their first time looking for a vendor with the skills to build an engaging and sophisticated online user experience. We recommend the following when meeting with potential candidates:

Ask to Meet the People Who Are Actually Going to Staff Your Project
Guard against "bait and switch" tactics. Some firms send the most personable and skilled people during the sales process, but on the day of

the project kick-off, the real team shows up and is neither personable nor skilled. Understand the make-up of the proposed team and the individuals' respective responsibilities.

Understand How the Firm Will Work with You Throughout the Project, a.k.a. "The Metholodogy" A logical and disciplined methodology allows for creativity while ensuring that timelines and budgets are met. Strong project management allows the client and the creative staff to focus on the solution. If the firm has no clear methodology, run, do not walk, to the nearest exit.

Dig Deep into the Former Work of the Potential Firm Look for previous experience in your industry or in the type of initiative you're undertaking, or both. Many design firms have a set style; this is fine if you like that style and it is appropriate, but if you can't see a broad enough range, move on. Also, ask for client references to learn how the firm worked with them.

Don't Get Wowed by Bells and Whistles The firm may show you a jazzy Flash presentation, but not one portfolio site similar to your project. Enjoy the Flash, but don't choose the firm. Also, don't pick a firm because the various members of the design team look the part; that is, stylishly attired, covered in tattoos, dyed-hair, etc.

Do Make the Online Experience for the User of Paramount Importance

Don't base your Web site's architecture on your organizational structure.

We run across this one often. When developing a user experience, organizational politics and other internal wrangling wreak havoc on site architecture. The end user should be considered king; all decisions should focus on inspiring the user to interact with the content, and enabling that user to act. Remember that users are also fickle. You have only a few seconds to engage their interest. When dealing with architectural issues and with page structure, do not let office politics prevent usability. Here are some helpful hints when making site architecture and page layout decisions:

Set Priorities for the Objectives and Measures of Success for the Site For many nonprofit organizations, these may include fundraising, education, and advocacy. Oftentimes, the answer is all of the above—and then some. That is acceptable, but you must prioritize, or the end result will be that the user does none of the above.

Stick to Your Guns Once you've set your measurable objectives, don't forget them down the road. A good firm will document your prioritized objectives and reference them frequently during the design process. Every decision on site architecture and the visual hierarchy of each page must reinforce the agreed upon objectives.

Conduct Focus Groups Identify existing and potential contributors to your organization, and ask them what they would want to see on your site. There are many market research firms that now offer Web site focus-group testing.

Do Use the Web to Extend Your Brand, Not Destroy It

Don't throw out all that you've done to build your brand through other channels, just because the Web allows you to create spinning logos so easily.

Remember, your logo is *not* your brand. Your brand is the user's total *experience* of your organization and its message.

A 1999 study conducted by Edgar, Dunn & Company for the International Olympic Committee (*Sport Business International*, February 1999) found that people attributed the following selected characteristics to the Olympic brand:

- Friendship
- Peace
- Fair competition
- Global
- Multicultural

These core attributes of the IOC brand are communicated through all media, whether Internet, television, products, or print.

Here is a test for your own brand and how well your Web site design reinforces it:

- Step 1. Use the lines below to list the top five attributes you want your brand to convey to the public. (Refer to the Olympic list as well as these additional examples: trustworthy, caring, dynamic, knowledgeable.)

_____

_____

_____

_____

_____

- Step 2. Review the imagery, content, and messaging of your site. Does it reflect the attributes you listed?

- Step 3. If the site reinforces your list, pat yourself on the back. If not, go back to the beginning of this chapter. It's time to hire a firm to redesign your site.

Do Recognize that a Web Site is Never Done; It Will Grow and Change with Your Organization

Don't let an intern with some Photoshop and HTML skills use it as his private sandbox.

The real work begins after the site is initially launched. Ideally, you've built a *database-driven site,* using a content management system with an administrative interface. Most content management systems include easy interfaces for adding and updating content through Web templates, so the integrity of the design and architecture remains intact.

However, with a *static HTML site,* post-launch is where the downward spiral begins. Often the organization assigns an inexperienced person to the daily upkeep of the site. This individual is often overburdened and underinformed about why certain decisions were made during the building process.

Make sure that you are best equipped to manage your site by getting these key items from your design firm at launch:

- A style-guide
- Original Photoshop files
- Typeface specifications
- The RGB values for your color palette

In addition, consider turning to your design firm for ongoing consulting in the maintenance of your site. It is in their best interest to keep the site on track, because they are as proud of it as you are.

Case Study: NARAL

A Web site can be attractive esthetically but miss the mark from the standpoint of usability (Exhibit 21.1). This frequently happens when the organization has a solid history of strong design for its print material but limited experience with the Web and the particular challenges it places on the user.

The online presence of NARAL (National Abortion and Reproductive Rights Action League) offers a classic example. In early 1999, The NARAL Foundation launched its Choice for America Web site to coincide with the launch of its "Choice for America" (CFA) television advertising and grassroots campaign. From a purely esthetic standpoint, the site was a winner. It integrated the look and feel of the television ads and direct mail so that the

AN AMERICAN RIGHT AT RISK

ABORTION & WOMEN'S HEALTH

CONTRACEPTION & EDUCATION

YOUR COMMUNITY

STORIES OF CHOICE

FACTS & NEWS

information

"Choice for America" is a grassroots effort to protect our right to choose, sponsored by The NARAL Foundation and supported by those who value freedom and independence.

TAKE THE CENSUS

QUIZ YOURSELF

action

SEND A POSTCARD

GET INVOLVED

Exhibit 21.1. 1999 NARAL Foundation "Choice for America" Web Site: Strong Design But Weak Usability.

organization was consistent in its messaging through multiple channels. The typography was sophisticated and classic: The teal, black, and tan color palette evoked a sense of calm, and the photographs reinforced the individual liberty and patriotism themes of the television ads.

The CFA site was separate from NARAL's public Web site, which was a rich resource of information for activists and contained important calls to action such as "donate," "send an e-mail to Congress," and "state legislation look-up." However, NARAL's primary URL (naral.org) was pointed to the foundation-funded CFA site. Hence, there were no clear calls to action on the home page for a new visitor to naral.org. Also, although the majority of the text on the home page was linked to further material, the text did not appear "clickable." Even if the user did manage to click on those links, the architecture made it difficult for users to find what they were looking for, or know what their choices were. Usability had been sacrificed for design.

In 2000, NARAL launched its new site (Exhibit 21.2), which achieves that elusive balance of strong design *and* usability, and integrated the two sites into one. The drop-down menus collect the many actions and issues that the user can access, making them each only a click away. The column at right is a collection of HTML "hot links" that the staff updates frequently to keep the content fresh. The layout communicates that this is an action center, where people can get informed and get involved. The single, large image of a woman and the teal and white colors set a welcoming and open tone. The "What's New" graphic area allows the staff to draw attention to

Exhibit 21.2. 2000 NARAL Foundation Web Site Combining Strong Design and Usability.

frequently rotating special campaigns. In addition, this design places
NARAL much higher in search engine results than the previous design.
This is because most search engines factor all HTML text (including that in
the drop-down menus) into their algorithms. So the second design contains
far more relevant text than the first, and thus scores higher in search
engines. And because most of the text is HTML, the page downloads
faster than its graphic-intensive predecessor.

Remember . . .

- Trust professional designers and their expertise.
- Choose a design firm with a proven track record.
- Make the online experience for the user of paramount importance.
- Use the Web to extend your brand, not destroy it.
- Recognize that a Web site is never done. It will grow and change
  with your organization.

Viral Marketing

Never have there been more effective means of spreading the written word than by e-mail and the Internet. E-mail is often characterized as "viral" in that e-mail messages can be easily disseminated, thus replicating like a virus and resulting in exponential numbers of people contacted. The term viral fundraising *refers to the practice of using e-mail and the Internet to attract, communicate with, and appeal to a larger audience of current and potential donors. This chapter explores the methods, messengers, rules, caveats, fears, and resources necessary for nonprofit organizations to make viral fundraising work for their organizations.*

BY NOON, Web site traffic had doubled. By 5:00 P.M., it had quadrupled. By evening, the Web server crashed under the load. What was happening?

The Webmaster found the answer in an unexpected place—an e-mail that began: "Here are some things our young visitors told us they 'learned' on their recent visit: 'George Washington's teeth were not wood, they were irony,' Lee, age 9; 'George Washington liked kids. He was the father of the nation,' Chris, age 8."

There were a dozen more funny comments in the e-mail. This innocent e-mail was now spreading all across the country, forwarded from one person to another, with no grand scheme.

Sound far-fetched? It's not. In fact, it's happening every day, and if you haven't yet received a humorous e-mail such as this one, you will.

But why all the hits on this nonprofit's Web site? Because at the bottom of the e-mail was a link back to the nonprofit's Web site that many readers clicked on hoping to find more funny comments from the kids. Unknowingly, this nonprofit had stumbled upon the power of "viral marketing."

What Is Viral Marketing?

Viral marketing is word-of-mouth communication spread via electronic means, at electronic speeds, by customers and others interested in your product or service. Because of the speed and ease of dissemination, the number of people contacted by viral marketing grows geometrically, rather than dying off, as word-of-mouth usually does. In effect, your users have become your marketers.

Viral fundraising is viral marketing with the goal of helping raise money for nonprofits. The means are similar, but the goals and messengers are different. In this case, your donors become your fundraisers.

But in both cases, the idea replicates like a virus, doubling every generation; thus the name.

Means and Methods

Someday we'll all be using hand-held communicators and mobile phones with graphics, but until then, there are two viral fundraising methods: e-mail and Web sites. I'll describe a number of practical methods that use these two channels of communication. You don't need to use them all at the beginning, or all of them at once, but the more you use, the more successful your efforts will be.

E-Mail Techniques

The following techniques will increase the effectiveness of your organization's e-mails.

Append a Signature If you don't know what an e-mail signature is, learn how to construct one, and then quickly create one for your organization. It's simple. An e-mail signature is a footer automatically appended to the bottom of each e-mail you send. Signatures are used to identify your organization and provide links back to your site. To set up a signature, follow the instructions in the Help menu of your e-mail program.

Provide Links to Your Home Page Your e-mail signature should contain a link to your home page. Links to home and other appropriate locations should also be included within the body of your e-mail, where appropriate.

Provide Links to Your Donation Pages If your e-mail message includes a call to action to make a donation, provide a phone number, an e-mail address, *and* a link to your online donation page (assuming you have one).

Forward E-Mails Ideally, your site should have a "tell others" capability that will enable visitors to initiate an e-mail about your site to their friends. The *New York Times* site and Salon.com are sites that illustrate this capability well. These sites let you "e-mail this story" to others. Regardless of whether you have that capability, always have a sentence in your viral e-mail that encourages the reader to forward it to others.

Web Site Techniques

You will drive traffic to your Web site as a result of your successful viral marketing efforts. When your visitors get there, you must be prepared for them. Use these techniques to engage your visitors:

Include Online Fundraising Capacity This is a must. If one of your goals is to raise money, the easier you make it for your online visitors to give, the more likely it is they will do so. There are many online fundraising service providers that can supply an easy-to-use, low-cost, online fundraising capability for your site.

Engage Web Visitors The essential idea is to make the visit worth the visitors' (and the nonprofit's) time—and at least to get their e-mail addresses (with their permission to contact them again).

Create an Affiliate Program A more involved and sophisticated technique is to create an affiliate program that will let your committed donors, and others, create links from their sites back to yours, typically to your gift shop. The most visible and highly developed example of an affiliate program can be found at Amazon.com. Thus far, this technique is rarely used by nonprofits.

The Messengers

Who will spread your message? It'll be your most committed friends and donors, and those that are respected and like to network. Let's call them *the fanatical 5 percent*. But consider yourself lucky if 5 percent of your support base is fanatical—it's probably less. Don't expect all your board members to be messengers: Some will be, some won't. You probably know a few people already involved with your organization who will be eager to spread your viral message and begin the viral response.

When *Los Angeles Times* columnist Patt Morrison told her readers that she was making a gift to Planned Parenthood in the name of George W. Bush on President's Day to protest his position against abortion, she had no idea what she was starting.

Readers started sending e-mail messages detailing her idea to family and friends. Those e-mail messages were then forwarded to hundreds, then thousands, then tens of thousands of e-mail accounts all across the country. This viral fundraising message brought in gifts from more than 15,000 donors, contributing a total of more than $600,000 for Planned Parenthood. This represented the organization's largest surge in contributions in recent history (Nicole Wallace, "Spontaneous Campaign Reaps Charity Windfall," *Chronicle of Philanthropy,* March 8, 2001).

You'll never know until you try, and some people will surprise you. It's likely that the people spreading the word will be highly influenced by the content of the messages being spread. For instance, a simple humor campaign will be spread by lots of people, committed or not, whereas a matching-grant campaign will mainly be spread by the committed.

What Topics Are Best?

It's still too early in the Internet and e-mail revolution to completely understand which topics work best for viral fundraising. We're all still learning by doing, but there are a few clear trends, which we'll refer to as HERO (Humor, Emergencies, Rewards, Opportunities). The letters of HERO are ordered from the most viral potential to the least.

Humor In the 2000 presidential election a humorous diagram of the Florida butterfly ballot crossed the nation in hours and made headlines in newspapers, magazines, and on prime time TV. Planned Parenthood's windfall is another great example.

Emergencies Recent earthquakes and hurricanes have generated millions of e-mails and dollars to help the victims. Emergencies, even small ones, have the potential to trigger a viral response. People will respond to genuine emergencies.

Rewards A classic example of offering a reward is Hotmail's offer for a free e-mail account that appeared at the bottom of every e-mail message sent by its users. This viral marketing campaign was wildly successful by gaining hundreds of thousands of subscribers for Hotmail in a very short time. You don't have to give out money or other costly items; the reward could be a link back to your site with more "funny comments from the kids." The possibilities are endless. The point is to reward the behavior you are seeking.

Opportunities Viral opportunities could include, for instance, the opportunity to name a new building, solve a puzzle, contribute to a challenge grant, and more. The only limit is the extent of your imagination. In your next capital campaign, for example, you might send a message offering all comers the opportunity to name a room or a special feature of a new building, requiring in return an e-mail address and a zip code. You could then follow up those entries from appropriate zip codes with information about the campaign—and an appeal for funds.

The Four Ns In addition to HERO, the Four Ns should help you trigger a viral response. Your effort should feature as many of the Ns as possible.

- New. It's going to be tough to generate a viral response to your annual fund unless you have a new twist.
- Novel. People spread the word about the unusual, not the commonplace.
- Newsworthy. If the media picks up your effort, your chances of a viral response increase greatly.
- Neat! You don't have to create a big-deal effort. Your message can be small, even a quote or paragraph, but it can't be boring.

Of course, even using all four tactics is no guarantee that you'll trigger a viral response.

Some Rules, Caveats, and Fears

There are some rules you *must* follow in order to be successful.

Rules
- No spam. Sending out 10,000 e-mails to strangers is *not* initiating a viral response; it's initiating a potential backlash. Get permission first. Start by e-mailing those closest to your cause and letting them spread the message.
- Tell the truth. Don't exaggerate. Be honest, and show integrity. Commercial ventures often don't, and the contrast works to your advantage.
- Get your administrative house in order. The links on the e-mail need to go to the right pages, your online donation system (if you have one) needs to work, and so forth.
- Gather your donors' e-mail addresses. E-mail is important now and getting more important every day. Get *permission* to e-mail them.
- Put your Web site and e-mail addresses everywhere. Put them on your business cards, in your newsletter, on the side of your building, in your case statement, *everywhere.*

- Make viral fundraising part of your strategy. Don't talk about it; just try it. It's not a science, and you'll never know if it will help until you try.
- Keep trying.

In addition, keep in mind the following caveats as you organize your efforts in viral marketing:

Caveats
- Only a few people will ever be "messengers." Don't let this discourage you. It's the nature of the medium.
- This is a new technique. It's not a science or even a discipline yet. Be patient.
- Don't expect windfalls.

New fundraising techniques come out, what, every fifty years? So it's no wonder that nonprofits are moving slowly to embrace e-mail and the Web, to say nothing of viral fundraising. Here are a few things that might be holding you back:

Some Fears and How to Work Through Them
- *I'll lose control.* The thought of turning one's donors into indirect fundraisers might be unsettling at the beginning, but it won't be in the long run. Learning to launch the effort, influence the response, and set the rules for donations is no different from what you're doing now. Only the medium has changed—and the speed at which the "word-of-mouth" message travels.
- *It won't work.* It might not work the first or second time. Don't be embarrassed if it doesn't work right away. We're *all* learning as we go.
- *It'll waste time.* In the short run perhaps, but not in the long run. Nonprofits that have seen their Web site traffic double overnight because of viral marketing have already seen the benefits.
- *It'll cost too much.* Don't invest lots of time and money in your first effort. Start small. Most of the requirements are things you need to do anyway, like launching a Web site and accepting online donations. Viral fundraising is an exercise in creativity, not cost.

Next Steps

Getting started is easy. Take the first two steps below, give them some thought, then move on to steps three and four.

1. Learn about online fundraising at [www.hitdonate.net]. Then download "Unleashing the Idea Virus" from [www.ideavirus.com] and read it.

2. Create a small viral fundraising campaign.

3. Unleash your campaign and see if anything happens.

4. Repeat steps 3 and 4 until something *does* happen.

Resources

A number of references are available for those wishing to learn more about viral marketing.

Books

• *Permission Marketing,* by Seth Godin (New York: Simon & Shuster, 1999). This is the first major book on "turning strangers into friends, and friends into customers" by using e-mail and the Web.

• *Unleashing the Ideavirus,* by Seth Godin (Do You Zoom, Inc., 2000). This book is a *must read* on the topic of viral marketing. Best of all, it demonstrates the viral technique by letting you download the entire book for free at [www.ideavirus.com]. You are then encouraged to "tell others" by e-mailing them copies of the electronic book also. Has it worked? Yes. Over 100,000 people have downloaded the book from the site, and many then bought the printed version, making it a bestseller. The "medium is the message" in this great example of viral marketing.

There are thousands of nonprofit-oriented Web sites. Here are a few of the best:

Web Sites

• Hitdonate [www.hitdonate.net]. The mother lode for information about online fundraising. It is practical, knowledgeable, and *will* result in increased online fundraising if you implement the recommended ideas. A must, visit today.

• Nonprofit Charitable Orgs [www.nonprofit.about.com]. This site is an excellent jumping off point for information about all aspects of running a nonprofit organization, Web fundraising, online donations, and much more.

• PhilanthropySearch [www.philanthropysearch.com]. A good search engine and resource site dedicated to philanthropy, charity, and the nonprofit sector.

For the latest information, search the Web using a search engine site. I recommend Dogpile.com, because with it you can search Yahoo, Excite, Lycos, and many more engines, all at once. Here are a few terms to try:

Search Terms
- Viral marketing
- Viral e-mail (or email)
- Opt-in
- Permission marketing
- Online fundraising
- Online donation

Two Examples of How Viral Marketing Can Work

A viral marketing campaign launched by the Toronto United Way in February 2001 resulted in over 250,000 hits on their Web site in a three-day period. Before the viral campaign, the site [www.clickforunited-way.com] was receiving fewer than a thousand hits a day. The trigger was a simple e-valentine sent to friends and family urging them to visit the site. For each visit a sponsoring company would donate $1.25. The campaign was a huge success and is a great example of an "opportunity" campaign.

A few minutes ago, as I was writing the last page of this chapter, I received a viral e-mail message forwarded to me from a friend. The e-mail was very funny, concerned the unfair labor practices of a major shoe company, and was authored by someone I've never heard of. It hit my e-mail, I read it, laughed, and immediately forwarded it on to five friends of mine. Something tells me that by later this afternoon, tens of thousands of people will have read this e-mail.

That e-mail featured three of the four Ns: It was new, novel, and neat. I'm sure that the shoe company will not be happy if it achieves the fourth N: newsworthiness. We'll see.

How Nonprofits Can Harness Technology to Build One-to-One Relationships

Nonprofits have always been concerned about developing strong contributor relationships, but their strategies have been one by one, rather than one to one. New technologies make it affordable for a company to customize its interactions with many or all of its customers, based on each individual's expressed preferences. By using the power of databases, the Internet, and other technologies, an organization can foster a long-term—and increasingly rewarding—relationship with a contributor.

SAVE THIS CHILD. *Preserve our wilderness. End the violence.* Nonprofit organizations have long been expert at tugging the heartstrings of caring individuals with their messages of charity, advocacy, and community service. But until recently, those messages had to be either delivered in a mass marketing effort to large groups of people, or delivered one by one, through fundraising events and personal contact.

In the past five years, new technologies have enabled organizations to shift from mass marketing to one-to-one personalized communications and offerings on a large scale. This shift is most visible today in the financial, travel, health care, and retail industries, but those are only the early adopters.

In the private sector, these new business strategies and tactics are commonly known as customer relationship management (CRM), also frequently referred to as "one-to-one marketing," a phrase popularized by the writings of Don Peppers and Martha Rogers (*The One to One Future,* Peppers and Rogers, 1993).

Nonprofits can also benefit greatly by applying CRM strategies and tactics to their contributors—donors, members, advocates, board members, or volunteers. Yet there are important differences between the private and independent sectors. It is useful to view CRM initiatives by nonprofits as *contributor* relationship management.

Nonprofits have always been concerned with developing strong contributor relationships, but their strategies have been one *by* one, rather than one *to* one. The exceptions lie in the field of direct marketing, where nonprofits have been on the forefront of segmentation marketing, in which the audience is segmented into like groups and the communication is tailored to that group's characteristics. This was the precursor of one-to-one marketing and CRM.

The core concept of CRM is deceptively simple: that new technologies make it affordable for a company or organization to customize its interactions with many or all its customers, based on each individual's expressed preferences. By using the power of databases, the Internet, and other technologies, a company can foster a long-term—and increasingly rewarding—relationship with a customer.

Few nonprofits have yet implemented CRM in any significant way. But a fundamental shift is occurring that nonprofits cannot ignore. New technologies such as the Web have empowered consumers. Consumers now have better access to information, geographic barriers are diminished, and transactions take place at lightning speed. The expectations of consumers have been raised about quality and personalization of service. This affects their attitudes, not only when they're shopping for consumer goods but also when they're considering making a donation, becoming a member, or volunteering—in short, whenever they think about relating in any way to a nonprofit.

As one nonprofit decision maker said, "We have twelve frontline fundraising staff servicing more than 100,000 annual donors. It is impossible to expect a personal level of service with this ratio. We don't even have the names of all these donors, yet we wonder why many of them lapse each year. If we employed one-to-one marketing techniques we would undoubtedly increase donor retention and be more effective fundraisers."

A Learning Relationship

The cornerstone of CRM is the concept of a "learning relationship" (Peppers and Rogers, 1993). Each time the customer interacts with the company, something new is learned about that customer's preferences, habits, or other characteristics. This information influences the next interaction, thereby adding value for the customer each time by making the experience easier, faster, or more rewarding in some way. Eventually, customers have "taught" the company so much about themselves that a competitor would have a difficult time giving comparable service.

For example, imagine a charity that relies on "honor donations" (in which the donation is made in honor of a loved one). Imagine then that the charity was able to store and leverage the information about the donor and the honoree, the occasion being honored, and more. Via technology, the charity could remind the donor a year later of a recurring event like a birthday, suggest new ways and different occasions for which to give, and simplify the donation process. This convenience would encourage the donor to provide even more information and make more frequent or larger donations. All this is possible today, but few nonprofits are implementing such strategies.

Lifetime Value Model

Organizations should calculate the lifetime value (LTV) of their customers by using a spreadsheet model that measures the value of a customer over the length of the relationship. The actual value of a nonprofit contributor equals the net present value of all future net revenue from that contributor, including the value of other donors recruited by that contributor.

For example, most membership organizations spend far more to acquire a new member than that member gives in first-time membership fees. Remember that the acquisition costs include the dollars spent on all the people that were exposed to the marketing communications but didn't join, as well as those that did. If it costs more to acquire members than they donate, why bother? Because some of those members will renew in future years, make further donations beyond their dues, participate in planned giving programs, make purchases with the organization, and recommend that others do the same.

The purpose of the Lifetime Value model is to prove the value of investments in efforts to acquire and maintain customer relationships, and to determine which contributors on which to focus more effort. Without it, "it's very much like a black hole," says one nonprofit executive. "You pour resources into communications, marketing, media relations, Internet. And it's very hard to see the benefits from that. It's all very soft. That's something organizations need to get a handle on to move forward."

Establishing an LTV model or formula for an organization requires approximations for many variables. Exact data on factors are not practical to gather. There is no one best model. An organization must choose what fits its own unique circumstances. Variables to include should be chosen because they are important and reasonably predictable. Those variables might include

- Initial contributor acquisition cost
- Costs to maintain relationship

- Profits from donations and membership fees
- Profit from referrals of other contributors
- Renewal rates or other predictor of loyalty or attrition
- Profits from products and services

Privacy Concerns

When an organization enters into a learning relationship with donors or members, it is implicitly asking them to trust that it will not misuse the information they provide. Yet currently, most organizations are not adequately addressing constituents' privacy concerns and are thus destroying—or at least endangering—that trust. This is the single greatest threat to the widespread success of CRM, because it requires willingness on the part of consumers to provide personal information. If they don't trust that their information will be used responsibly, they will not provide it.

According to a report to the U.S. Federal Trade Commission, 92 percent of Americans are concerned about the misuse of their personal information. It is critical that every organization develop and adhere to a privacy policy that minimizes risk and treats data about individuals as privileged information. The following are tactics an organization should adopt:

- Publish the organization's privacy policy in clear, straightforward language on the Web site and in other communications that ask for data, such as direct mail
- Limit internal access to data to a need-to-know basis
- Enable customers to view and control the information collected about them
- Respond promptly and responsibly to complaints from customers that their information has been improperly used
- Join and adhere to the guidelines of one of the well-known privacy watchdog groups such as TRUSTe or BBB Online.

Relevant Information Technologies

Recent advances in technology enable the application of CRM practices. The choices can be overwhelming. One nonprofit decision maker said, "The time it takes to identify and evaluate possible tech solutions is intense! This does not include the time required to purchase and install, implement across the company, and then train staff on proper application. This time-intensive nature of IT continues to be a challenge—but we feel it is well worth the cost."

Most important, a decision maker must remember that technology is only a means to an end, not the end itself. First and foremost, a strategic plan is needed. Only after an organization has determined its strategic objectives can appropriate technologies be identified. There are many technological tools that can be employed in relationship management; however, the following two are of primary importance.

Databases

The gathering of information about individuals, and more important, the ability to access and sort that information, lie at the heart of CRM. A single database—or the integration of multiple databases—allows the organization to speak with one voice and enables its message to be relevant to the customer. Without a solid database foundation, CRM is not possible. Fortunately, database systems continue to increase in functionality and processing power while decreasing in cost, thereby making more advanced solutions affordable for most nonprofits.

One nonprofit executive said, "We didn't invest in databases to the level we should have, and we're suffering terribly for that. The corporate culture was such that there was no commitment. As a result, we've lost many opportunities. We spend a lot of money doing things the old-fashioned way, and we're not able to communicate with our donors the way we should. We have many databases instead of one. If a [for-profit] company made the sort of decisions we've made, they would have gone belly up by now."

CRM requires a centralized database, or integrated database system, that can access data from multiple sources, such as Web sites, transactions, call centers, and third party data. This provides a complete view of the contributor, who may interact with the organization through multiple channels. Then, the interactions with the contributor can be customized based on the relevant information about that individual, and the customer can be reached at the appropriate place and time, in the appropriate manner.

However, because of the complexity and cost involved in integrating all these data into one central database, few nonprofits have yet pursued this course. As the technology becomes easier to use and as competitive pressures rise, more and more organizations will take the plunge.

The Internet

Nonprofits, like their private sector counterparts, have turned to the Web to interact with their audiences. Says Phil Gutis, the American Civil Liberties Union's (ACLU) director of legislative communications, "It's extraordinary to me how the public is turning to the Web as a way of venting, stating its opinion, and asking questions. . . . We've shown you can get members through the Web site, and the costs are small compared to other methods. But an organization has to have somebody that's willing to take that initial risk."

Although CRM tactics are not limited to the Web, an organization's Web site is the most public display of its relationship marketing approach and capabilities. Careful study of innovative Web sites is an excellent way to learn from the best. For example, here's one nonprofit organization that has taken outstanding first steps toward CRM.

Case study: WWF

Check out [www.panda.org] (Exhibit 23.1). The World Wide Fund for Nature, the world's largest independent conservation organization, known internationally as WWF, maintains over forty connected sites representing national offices and major programs in a multitude of languages. The cornerstone of this network is the international site at [www.panda.org].

The site includes a powerful application called Panda Passport, in which users can fully customize their experience based on geography, issue, species, and type of involvement desired (advocacy, education, financial support). Panda Passport allows WWF to communicate with its support base as individuals. The user is rewarded for providing additional information and taking action, and the online experience is enriched as the site "learns" more about the user.

The organization regularly communicates with over 80,000 individuals in 131 countries through its e-mail lists. WWF saw its online donations double from 1998 to 1999. Most important, WWF's innovative online efforts have transformed the organization's brand and launched relationships with thousands of individuals younger than the average age of traditional WWF members, a critical strategic need for WWF's future growth and success.

Customer Communications, Service, and Fulfillment

A common error that many organizations make when first experimenting with CRM is to forget that a relationship means *two-way* communications. If you don't respond to a contributor's communications, you are essentially saying, "I want to have a dialogue with you, as long as I do all the talking!" An appropriate infrastructure to handle inquiries, updated customer data, comments, and complaints is critical to the success of CRM. Inquiries that have a standard format or repetitive information should be shifted from human operators to technologies such as the Internet, wireless personal digital assistants (PDAs), and electronic data interchange (EDI) systems.

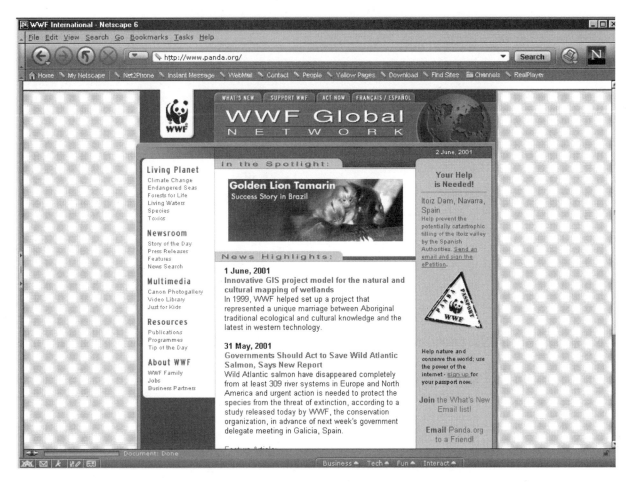

Exhibit 23.1. WWF Links Content to Giving.

However, technology will not eliminate the need for human interaction, nor should it. Most nonprofits currently have some sort of call center (in-house or outsourced) that handles the bulk of customer transactions and inquiries via telephone. In many cases, the call center is the primary voice for the organization, and thus it is critical that it be well equipped and staffed. In addition, call centers provide marketers with an opportunity to learn from customers directly rather than through focus groups and other forms of market research.

Leadership and Investment Required

A nonprofit's constituents can usually be divided into two groups: those that are served or advocated for (recipients of emergency aid, health care services, legal defense), and those who contribute (members, donors, volunteers). Traditionally, nonprofits have focused on the needs of the first group only, and not the second. There is a cultural attitude throughout much of the sector that it is the contributors' responsibility to give, and no services from the organization are required in return. As one nonprofit leader said, "The whole question of responding to our members' concerns is not a high priority. Can we rely on the fact that every year our income grows anyway?"

Mission-focused, *external* metrics are top-of-mind for nonprofits: win-loss rates in court, number of families served, alcoholics treated, rescue dogs placed, laws passed, and so forth. At the same time, nonprofits must measure their internal efforts to raise funds, acquire and retain members, secure grants, and all the other resource development efforts that keep an organization growing.

The application of CRM practices in a comprehensive manner has implications for virtually every department of an organization, and thus requires considerable commitment and leadership from the top of the organization.

This does not mean that every decision maker at every nonprofit should immediately jump up and yell, "CRM or die!" For organizations relying primarily on funding from major donors and foundations, those one-to-one relationships can and should continue to be cultivated one *by* one through personal interactions. However, organizations that rely on large numbers of contributors—through memberships, sales of products, subscriptions, and low-dollar donations—should make CRM the cornerstone of their strategic plans.

How to Proceed?

Commit to the inherent value of contributor relationships. Without a firm and clear mandate from the top, organizations will abandon the effort before the benefits are achieved. You need to adopt a strategic plan, identifying measurable objectives and desired outcomes, before you can pursue tactical steps.

Inventory your organization's current tools and process for gathering information and communicating with contributors to develop a gap analysis.

Invest in the necessary staff and tools to fill the gaps, setting priorities among choices based on the objectives identified in your strategic plan. Most organizations should focus their initial attention on their database capabilities, their online efforts, and their call center.

Protect the privacy of your contributors by putting responsible privacy policies in place and enforcing them. CRM requires considerable trust from your contributors, which can be eroded or destroyed by careless or malicious abuse of their personal data.

Measure the outcomes of your efforts. This requires that you first gather benchmarks before the initiatives are launched, so that you have quantitative proof of their results. Develop a Lifetime Value model that is appropriate for your organization. This model will give a clear picture of untapped opportunities, and where resources need to be redistributed.

As measurements demonstrate a return on investment, internal buy-in will increase and staff will become enthusiastic. Contributors will provide valuable input on further improvements. With strategic application of technology, mutually beneficial one-to-one relationships between nonprofits and their contributors are within reach.

References

Johnston, M. "Study: Online Privacy Fears Growing." Reported on [CNN.com], July 11, 2000.

Peppers, D., and Rogers, M. *Enterprise One-to-One: Tools for Competing in the Interactive Age.* New York, Doubleday, 1993.

New Paths to Giving Through Charity Portals

The emergence of commercial giving portals, affinity shopping sites, and other Web-based services that assist nonprofits in raising money online has added a new creative energy to fundraising. However, if you decide to work with one of these services, you should have minimal expectations about the income they will generate for your organization. Of the hundreds that sprang up in 1999 and 2000, more than half have closed or become inactive. It can be hard to tell because a Web site can live on after an organization has died. Many of the remaining services are near failure. Be careful to keep your own mission and mandate— and your own fundraising efforts via your Web site and e-mail messaging program—as the primary focus.

INNOVATION ABOUNDS in fundraising. From walkathons and celebrity dinners to corporate challenges and neighborhood bake sales, the creativity of nonprofit fundraisers has triumphed many times over donor fatigue and public cynicism, and the funds keep rolling in.

A quick look around the Internet finds nonprofits engaged in all sorts of creative and resourceful online fundraising ideas. Online charity auctions, shopping malls where nonprofits get commissions, and "click here to give" buttons—these are all part of the new face of online fundraising, where your supporters can choose from a variety of ways to demonstrate their financial support for your organization.

What Kinds of Services Are Offered?

Charity portals, such as Helping.org (one of the few nonprofits) and GiveForChange.com, seek to attract visitors who can choose from hundreds or thousands of nonprofits working in many fields, learn more about them, and make online credit card donations. The affinity shopping sites group dozens or hundreds of e-commerce sites, such as amazon.com and landsend.com. Visitors can designate a nonprofit, which then gets a percentage, typically 5 to 10 percent, of each sale. Auction sites allow nonprofits to run online auction sites, selling both items they have collected and items obtained by the auction site. (Both eBay and Yahoo auctions also offer charity events.) Click-to-donate sites enable visitors to make a very small donation (funded by site advertisers) every time they visit.

Another type of service, known as application service providers or ASPs, host sophisticated applications, such as donation transaction processing, e-mail messaging, or donor databases, on their computer servers. They do the installation, maintenance, and upgrading; the nonprofit basically "rents" the services for a monthly fee or per-transaction fee, and the ASP customizes the pages to make them look more or less like the organization's own Web site.

Most of these services operate fully developed end-to-end services that take care of all aspects of a particular form of online giving, including the following:

Front-End Design Typically a portal has a predesigned page or template that provides a "public face" to the service. The level of customization can vary from portal to portal, but in general you should be able to provide a logo and a short piece of text that can be used on your page.

Back-End Programming and Technical Maintenance The programming requirements for the implementation of online fundraising services can be complicated. Portal providers take this headache out of the hands of nonprofits—including making periodic upgrades or adding new options.

Online Marketing Though some of the charity portals and shopping sites have invested in building their brand names and driving traffic to their Web sites, nonprofits should expect to lead their own marketing efforts to bring people to these sites.

Customer-Donor Support Charity Web portal providers should have technical and customer support staff ready to field inquiries about the workings of their services. However, if donors use a portal to give to your organization, you should be ready to service them.

Security Charity Web portals recognize that donors are concerned about the security of online transactions, and they put considerable effort into maintaining online transaction security.

Transaction Processing Some portals are able to help their nonprofit partners process online contributions by setting up automated deposit links to their merchant or bank accounts. That way, online donations are deposited directly into a nonprofit's bank account. Other portals hold all contributions designed for the nonprofit and make a single payment every month or quarter. (Take special note of the frequency and minimum levels required before any funds will be transferred to your account.)

The governing assumption is that a charity portal handles all the setup and technical work, and the nonprofit provides the philanthropic content to engage visitors. Hence, you should approach portal providers more as partners than suppliers. The relationship between a nonprofit and a portal should be built around *quid pro quo* agreements that lay out clear terms, conditions, and obligations for both parties.

Why Use One of These Services?

The services provide a turnkey, ready-to-go solution for nonprofits that want to add new ways for supporters to make financial contributions through the Internet. Nonprofits don't usually have the staff and technical capacity to develop and manage their own online shopping malls or charity auctions.

For example, an organization wanting to set up an online charity auction would find it daunting to attempt it on its own. The project would require months of staff time. However, by partnering with a service provider, the nonprofit can have an online auction ready to go in just a few short days and with very little investment of staff time.

Shopping sites, auction sites, and others can also help an organization reach two online audiences that they may otherwise have trouble reaching with their online fundraising:

- Existing donors who already support your organization but who have not yet responded to your other online fundraising attempts. Giving these supporters a new option to show their support may encourage them to engage in some online fundraising activity on behalf of your organization. (The key to successful fundraising online is the same as it is off-line: emphasizing relationship-building, cultivation, and stewardship.)

- New donors continue to be attracted to the Internet and many find giving online to be convenient. Some portals attract new visitors as a result of their advertising, or in response to news items featuring the portal. Visitors to these sites, such as The Hunger Site, may be new to online giving.

Cautions

Unfortunately, few nonprofits have raised significant revenue from any of these sites, even from well-capitalized dot-com sites that spent millions on marketing. One of the biggest players in this field, Charitableway, closed its doors in early 2001 after having raised more than $43 million in venture capital. The company first tried running a charity portal; when that failed, it turned to offering a sophisticated online workplace giving system to United Ways and corporations. Although Charitableway was having some success with the workplace giving model, the venture capitalists were running out of patience in their quest for profitability.

Many nonprofits have invested considerable staff time either in sorting through the hundreds of offers from aggressive dot-coms or in creating content and promoting their online dot-com partners. Often this time could have been better spent in improving their own Web sites, developing an effective e-mail marketing program, and driving traffic to the organization's own site.

In partnering with commercial suppliers, there are always issues of concern for nonprofits. In working with these suppliers, there are five specific concerns that nonprofits should seek to address in contract negotiations:

- Control and content ownership. Keep in mind that when you set up a page on a portal site, you are putting your content on a server you won't have direct control over. You need to exact a clear commitment from the portal to keep the site's content up-to-date according to your organization's needs.

- Brand association. You also need to be concerned about how your organization's identity—name, logo, and so on—is presented to your supporters. You need to reach a clear understanding with your portal partner on exactly how the portal may present the nonprofit's name and logo on their site. (See Resource A, The ePhilanthropy Code of Ethical Online Philanthropic Practices, Section C: Disclosures, number 2.)

- Data privacy and access. Portal sites gather data on all site visitors who engage in online fundraising. It's vital that you have a clear understanding with your portal provider on the disposition of donor data: Who owns it? How will the nonprofit get access to it? Does the portal intend to sell or use the donor list for its own marketing purposes?

- Bankruptcy and buyout contingencies. It's an unpleasant reality these days that numerous dot-coms are going out of business. Unfortunately, therefore, you should be especially concerned about receiving guarantees on the disposition of your donor data and on the treatment of outstanding financial transfers in the event the company ceases operation. Arrange regular (biweekly or monthly) downloads of donor data and settling of accounts to minimize the risk of loss. Be aware as well that there may be different settlement terms in effect in the case of a buy-out or merger. The time to find out what those terms are is at the beginning, not after the fact.

• Marketing. Unless your organization's Web page is given some special prominence on the portal, you shouldn't expect to receive more than a handful of new visitors through the portal's own marketing. Instead, you should rely on your own marketing strategies and view your partnership with a portal as more of a facilitating tool that makes things easier for your supporters to give online.

Types of Fundraising Portals

Fundraising portals cover a variety of online giving activities. I'll list a few of the major categories in this section and give a few examples of each type. For an up-to-date listing of portal providers to the nonprofit sector, visit The Nonprofit Matrix at [www.nonprofitmatrix.com] (Exhibit 24.1). Take care, though. The site includes a comprehensive listing that may contain providers that are no longer active.

Giving Portals

Giving portals approach the world of online giving as central receiving stations for gifts to a variety of charitable organizations. A giving portal spends a lot of its energy building a public profile as a place where Web surfers can go to make safe, secure, online donations. Giving portals allow donors to pick and choose from local, regional, and national charities to receive their gifts. The leading American giving portal is Helping.org, which is supported by the AOL Time Warner Foundation. Helping.org, which also includes an excellent nonprofit resources center, had raised about $3 million in early 2001. GiveForChange.org, run by the Working Assets company to raise money for progressive social change groups (and market Working Assets), has been one of the more successful donation portals. Many others, including Charitableway.com and AllCharities.com, have failed or dramatically changed their business models.

Some giving portals have a particular issue or geographical focus. For example, [www.conservenow.org] is a portal for online donations to environmental organizations, whereas [www.animalfunds.org] (see

Exhibit 24.1. The Nonprofit Matrix Web Site.

Exhibit 24.2) supports only animal rights organizations. Both of these organizations focus primarily on traditional workplace giving, although they do allow online donations to their affiliated groups.

Nonprofit organizations can usually register with giving portals at no charge and will thus be included in the lists of potential recipient charities. Some giving portals, such as Helping.org, will even provide you with a graphic "button" that you can place on your own Web site to provide an easy link to the donation page.

Affinity Shopping Portals

Organizations can share in the proceeds of the online shopping habits of their supporters by setting up shop with an affinity shopping portal, which channels shoppers to hundreds of online stores, including leaders such as amazon.com and landsend.com. The online stores pass along commissions of 1 to 20 percent to the malls, which share them with the

Exhibit 24.2 A Giving Portal.

designated nonprofits. In most cases, organizations need only register with an affinity shopping network, and they will be added to the list of available organizations for online shoppers to select as the beneficiaries of their online purchases.

At iGive.com a percentage of every purchase benefits a charitable organization (Exhibit 24.3). Some affinity shopping portals focus on a particular group of beneficiary organizations. For example, [www.schoolpop.com] and [www.schoolcash.com] allow parents and community members to direct their affinity earnings to support their local schools.

The "affinity rewards" percentage that the nonprofit receives from an online sale varies according to different vendor arrangements, from 1 percent to as high as 20 percent. The shopping portal itself takes part of the commission paid by the stores. So far the reported revenues for non-profits from affinity shopping portals have been very low. (See Resource A, Section E, 2.)

Exhibit 24.3. An Affinity Shopping Portal.

Online Charity Auctions

Charity auction sites work just like the for-profit online auctions, such as eBay [http://pages.ebay.com/charity/index.html], but part of the proceeds go to a designated charity. Online charity auctions may be time-limited, minimum-bid reserved, silent, or open just like traditional charity auctions.

Generally, you're free to select items from the portal provider's inventory to include in the auction and can add any of your own items to the auction. (The portal will collect a commission on all sales of its own items but usually charges a small fee, but no commission, on items you supply.)

Some online charity auction portals specialize in a particular kind of auction or promotional vehicle. [www.benefitevents.com], for example, specializes in original art pieces (Exhibit 24.4); [www.allstarcharity.com] auctions items donated by Hollywood celebrities. Unless your organization can collect high-value items to auction on one of these sites, it's hard to raise a lot of money. Whereas bidders at an organization's auction event usually bid high to benefit the organization, most online bidders are looking for low prices. If you can get Madonna's dress or Sammy Sosa's mitt, you might make some money, but that round-trip ticket to Miami will only bring in $200 online.

Affinity Portals

Affinity portals are designed as gateways to the Internet for membership-based organizations. In working with such a portal, you would encourage your members to set their Web browsers to use the customized affinity portal page as the default home page for their browsers

Exhibit 24.4. Online Auction at BenefitEvents.com.

(that is to say, the first page that their browser opens each time it is started). This gateway page presents content from your organization, plus a variety of useful information and links that Internet users typically get at a commercial portal such as Yahoo: latest news, weather, sports, stock market, online shopping, and so forth.

While the nonprofit receives a small share of the advertising and e-commerce commissions (if there are any) generated by its site, these portals are primarily for delivering member services and building relationships, not fundraising. [www.MyAssociation.com], now known as BlueStep.net, and [www.wego.com] are leading affinity portal providers.

Alumni Portals

Alumni portals are a specialized form of affinity portal that cater specifically to university alumni associations. Associations pour their content into sites using the portal's infrastructure, features, and functionality, then try to direct their members to use the site as their main "homepage" gateway to the Internet.

As with any affinity portal, individual visitors may select the information they want to include regularly on their personal homepage: news, sports, weather, links to shopping. In the case of the alumni portals, the categories of information are more tailored to a young, college-university graduate demographic. The alumni portal contributes a (small) percentage of the commercial revenue from the Web page, if any, to the alumni organization.

There are many companies currently competing in this subsector of the nonprofit world. [www.Zuniversity.com] and [www.eAlumni.com] are a couple of examples.

Click Donations

In June 1999 The Hunger Site [www.thehungersite.com] appeared with a new and innovative way to raise money online for nonprofit organizations. (At press time for this book, the future of The Hunger Site was in question.) Web site visitors could make a (modest) donation to the United Nations World Food Program just by clicking on a button and viewing an advertiser's banner. By presenting the banner ads within the context of making a donation, The Hunger Site created a new sponsorship model that opened the door to nonprofit Web sites tapping into the huge online advertising marketplace. Advertisers paid fees that amounted to the cost of part of a cup of rice for every click.

It's not surprising that in the year or so that followed, a number of click-to-donate sites have appeared supporting a gamut of good causes. A few click-to-donate portal sites, such as 4GoodnessSake.org and Quick-Donations.com, appeared that offer links to many click-to-donate sites.

Building Your Base Through Advocacy Campaigns

One of the most effective ways to build a "prospect" list of potential online donors is through online advocacy campaigns that seek to engage people in some sort of action by means of the online medium: actions such as sending an e-mail or a fax to an elected official or a corporate target, signing an electronic petition, receiving regular action alerts by e-mail, or forwarding e-mail action alerts to friends. Online advocacy campaigns have two goals: (1) to encourage people to participate in the online advocacy event, and (2) to sign them up to receive future communications by mail or e-mail. These future communications will probably include donor fundraising and membership appeals.

AS YOU'VE SEEN in many of the chapters of this book, fundraising on the Internet involves much more than just putting a "donate now" button on your Web site. Though it's important to have donation transaction tools in operation online, it is also critical to offer engaging campaigns to persuade people to become involved in your activities—and eventually become donors. Online advocacy campaigns are one of the best tools available to offer involvement opportunities that will add new donors and increase the tendency of existing donors to renew their support.

The actions that online advocacy campaigns encourage include sending an e-mail or a fax to an elected official or a corporate target, signing an electronic petition, receiving regular action alerts by e-mail, or forwarding e-mail action alerts to friends, coworkers, and family. In addition to increasing the flow of communication to elected officials and other advocacy targets, online advocacy campaigns help you identify supporters you can continue to cultivate and, in at least some cases, convert into donors.

Online advocacy campaigns have two goals: (1) to encourage people to participate in the online advocacy event, and (2) to sign them up to receive future communications by mail or e-mail. These future communications will probably include donor fundraising and membership appeals.

Two Examples

Here are two recent examples of online advocacy campaigns and how they helped build the base for the organizations that undertook them:

When Senator John Ashcroft was nominated for attorney general by President Bush in early 2001, an online advocacy campaign organized by the Million Mom March organization generated 50,000 faxes that were sent to U.S. senators through the StopAshcroft.com Web site (Exhibit 25.1). The campaign, combined with numerous off-line activities, resulted in aggressive questioning in the Senate of Senator Ashcroft's policies on gun control, and the addition of 20,000 names, addresses, and e-mail addresses to the Million Mom March's donor database.

The Lindesmith Center–Drug Policy Foundation capitalized on the success of the hit movie *Traffic* in early 2001 to create the StopTheWar.com campaign with a Web site, online marketing, and e-mail newsletter campaign to stimulate conversation about the fundamental flaws in the war on drugs (Exhibit 25.2). The campaign generated four thousand faxes to President Bush, coverage in major print and online media, and the addition of over ten thousand e-mail addresses of sympathetic constituents who may be cultivated and eventually converted into donors.

As both these examples demonstrate, an online advocacy campaign can deliver real-world results (in these cases, sending faxes to political targets and mobilizing people) and also attract potential new donors to the organization. However, activists are not yet donors. The organization must next cultivate these activist-prospects with ongoing e-mail communication and send them fundraising appeals that offer them the chance to take action of a different sort.

Creating an online advocacy campaign requires careful planning so that you can make effective use of your Web site and your e-mail bulletins or newsletters to disseminate your campaign message. You'll also need to consider the technology requirements of setting up an advocacy campaign and connecting it to your donor prospecting and cultivation efforts.

Exhibit 25.1. The Million Mom March Organization's Web Site.

Integrate Your Online and Off-Line Efforts

To ensure the success of your online advocacy campaign, it's important that you coordinate your online and off-line efforts. Discuss the online component of your campaign early in your planning. Consider budgetary, implementation, and staffing issues. Your online campaign needs to be "on message" with the rest of your campaign efforts; that is, any Web pages or e-mail messages that you create must contain the same (or reasonably similar) information as any print or other media that you are creating. To the extent possible, they should all contain the same logos, themes, slogans, and colors.

Identify clear and specific goals and audiences for your online advocacy efforts. Your campaign in the off-line world may have a number of goals and components. You need to determine realistically how many of these goals can be reached through action in the online medium.

Identify Your Fundraising Goals

Identify your fundraising goals as they relate to your online advocacy efforts. Since one of your organizational goals is to deliver potential new donors to the organization, you will need to plan for how you will follow up with communications that educate, cultivate, and involve, as well as solicit gifts.

When you're conducting your online advocacy campaign—for example, asking people to send a fax to a political target—decide whether you want to include a fundraising appeal in the early outreach efforts. Typically, nonprofits don't do so because they don't want to detract from the intended advocacy effort. In such cases, the fundraising goal becomes simply one of building your prospective donor file.

Review your donor database needs prior to conducting your online advocacy campaign. As you're signing people up for your campaign, you'll need to enter their names, contact information, and e-mail addresses in your in-house database systems. Review your donor coding system so that you can tag these new records appropriately.

When you do follow-up mailings or e-mailings, you will want to make reference to your initial contact with them. An example might be: "Earlier this Spring, you were one of 50,000 Americans who sent faxes from the StopAshcroft.com Web site to President George Bush opposing

Exhibit 25.2. The Lindesmith Center–Drug Policy Foundation's StopTheWar.com Web Site.

the nomination of Senator John Ashcroft for U.S. Attorney General. We're contacting you today to ask for your continued support to . . . "

Identify Appropriate Staff to Manage Your Campaign

Staffing your online advocacy efforts is critical. Often, these staff members may not be the same as those who manage your off-line campaign. You'll need people with skills and experience to update your Web site, write and send out e-mail bulletins, do online marketing, and work with various Internet companies to manage any technology components of your advocacy campaign. You may find that you do not have adequate in-house staff to do this work and will have to hire a consultant or a firm to help you.

Another staffing issue to consider is the need to integrate your online advocacy efforts with your donor management system. Since one of your organizational goals is to deliver potential new donors to the organization, you'll need to merge these new names, addresses, and e-mail addresses into your in-house donor management system. Whether you have in-house staff managing your donor file or out-source that function to a consultant or a service bureau, you'll need to involve them early in your planning and implementation.

Review Your Internet Technology Needs

A review of your technology needs will help you budget in advance of your campaign and anticipate any hardware or software issues that you'll have to take into account during the planning and implementation phases.

You'll need to acquire the appropriate Internet tools to be able to do online activism on your Web site. Such tools are available online from a number of application service providers (ASPs). Currently, the leading providers in this field are

Capitol Advantage	www.capitoladvantage.com
GetActive Software	www.getactive.com
CapitolConnect	www.capitolconnect.com

With these online services you can create issue-specific Web pages where users input their zip codes and contact information to generate communications (via e-mail, fax, or mail) to their elected officials or other designated targets. The organization sets up a prewritten letter that users can then send as-is or edit by adding personalized text. The letter can then be sent as a fax, an e-mail message, or printed out and mailed with a postage stamp.

When you're planning your campaign, you will need to choose the targets of the advocacy campaign. Each one of these ASPs will have the necessary tools to make your selection process go quickly and easily.

Users may also use these systems to identify their elected officials, get contact information, view committee assignments and voting histories, and find background information about bills.

These ASPs have a lot of experience working with nonprofit organizations, and they'll be able to show you examples of how other organizations have used their products and services. Be sure to review the pricing plans for these services very carefully. You need to consider one-time sign-up fees, ongoing monthly fees, and any other fees relating to your needs with the project.

The ongoing fees for using one of these services may be scaled depending on how many people use the system. This will inject an element of uncertainly when you're budgeting for the project. It may be helpful to talk to other organizations that have conducted online advocacy campaigns to try to anticipate the response rates for such an effort.

Offer Incentives

You may want to offer an incentive for people to take the desired action in your online advocacy campaign, such as entering a raffle to win tickets to a show or a free DVD. Incentives like these may be effective at drawing in new names, but the long-term value of those names may not be as high, especially with a free product offer. People attracted by these incentives may not be as committed to your cause, and therefore not as likely to take another action or make a donation without further incentive.

Prepare Your Organization's Web Site for Online Advocacy

Your Web site will be ground zero for your online advocacy campaign. Once you have acquired the necessary activism tools, you'll need to plug them into your Web site. If you're working with an ASP, you'll get the necessary information from them to make this process go smoothly. You'll want to promote your online activism prominently on the home page and other appropriate pages of your Web site.

Two More Examples

The American Lung Association of California [www.californialung.org] promotes its campaign through small and regular features on its home page (Exhibit 25.3). The Association invites people to join its advocacy network and take action on the most recent action alert. Users input their contact information, which is remembered by the system the next time they log in with their e-mail address and password. The Association uses GetActive Software's service.

Bread for the World [www.bread.org] promotes its campaign right at the top of its home page (Exhibit 25.4). If you opt to participate in the campaign, the Web site asks for your zip code, then it displays a customized page with your geographic information. Users who input their contact information are recognized by the system the next time they log in with their e-mail address and password. Bread for the World uses Capitol Advantage.

Use E-mail Activism for Effective Online Advocacy

To deploy your online advocacy campaign effectively, create and disseminate e-mail bulletins and e-mail urgent actions to mobilize people who are interested in your issues. At every opportunity, invite people to subscribe to receive action alerts by e-mail. Make it clear to subscribers during any e-mail sign-up process that you will be sending them e-mail updates. By opting in, they won't be surprised later when receiving follow-up e-mails from your organization. But whenever you send an e-mail action alert, be sure to include information about the campaign and

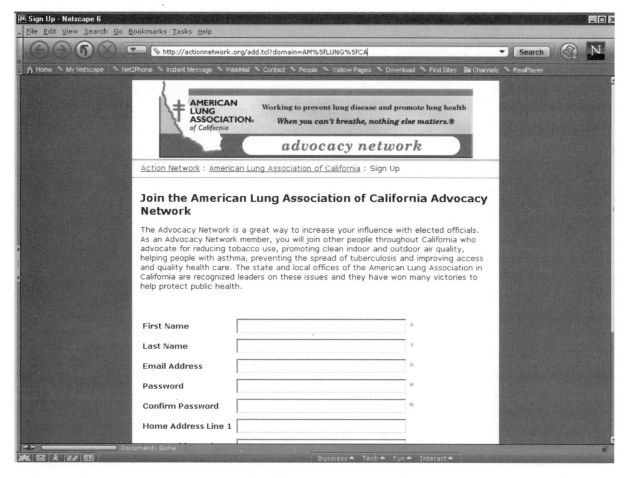

Exhibit 25.3. American Lung Association Advocacy Network Sign-Up.

a link to the page on your Web site where people can take the action you want.

With sophisticated systems such as the one from GetActive Software, you can send personalized e-mails to your activists that are preconfigured so that recipients can take action either by replying to the e-mail or by clicking through to a Web page that contains a pre-filled letter to the campaign target. All recipients need do is edit the letter (if they wish) and click "Send."

Promote Your Online Advocacy Campaign

To make your online advocacy campaign successful, effective promotion is important. Begin by integrating the online component into your off-line efforts so that you can make the most of your ongoing outreach efforts. Printed newsletters, flyers, radio interviews, and other public relations opportunities should inform your constituents that you're using your Web site and your e-mail action alerts to engage people in

Exhibit 25.4. Bread for the World Crosslink.

your campaign. Develop banner ads and place them with like-minded and high-traffic Web sites, and ask other organizations to mention the campaign in their newsletters.

In addition to asking visitors to take action and make a donation, encourage them to e-mail their friends about the campaign. Word-of-mouth marketing is just as effective online as it is off-line, and it's easy to incorporate a "tell-a-friend" tool into your Web site that lets visitors input the e-mail addresses of up to five friends and provide a prewritten message that they can edit if they want.

When you develop a high-profile campaign, you can either drive traffic through your own home page or create a special page or mini-Web site with its own (clever) domain name, like StopAshcroft.com or StopTheWar.com.

Follow Through with Your Online Advocacy Campaign

To turn your advocacy campaign into a fundraising success, appropriate follow-through is essential with the people whose names and contact information you've acquired during the campaign. Whether you've enlisted 4,000 or 400,000 people, update them on the progress and successes of your campaign.

If you have their e-mail addresses, create and disseminate an ongoing e-mail bulletin that updates them electronically on your efforts; if all you have is a street address, send an inexpensive print newsletter. Since their initial contact with you was on the occasion of an advocacy campaign, it's important to close the loop on the effort—and then to offer additional ways they can help you make the world a better place. You might want to propose additional advocacy activities, invite them to volunteer, or suggest a fundraising gift to support your ongoing efforts. The whole idea is to turn these potential donors acquired during an online activism campaign into actual donors and eventually into renewing donors.

Measure Your Success

The success of your online advocacy campaign and of your fundraising efforts can be measured in a number of ways.

1. Track the number of people who came to your Web site during the course of your online advocacy campaign. One of your goals is to increase the number of visitors to your Web site, and you need to track your progress in that respect.

2. Track the number of people who took part in your advocacy campaign, either by sending a fax or e-mail or by signing your e-petition.

3. Track the number of people who provided you with contact information such as name, address, and e-mail address, since you will be following up with these people to encourage them to become donors.

4. Over a longer period, track the number of people you were able to convert into donors, but this requires you to code these people appropriately in your donor management system.

Case Studies

Comic Relief:
Red Nose Day

On just one night in March this year, the Comic Relief Web site [www.comicrelief.com] took in £3 million (US $5 million) in its Red Nose Day fundraising drive. This, according to them, smashed all World Wide Web records. And the number of users turned the site into one of the world's busiest e-commerce sites. During one night of TV, a record-breaking 96,000 transactions were processed.

By contrast, in its last campaign two years ago, Comic Relief received only £460,000 online, 1.6 percent of their online and off-line total of £35 million.

This rise is truly meteoric. It obviously marks a big change in attitudes to online giving in the United Kingdom, and it indicates the huge potential for charities if they can get their Web presence right.

Online donations formed a markedly high 10–15 percent of the £23 million total donations on the night, some of which were made off-line by large corporations and the rest from credit card donations over the phone. (Donations currently stand at around £50 million.)

In a press release, Amanda Horton-Mastin, Comic Relief's marketing director, commented that, "The most interesting aspect is that unlike phone donations, there was less correlation between the TV content and the pattern of donations made online. In fact, our analysis shows that the response to Red Nose Day online most matched the pattern of day-to-day life for the majority of people. There was a surge of interest online just before people were leaving the office, again during News at Ten, and finally post 11:00 P.M., when people were returning from an evening out."

It's also interesting to counterpose the success of Comic Relief online with the apparent stagnation of a second BBC-backed telethon, Children in Need, which in November 2000 raised £132,014 online [www.bbc.co.uk/cin/] compared to £130,000 in 1999 (1 per cent of an online and off-line total of £11.6 million).

Note: Adapted with permission from a posting by Graham Francis on [www.hitdonate.net].

Comic Relief's e-charity project was made possible through the involvement of title sponsor Cisco Systems, a worldwide leader in networking for the Internet. The architecture was designed to take up to 200 donations per second.

The peak period for donations was between 9:30 P.M. and 10:30 P.M. on March 16, with over 47,000 being registered in this hour, although the overall average number of online donations per second during the eight-hour television show was 12,000—equivalent to three donations per second.

Within the five-week campaign, [www.comicrelief.com] registered more than 100 million page requests, with over 80 million in the final week, making it one of the world's most visited sites between February 6 and March 17. On Red Nose Day itself there were 20.9 million page requests, using a bandwidth of up to 50 Mbit.

[www.comicrelief.com] was built with some of the most developed and reliable back-end technology available from Cisco Systems, Oracle, Compaq, and other participating companies. The equipment ensured that even through the most intense traffic period between 9:30 P.M. and 10:30 P.M., the hardware remained completely reliable.

TODD COHEN

Harvard and Wake Forest Universities

Harvard University

Harvard University is banking on e-mail and the Web to do a better job at raising money. After using its Web site for several years to keep alumni informed and explain its development activities, Harvard now plans to embrace e-mail to reach donors and drive them to a redesigned Web site that will be launched January 1, 2001.

"Over time, as people become more comfortable with online banking and with making purchases online, we believe that they will make many of their charitable gifts online," says Andy Tiedemann, director of communications for alumni affairs and development at Harvard.

Harvard is one of America's premier fundraising organizations. In December, it completed a seven-year, $2.6 billion capital campaign.

In the year ended June 30, 2000, Harvard College and Harvard's Graduate School of Arts and Sciences raised an estimated $164 million in their annual fundraising drive and capital campaign, up from $127 million a year earlier.

Those annual totals include more than $4.5 million raised through four direct mail appeals each year to a donor base of 126,000 alumni. The appeals cost a total of $125,000, an amount that Harvard hopes to reduce by adding e-mail appeals.

To test alumni receptivity to e-mail, Harvard last spring sent a series of e-mail messages to more than 59,000 alumni of six undergraduate classes. Of the total, only 2 percent said in replies that they didn't want to receive e-mail from Harvard.

One test e-mail message from Harvard solicited funds from 4,000 alumni. Of those, 200 replied with contributions totaling $38,000.

"One person sent a $10,000 gift and said, 'I only want to be solicited by e-mail,'" Tiedemann says.

Harvard now plans to add at least one e-mail fundraising appeal to the four direct mail appeals it has made each year. Harvard has 90,000 e-mail addresses for graduates.

"Our long-term goal would be to replace some of our mail campaigns with e-mail campaigns," Tiedemann says.

"E-mail is less costly than regular mail and generates a much quicker response," he says.

Harvard also is revamping its Web site, which now lets visitors make a contribution using a credit card. In January, Harvard will add the option of downloading a pledge form that can be completed and submitted with a check by regular mail.

A third option—coming soon—will allow donors to transfer stock electronically to Harvard. In the year ended June 30, 44 percent of Harvard's $483 million in gifts were stock transfers.

Tiedemann estimates that Harvard in the fiscal year ended June 30 received more than 350 gifts online totaling less than $100,000, compared to more than 83,000 gifts overall totaling $485 million.

"We're in roughly the same place that all nonprofits are in," he says. "We all envision that this will make a big difference. We envision that this will become a significant portion of our fundraising strategy. But right now it's sort of a giant experiment."

Wake Forest University

In Wake Forest's 2000 fall fundraising telethon, fundraising officials sent e-mail appeals on September 1 saying anyone sending a gift by September 28 would not get a phone solicitation later.

By September 22, 349 donors had made gifts totaling $127,854, compared to $33,362 from 122 donors in the same three-week period last year—when e-mail was not used.

The e-mail campaign underscores Wake Forest's effort in recent years to build Web technology into its overall fund-raising strategy.

"It changes the way in which we can communicate with alumni and friends and others in almost every way," said Bob Mills, associate vice president for advancement.

Three years ago, the advancement office created an "advancement technologies" unit to put computers, e-mail, and the Web to work building relationships and raising money.

In the fall of 1997, the unit launched a Web feature allowing people to make gifts online. Web donations totaled only $3,200 in the 1997–1998 school year but grew to $14,985 the next year and to $80,546 last year.

In June 1999, Wake Forest made its first e-mail fundraising appeal— a reminder to people who had made pledges during the school year but hadn't sent in their gifts. In just two weeks, the school received funds from roughly three of every ten people receiving the e-mail.

"But aggregate numbers alone don't capture technology's impact on fundraising," said Tim Snyder, Wake Forest's director of advancement technologies.

Last December 29, for example, the school received a number of online gifts, including one for $10,000—its biggest gift ever over the Web. The next day, the school received several more online gifts, including one for $25,000.

"What that says to me is that people are now more comfortable making significant transactions on the Web," said Snyder.

"The Web also is a powerful tool to keep in touch and even reconnect with alumni," he said.

Two years ago, a Wake graduate living overseas who had lost touch with the school for seven or eight years found its Web site and sent an e-mail message.

One thing led to another, and when the alumnus finally visited the school less than a year later, he stopped by the development office to drop off a $40,000 check, pledging to give $10,000 more over five years.

"That's the power of the Web that isn't measured if you're just counting dollars that come in online," Snyder said.

The school plans to increase its use of e-mail to communicate with alumni, family, and donors—in some cases using e-mail to replace traditional mailings. It also will add Web features to recognize significant donors and help prospective donors plan large gifts.

Mills, the associate vice president for advancement, estimated that annual fund dollars "will be raised almost totally online within five years."

And Snyder said that three of every four dollars raised a decade from now "will be significantly influenced by an experience that took place on the Web."

"Yet while technology can be a powerful fundraising tool," he said, "it is best used to support the larger challenge of building relationships."

"You need to view your technology outreach program as part of your overall fund-raising strategy," he said.

The Heifer Project International

Since 1944, when Heifer Project International (HPI) first shipped cows to impoverished families, the organization knew that livestock offered some of the best resources for ending the cycle of chronic hunger and poverty that plagues two-thirds of the planet. Over the last five decades, HPI has helped four million small-scale farm families on five continents and 115 countries become self-reliant by providing livestock, training, and agricultural tools.

In 1997, HPI recognized the importance of the Web as an additional avenue for engaging and educating the public on hunger and poverty and for raising funds to support its programs. HPI sought to use an enhanced site as a value-added communication tool among existing donors and supporters of HPI, and among potential, new audiences online. They needed a provider who could help the organization develop and execute a plan to recruit and retain a broader audience.

HPI had a Web site [www.heifer.org], but it needed a full-service development partner with the expertise to realize its online goals of raising awareness, disseminating valuable information to the large and growing Internet audience, and raising funds through an online gift catalog. HPI chose Commerce One.

A New User Interface

Commerce One completed an overhaul of both graphic design and overall site architecture, which allowed for an increase in the breadth and depth of informational content and special features, and a more compelling homepage to engage visitors and encourage them to interact with HPI.

The user interface on the new site created a robust sense of HPI and its cause through earthy colors and textures, and powerful images of

Note: Used with permission from Heifer Project International.

women, children, and animals. The "Gift Catalog" was the centerpiece, with every page featuring a catalog icon and link. Special rotating content features such as "Hunger Facts" and "HPI Around the World" infuse the stable elements of the home page.

The "Giving Programs" section encourages participation and offers special challenges for church groups, schools, and civic clubs. The "Get Involved" section features information on educational and volunteer opportunities in HPI's regional centers. An "Ending Hunger and Poverty" section conveys HPI's success stories as well as the continuing challenges it faces in community development, women in development, the environment, and sustainable development.

Heifer Project's "Gift Catalog"

The "Gift Catalog" area is a primary means for user interaction and support. Every page features a story of HPI's work, interactive graphics, a strong call to action, and links to secure donation forms. A gift catalog application that includes a shopping cart feature allowing visitors to pick and choose among its options offers automatic processing of credit card donations and allows users to preview their orders before proceeding to check out. Text and images accompany each animal option, reinforcing the importance of the gift and describing how it will be used to help families achieve self-sufficiency. Users can donate on their own or in honor of another person, and the HPI site offers Web-based gift cards, or "honor cards," which donors can send to their gift honorees.

From the site's launch in mid-1998 and continuing through to the present, HPI has integrated online marketing efforts with site development in an effort to raise awareness and acquire new site visitors and donors. In 1999 the organization executed two major marketing initiatives: a rapid-response campaign in the aftermath of the Kosovo conflict, and a traditional holiday, online-fundraising plan that extended from October through December 1999 and built upon previous holiday efforts in 1998.

In both cases, HPI conducted extensive online public relations initiatives that included the distribution of online press releases, targeted pitches to key media representatives, participation in relevant mailing lists, and submissions to the top awards sites and newsletters. During the holiday campaign, Commerce One and HPI developed an opt-in e-mail advertising campaign targeted to subscribers of Christian and holiday gift-giving mailing lists. They also developed an outbound communication plan to encourage repeat visits and repeat donations by existing site visitors and previous online donors.

300 Percent Return in Year One

In its first year of operation online, HPI realized a 300 percent return on its Web investment. A comparison with off-line giving methods showed that the average online gift value was higher than the average gift value for mail, inbound phone, and fax orders. Analysis has shown that nearly 50 percent of Web givers were new donors to the organization.

Site traffic increased more than 400 percent during the 1999 holiday season. Heifer Project saw a 74 percent increase in individual user sessions from October to November, and another 136 percent increase from November to December.

An opt-in e-mail marketing campaign during the 1999 holiday season yielded a 3 percent overall response rate. The outbound communications to existing site visitors and donors yielded response rates higher than 10 percent.

Dedicated and sustained online public relations and marketing efforts generated a number of placements and site mentions in high-profile publications such as *Time*, Time.com, CNN.com, the *New York Times* (print and online), the *Washington Post*, and *Newsweek*.

Moving forward, HPI will continue to refine and develop its online fundraising capabilities, including testing the connections between direct mail and the Web site. The organization continues to explore ways to integrate online marketing and public relations with HPI's off-line promotional efforts—including direct mail and traditional advertising—to enhance the donor experience and broaden its current base of supporters.

Stanford University

In October 1998, the Stanford Alumni Association and the Stanford News Service distributed the first issue of @Stanford, a free monthly e-mail newsletter of campus news and research. Each issue takes about a minute or two to skim and consists of headlines with brief summaries and links to the full stories on the Stanford Web site. (See, as of this writing, [www.stanfordalumni.org/jg/online_services/mailing_lists.html#atstanford].)

Context: Online Usage Among Alumni

To begin with, almost all alumni are now online. As of November 2000, 100 percent of alumni under forty, and 97 percent of alumni forty to fifty-nine had access to the Web; 98 percent of both younger and middle-aged alumni had e-mail addresses. More than eight out of ten alumni sixty or older had both e-mail and the Web in November 2000. (It's likely that access among alumni from other four-year colleges and universities is similar to what it is among Stanford alumni.)

Although access to the Web will soon be almost universal among alumni, not all of them visit their alma mater's Web sites. As of November 2000, 71 percent of Stanford alumni with Web access (or 68 percent of all alumni) had visited a Stanford site. Moreover, alumni do not visit the university sites as frequently as they visit other sites: In November 2000, only 41 percent of alumni with Web access said they visit a Stanford site even once or twice every few months—and just a fifth said they visit at least once a month.

As of November 2000, 30 percent of Stanford alumni were receiving @Stanford. Most recipients were added to the distribution list if Stanford had their e-mail addresses. As the likelihood of having their e-mail addresses decreased with age, so too did the likelihood of receiving @Stanford: 46 percent of younger alumni were receiving it, compared to 23 percent of middle-aged alumni, and only 8 percent of older alumni.

Nondonors and lapsed donors were as likely to receive @Stanford as current donors were. Indeed, recipients were fairly reflective of the alumni population as a whole in all ways except age.

Because most recipients were under forty, the only differences reported in this chapter are those that are independent of age.

Communications

For the most part, @Stanford is achieving its primary goal as an effective communications vehicle. Alumni who receive it feel better informed than alumni who do not receive it, and in many (but not all) ways, they actually are better informed. In November 2000, recipients were more likely than nonrecipients to have read something in the past year that made them proud of their Stanford affiliation, to be able to name the University's new President, to feel Stanford does an excellent job at keeping them informed, and to have read about four of the seven news items tested in the survey. @Stanford is also enhancing the university's overall communications program by stimulating usage of Stanford Web resources. Among alumni with Web access, @Stanford recipients are not only much more likely than nonrecipients to have visited a Stanford Web site (94 percent versus 64 percent in November 2000), but they are three times as likely to have book-marked a Stanford Web page and also visit more frequently (63 percent of recipients visit at least once or twice every few months, compared to only 35 percent of nonrecipients). Moreover, a fifth of recipients said they had forwarded an issue of @Stanford, and a fifth said they had forwarded a link—so @Stanford is further augmenting University communications by means of "viral marketing."

Feelings and Perceptions

By keeping alumni better informed—especially about research and other positive contributions the university is making to society—the University hopes that @Stanford might engender more favorable perceptions of the institution, more positive feelings about it, greater pride in it, closer emotional connection to it, and ultimately greater support for it.

As of November 2000, however, most perceptions of Stanford that were tested in the survey did not differ between alumni who did and did not receive @Stanford. Recipients were no more (or less) likely than nonrecipients to give Stanford a very strong recommendation, or to agree with the positive statements about Stanford that were tested. Nor did they rate Stanford more favorably at serving their needs and interests overall or at valuing its alumni.

Similarly, personal feelings about Stanford did not differ between recipients and nonrecipients. For instance, recipients did not feel more (or less) strongly that Stanford has been a strong factor in their lives or feel a greater affinity with their graduating class. Of course, these are feelings one would not realistically expect a newsletter to have much of an influence upon.

However, recipients were clearly more likely than nonrecipients to have very positive feelings about Stanford now (72 percent versus 58 percent) and may have been more likely to feel a great deal of pride in their Stanford degree, a great emotional connection to Stanford, and that they do not only hear from Stanford when it's asking for money.

Alumni Giving

Previous research has consistently suggested that alumni who are most aware of what's happening at Stanford—and the positive impact Stanford has on the world we live in—are more likely to be donors. Simply put, these alumni have a keener appreciation of what Stanford is doing to deserve their support. And since @Stanford correlates in many ways with greater awareness, it is not unreasonable to hypothesize that it would have positive correlations with giving.

And indeed it does. The FY2000 giving records of the 20,951 alumni who had been receiving @Stanford for at least a year (since September 1999) were compared with the giving records of all other alumni. Alumni who earned their degree in 2000 were excluded from the latter group to ensure comparability.

The database was first examined by participation (whether or not a gift was made in FY2000). The participation data was sliced and diced twenty-eight ways; in every way, a greater percentage of recipients than nonrecipients made a gift to Stanford in FY2000.

The following data come from the actual giving records, not from a survey:

- Among all undergraduate and dual degree holders, about half (49 percent) of the recipients made gifts in FY2000 compared to only a third (34 percent) of nonrecipients (Figure C4.1).

- Among those who had made gifts in FY1999, a slightly greater percentage of recipients (78 percent) than nonrecipients (73 percent) renewed their support in FY2000.

- But most of the difference comes from lapsed and nondonors. Among lapsed donors (those who had made gifts prior to, but not in, FY1999), 32 percent of recipients made gifts in FY2000 compared to 22 percent of nonrecipients. And among those who had never made gifts prior to FY2000, 13 percent of recipients gave for the first time compared to just 5 percent of nonrecipients.

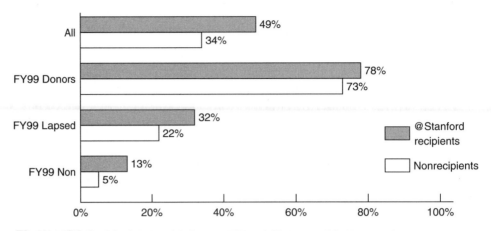

Figure C4.1. Undergraduate and Dual-Degree Alumni—Donors in FY2000.

Moreover, the differences are not limited to certain demographic groups but are seen across the board: FY2000 participation was much greater among recipients than nonrecipients regardless of class year, gender, or school (Figure C4.2).

Similar differences are seen among alumni with only a graduate degree from Stanford.

In addition to participation, the FY2000 data were also analyzed another twenty-eight ways to examine the average amount of the gifts made. And again, among undergraduate and dual-degree holders, the average gift was greater from recipients than from nonrecipients in almost every way (Figure C4.3). The gifts that were made by undergraduate and dual-degree holders in FY2000 were larger from recipients than from nonrecipients regardless of

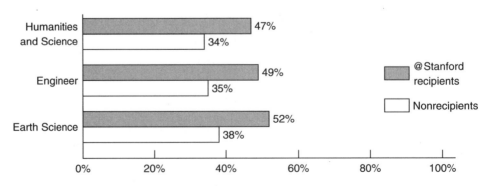

Figure C4.2. Undergraduate and Dual-Degree Alumni—Donors in FY2000.

- FY99 giving behavior (donors, lapsed donors, and nondonors)
- Class year
- Gender
- School (with the exception of Earth Sciences)

However, among graduate-only degree holders, average gifts were not greater among recipients. So, whereas @Stanford correlates with greater participation in every way for all alumni, its correlation with the amount given is less consistent.

Conclusion and Recommendations

E-mail newsletters can indeed play a positive role in institutional advancement by improving the effectiveness and reach of the institution's communications efforts, helping inform feelings and perceptions of the institution as it is now, and even increasing financial support for the institution. Therefore, I recommend the following:

First, recommend that Stanford, and other institutions with such newsletters, do all they can to increase awareness of, and subscription to, the newsletters. They might start by featuring them more prominently on their Web sites. If university policy permits, all alumni and friends should be automatically subscribed whenever their e-mail addresses are obtained. Just as most alumni appreciate receiving Stanford magazine without specifically asking for it, they also appreciate receiving @Stanford. Quantitative data from the surveys, as well as qualitative comments made in focus groups, indicate that alumni do not

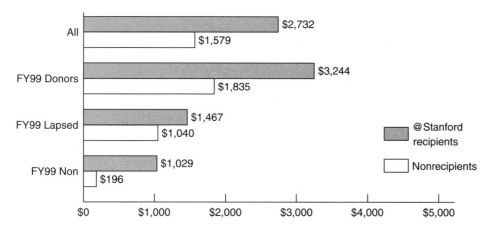

Figure C4.3. Undergraduate and Dual-Degree Alumni—Average Gift in FY2000, Excluding Gifts of $1 Million or More.

perceive @Stanford as spam. And for those who don't want it, unsubscribing is quick and easy.

Second, I recommend that serious effort should also be made to expand distribution beyond the alumni and campus populations. Key constituencies that should be included are parents of current and former students, residents of the neighboring communities, and opinion leaders and government officials throughout the state. Because these newsletters can increase awareness and help inform perceptions of the University, they could help build a stronger base of community support and enthusiasm, which would be of great value when community support is needed on town-gown issues.

The main challenge for e-mail newsletters may be to better serve the diverse interests of alumni and friends while maintaining both the brevity and the breadth of the newsletter. It may help to produce a customizable supplement to the main newsletter as well as regional events bulletins—especially since there is great interest in both. To be most effective, however, content and timing of all lists will need to be coordinated.

Like all online resources, e-mail newsletters are still evolving. So experimenting with, and market testing, various formats is also advisable. Again, this would be especially valuable if the results were published or otherwise shared.

Resources

ePhilanthropy Code of Ethical Online Philanthropic Practices

The ePhilanthropy Foundation exists to foster the effective and safe use of the Internet for philanthropic purposes. In its effort to promote high ethical standards in online fundraising and build trust among contributors in making online transactions and contributions with the charity of their choice, it offers this code as a guide to all who share this goal. Contributors are encouraged to be aware of non-Internet related fundraising practices that fall outside the scope of this code.

Ethical Online Practices and Practitioners will

Section A: Philanthropic Experience

1. Clearly and specifically display and describe the organization's identity on the organization's Web site.

2. Employ practices on the Web site that exhibit integrity, honesty, truthfulness and seek to safeguard the public trust.

Section B: Privacy and Security

1. Seek to inspire trust in every online transaction.

2. Prominently display the opportunity to have donors' names removed from lists that are sold to, rented to, or exchanged with other organizations.

3. Conduct online transactions through a system that employs high-level security technology to protect the donor's personal information.

4. Provide either an "opt in" or "opt out" mechanism to prevent unsolicited communications or solicitations by organizations that obtain e-mail addresses directly from the donor, and require the "opt in" mechanism before the donor's e-mail address may be sold, transferred, or otherwise distributed to a third party for communication, advertising, or promotion purposes.

5. Protect the interests and privacy of individuals interacting with their Web site.

Section C: Disclosures

1. Disclose the identity of the organization or provider processing an online transaction.

2. Guarantee that the name, logo, and likeness of all parties to an online transaction belong to the party and will not be used without express permission.

3. Maintain all appropriate governmental and regulatory designations or certifications.

Section D: Complaints

1. Provide protection to hold the donor harmless of any problem arising from a transaction conducted through the organization's Web site.

2. Promptly respond to all customer complaints and employ best efforts to fairly resolve all legitimate complaints in a timely fashion.

Section E: Transactions

1. Ensure contributions are used to support the activities of the organization to which it was donated.

2. Ensure that legal control of contributions or proceeds from online transactions are transferred directly to the charity or expedited in the fastest possible way.

3. Companies providing online services to charities will provide clear and full communication with the charity on all aspects of donor transactions, including the accurate and timely transmission of data related to online transactions.

4. Stay informed regarding the best methods to ensure the ethical, secure, and private nature of online ePhilanthropy transactions.

5. Adhere to the spirit as well as the letter of all applicable laws and regulations, including but not limited to charity solicitation and tax laws.

6. Ensure that all services, recognition, and other transactions promised on a Web site, in consideration of gift or transaction, will be fulfilled in a timely basis.

7. Disclose to the donor the nature of the relationship between the organization processing the gift or transaction and the charity intended to benefit from the gift.

Ten Rules of ePhilanthropy Every Nonprofit Should Know

- Rule 1: Don't become invisible

  If you build it, they won't just come. Building an online brand is just as important and just as difficult as building an off-line brand.

- Rule 2: It takes "know how" and vision

  Your organization's Web site is a marketing and fundraising tool, *not a technology tool*. Fundraisers and marketers need to be driving the content, not the Web developer.

- Rule 3: It's all about the donor

  Put the Donor First! Know your contributors; let them get to know you.

- Rule 4: Keep savvy donors; stay fresh and current

  Make online giving enjoyable and easy. Give the donor options. Use the latest technology. Show your donor how their funds are being used.

- Rule 5: Integrate into everything you do

  Your Web site alone will do nothing. Every activity you have should drive traffic to your site.

- Rule 6: Don't trade your mission for a shopping mall

  Many nonprofit Web sites fail to emphasis mission, instead turning themselves into online shopping malls, without even knowing why.

- Rule 7: Ethics, privacy, and security are not buzzwords

  Many donors are just now deciding to make their first online contribution. They will expect your organization to maintain the highest standards of ethics, privacy, and security.

- Rule 8: It takes the Internet to build a community

  Many nonprofits (particularly smaller ones) lack the resources to communicate effectively. The Internet offers the opportunity to cost-effectively build a community of supporters.

- Rule 9: Success online means being targeted

  The Web site alone is not enough. You must target your audience and drive their attention to the wealth of information and services offered by your Web site. Permission must be sought before you begin direct communication via the Internet.

- Rule 10: ePhilanthropy is more than just e-money

  ePhilanthropy is a tool to be used in your fundraising strategy. *It should not* be viewed as quick money. There are no shortcuts to building effective relationships. But the Internet will enhance your efforts.

Web Hosting

Web site hosting is a commodity. This means the products and services that make up what we call hosting are largely the same regardless of the companies that offer them (most often called ISPs, or Internet service providers). It also means that there should not be significant differences in price, as long as you are comparing "apples to apples," which most nonprofits are not. That said, there can be vast differences in levels of service and prices among ISPs. Speaking in lay terms, the hosting industry can be divided into three or four categories:

Level-One or Top-Tier ISPs These are the "biggies," often part of well-known telecommunications companies or large, stand-alone ISPs. Typically, these companies have spent in excess of $100 million on their hosting and data centers. This expense is reflected in the level of service, which is high; the level of technical sophistication, also high; and in the price—you guessed it, the highest in the industry. Probably the top 50,000 501(c)(3)s—those with revenues over $1 million annually—are in the market for the hosting services offered by top-tier ISPs, along with organizations or campaigns that have special, or heightened, technology needs. *Note:* Top-tier ISPs rarely offer anything but hosting on a dedicated server, something the majority of nonprofits do not need. Examples include Digex, UUNET, and AT&T.

Middle-Market ISPs This is probably the sweet spot for the nonprofit sector. Offering both dedicated and shared hosting solutions, these ISPs are geared toward small- and medium-sized businesses, including non-profits. Examples include Interland, VERIO, and Applied Theory.

Low-End or Free ISPs These organizations have succeeded in signing up thousands of small nonprofits. There is high variability in the reliability and level of service these companies provide, and there are considerable risks. (One company we visited literally had servers on particle board and cinder blocks in a shed.) For nonprofits with Web

263

sites that are not mission-critical and that may not be heavily used, low-end ISPs can be a viable option. Be extremely diligent when selecting a low-end provider, however. Also consider supplementing low-end hosting with a higher-end online transaction provider. Examples are too many to mention, but a search on "local Internet service providers" is usually a good place to start.

The hosting needs of the majority of nonprofits are, relatively speaking, straightforward. Most fall into the second and third categories described above. What should you look for? From an e-philanthropy standpoint, reliability, security, and data management (that is, data storage, access, transfer, and so forth) are among the key services offered by ISPs. Supplemental services to look for include some kind of reporting on Web site activity (for example, WebTrends) and transaction processing; many ISPs will "bundle" both services for you as part of your monthly service agreement.

One final note: Be aware of what happens if you want to move your hosting somewhere else. Ask questions like the following:

- Will the ISP help you with migration?
- If so, what will the costs be?
- Are there any scripts or other programs that cannot be taken with you?
- If you can take them with you, is there a cost associated with that?
- What about the contract? Does the contract hold you liable for hosting costs through the life of the contract, or can you give thirty, sixty, or ninety days' notice?

RESOURCE ▼
▼

D

▲

Tips for Creating Effective Vendor Contracts

An effective contract can provide part of the foundation for a strong (and predictable) relationship with an outsourcing vendor or partner. A poorly written contract can seriously undermine a vendor relationship and even project outcomes. In addition, the use of Internet technology introduces a number of new dynamics into the contracting process, including source code issues, intellectual property rights, and termination clauses. What follows is a checklist for outsourcing contacts. It is a mere glance at some of the things your contract with a Web site or related vendor should accomplish:

• The contract should clearly distinguish between a fixed-fee and time-and-materials (T&M) approach (or some hybrid). With a fixed-fee contract, it's important that you work closely and as transparently as possible with vendors to manage your expectations. Time-and-materials contracts can make nonprofits vulnerable to runaway project costs. Studies show that the majority of technology projects go over budget.

• The contract should clearly state under what circumstances additional hours or tasks can be undertaken by the vendor. One possible solution to the above quandary is to make the contract T&M with a cap. This way, no additional work or costs can be incurred without your understanding and approval in advance (usually in writing).

• The contract should clearly delineate whose intellectual property rights are whose. Who owns the project materials? Who owns the code used to create the Web functionality? If you have rights to the code (or other materials), what "use" rights do you have? For example, can you share the products of the project with your chapters? Can you sell it to them?

• The contract should clearly describe the deliverables you are paying for. In part because the business of creating technology solutions is new and in part because contractors and vendors are not always working from a common understanding of terms and concepts, it is important that a contract (or accompanying task order) lay out explicitly what tasks will be undertaken and what deliverables will be produced. This will hold your vendor accountable and protect you in the event that deliverables do not meet stated criteria.

• The contract should clearly define what constitutes "approval." Some companies have developed formal sign-off sheets that require customers to sign off on project "deliverables" or phases. This generally affords protection forward smoothly by delineating one deliverable or phase from the next.

• The contract should clearly articulate the terms of payment. Will you pay according to milestones (that have been approved) or on a monthly basis? Each payment arrangement has implications for the project and its progress and outcomes.

• Finally, the contract should clearly state the conditions of contract termination. How much notice do you have to give to terminate? For what reasons can you terminate? Most important, what are the obligations of both parties upon termination? Invariably, you will need assistance from the vendor after you have decided to terminate and their cooperation should be ensured (especially if they have gone out of business or been merged with or acquired by another business).

RESOURCE

E

APRACode of Ethics

Association of Professional Researchers for Advancement (APRA) members shall support and further the individual's fundamental right to privacy and protect the confidential information of their institutions. APRA members are committed to the ethical collection and use of information. Members shall follow all applicable federal, state, and local laws, as well as institutional policies, governing the collection, use, maintenance, and dissemination of information in the pursuit of the missions of their institutions. APRA members shall respect all people and organizations.

Code of Ethics

Prospect researchers must balance the needs of their institutions to collect, analyze, record, maintain, use, and disseminate information with an individual's right to privacy. This balance is not always easy to maintain. The following ethical principles apply, and practice is built on these principles:

I. Fundamental Principles

A. Confidentiality

Confidential information about constituents (donors and nondonors), as well as confidential information of the institutions in oral form or on electronic, magnetic, or print media are protected so that the relationship of trust between the constituent and the institution is upheld.

B. Accuracy

> Prospect researchers shall record all data accurately. Such information shall include attribution. Analysis and products of data analysis should be without personal prejudices or biases.

C. Relevance

> Prospect researchers shall seek and record only information that is relevant and appropriate to the fundraising effort of the institutions that employ them.

D. Accountability

> Prospect researchers shall accept responsibility for their actions and shall be accountable to the profession of development, to their respective institutions, and to the constituents who place their trust in prospect researchers and their institutions.

E. Honesty

> Prospect researchers shall be truthful with regard to their identity and purpose and the identity of their institution during the course of their work.

II. Suggested Practice

A. Collection

1. The collection of information shall be done lawfully, respecting applicable laws and institutional policies.

2. Information sought and recorded includes all data that can be verified and attributed, as well as constituent information that is self-reported (via correspondence, surveys, questionnaires, etc.).

3. When requesting information in person or by telephone, it is recommended in most cases that neither individual nor institutional identity shall be concealed. Written requests for public information shall be made on institutional stationary clearly identifying the inquirer.

4. Whenever possible, payments for public records shall be made through the institution.

5. Prospect researchers shall apply the same standards for electronic information that they currently use in evaluating and verifying print media. The researcher shall ascertain whether or not the information comes from a reliable source and that the information collected meets the standards set forth in the APRA Statement of Ethics.

B. Recording and Maintenance

1. Researchers shall state information in an objective and factual manner; note attribution and date of collection; and clearly identify analysis.

2. Constituent information on paper, electronic, magnetic, or other media shall be stored securely to prevent access by unauthorized persons.

3. Special protection shall be afforded all giving records pertaining to anonymous donors.

4. Electronic or paper documents pertaining to constituents shall be irreversibly disposed of when no longer needed (by following institutional standards for document disposal).

C. Use and Distribution

1. Researchers shall adhere to all applicable laws, as well as to institutional policies, regarding the use and distribution of confidential constituent information.

2. Constituent information is the property of the institution for which it was collected and shall not be given to persons other than those who are involved with the cultivation or solicitation effort or those who need that information in the performance of their duties for that institution.

3. Constituent information for one institution shall not be taken to another institution.

4. Research documents containing constituent information that is to be used outside research offices shall be clearly marked *confidential.*

5. Vendors, consultants, and other external entities shall understand and agree to comply with the institution's confidentiality policies before gaining access to institutional data.

6. Only publicly available information shall be shared with colleagues at other institutions as a professional courtesy.

III. Recommendations

1. Prospect researchers shall urge their institutions to develop written policies based upon applicable laws and these policies should define what information shall be gathered, recorded, and maintained, and to whom and under what conditions the information can be released.

2. Prospect researchers shall urge the development of written policies at their institutions defining who may authorize access to prospect files and under what conditions. These policies

should follow the guidelines outlined in the CASE Donor Bill of Rights, the NSFRE Code of Ethical Principles, and the Association for Healthcare Philanthropy Statement of Professional Standards and Conduct.

3. Prospect researchers shall strongly urge their development colleagues to abide by this Code of Ethics and Fundamental Principles.

Using E-Mail Effectively

E-mail is a vital and inexpensive tool for promoting nonprofit organizations, cultivating, educating, and activating supporters, and resoliciting donors. These recommendations can help you get the most from e-mail.

1. *Collect e-mail address everywhere from everyone.* Collect e-mail addresses on every page of your Web site (offer a free e-newsletter), in your direct mail, at events, in the media, in person.

Remember: The ePhilanthropy Code of Ethics requires you to let supporters "opt in" to receive your e-mail and "opt out" whenever they want to stop.

2. *Don't send unsolicited e-mail or "spam."* While it's acceptable to rent or exchange direct mail lists, it's not acceptable to buy e-mail addresses from other organizations or companies unless the people on those lists have "opted in" to receive mail from third parties. By the same token, don't share your supporters' e-mail addresses with anyone else unless you have received explicit permission from them to do so.

3. *Don't over-message your supporters.* Don't bother your supporters with too many messages or messages that aren't relevant for them. The great advantage of e-mail marketing is its ability to help you develop relationships via informal and inexpensive communications; but don't abuse the trust you are trying to build.

4. *Don't be afraid to ask for gifts.* While most of your e-mail messages will cultivate, educate, or move to action, it's also OK to ask donors or prospects to make a gift (and to remind them of how important their last gift was in achieving your organization's mission).

An e-mail acknowledging a recent gift might include information on how gifts have been used successfully to support the population you serve. You can also invite the donor's feedback with a short survey or request for comments.

5. *Be ready to answer your e-mail messages.* E-mail and the Web make it easy for your donors and other supporters to contact you with questions, concerns, or problems. To answer all those e-mails requires a well-organized system and staff assigned to the task. What's more, people expect a quick answer—24-hour turnaround or faster—to their e-mails. Make sure you allocate resources within your organization to respond, and provide a telephone number on your Web site for people who want live assistance.

These recommendations are based in part on the ePhilanthropy Code of Ethical Online Philanthropic Practices (Resource A) and the Ten Rules of ePhilanthropy Every Nonprofit Should Know (Resource B).

The Gilbert E-Mail Manifesto

Repeat after me: "E-mail is more important than my Web site!"

I can't stand it anymore. I've listened to too many four-hour workshops about online fundraising in which it's all about Web sites, Web sites, Web sites. I've been to too many technical assistance sites that have class after class on Web design. I've heard too many nonprofits obsess about their Web sites.

I ask leaders of nonprofit organizations if they have an e-mail strategy, and their usual response is something on the order of "Huh?" They are spending enormous amounts of money and staff time on their Web sites, but it's the rare exception that the organization even has enough of an e-mail strategy to have a newsletter.

They are wasting their money. I'm serious.

Why is this happening? Is it because Web sites are pretty, and e-mail is mostly text? Is it because people love graphic design? Is it because this is the approach that is pushed by the consulting firms? Or is it perhaps because thinking about e-mail is a little more difficult, as it is a constantly moving target?

I don't know the reasons for sure, but I do know that something can be done.

I have been recommending "Three Rules of E-Mail" to help nonprofit organizations develop a genuine Internet strategy and avoid being seduced by their own Web presence:

Rule 1: Resources spent on e-mail strategies are more valuable than the same resources spent on Web strategies.

Rule 2: A Web site built around an e-mail strategy is more valuable than a Web site that is built around itself.

Rule 3: E-mail–oriented thinking will yield better strategic thinking overall.

Nonprofits that truly embrace these three rules will reach a genuine
breakthrough in their online presence. They will seize the initiative from
technologists and guide their own technology on their terms.

Let me elaborate. For each of these principles I will scratch the sur-
face as to why it's true and how it might be applied. Each of these is
worthy of several workshops in its own right.

*Rule 1: Resources spent on e-mail strategies are more valuable than the
same resources spent on Web strategies.* However unglamorous it might be,
e-mail is the killer application of the Internet. It is person-to-person
communication—the one thing that breaks down barriers faster than
anything else on the net. Consider these facts:

- Everybody on the net has e-mail, and most of them read most of
  their messages.
- People visit far fewer Web sites than they get e-mail messages.
- E-mail messages are treated as "To Do" items, while bookmarks
  are often forgotten. E-mail is always a call to action.
- E-mail is handled within a familiar user interface, whereas each
  Web site has to teach a new interface.
- E-mail is a very personal medium.

Stop obsessing about how many hits your Web site gets—and start
counting how much e-mail interaction you have with your stakeholders. Stop waiting for people to discover your Web site, and start discovering their mailboxes.

*Rule 2: A Web site built around an e-mail strategy is more valuable than a
Web site that is built around itself.* On some nonprofit list, somewhere,
there are people asking right now how to get more traffic on their Web
sites. And other people are answering by telling them how to put META
tags in their sites, so they'll get listed in search engines. This is so tired!

My answer to this overused question is simple: Send them there with
e-mail!

Obviously, this means there has to be a purpose for them to go to the
Web site that cannot be fulfilled with the e-mail message itself. Some of
the obvious ways that a Web site can supplement your e-mail strategy
include

- Gathering e-mail addresses in the first place
- Archiving your relationships with stakeholders (for example, collecting the results of surveys)

- Serving as a library to back up your smaller e-mail communications

- Providing actual online tools for your stakeholders

- Providing Web forms that allow you to structure your communication and pull it into databases

Rule 3: E-mail–oriented thinking will yield better strategic thinking overall. Last year, the most common question I was asked by journalists reporting on the Internet and nonprofits was about the role of the Internet in fundraising. My response was always the same:

- The ability to process credit card transactions is the equivalent of having a checking account. It's not very interesting, and it's not actually fundraising.

- The true power of the Internet for fundraising (or any other stakeholder relationship) is the power of personal communication combined with the power of scale. Nonprofits know how to mobilize people on a personal level. By using the Internet appropriately, they can do so on a scale never before possible.

Understanding e-mail will make this possible. True, not all personal, online communication takes place through e-mail, but e-mail is the canonical "closed-loop relationship" that direct marketing managers understand so well. Applied well, it will allow nonprofits to succeed on a whole level.

Repeat after me: "E-mail is more important than my Web site!"

ePhilanthropyFoundation's GLOSSARY OF TERMS

This glossary of terms has been compiled from a variety of sources (noted in parentheses) by the ePhilanthropyFoundation.Org.

Acrobat (Source: Adobe.com). Acrobat® is a program made by Adobe that allows you to convert any document to a Portable Document Format (PDF) file (a type of file that is commonly posted on the Web for download). Anyone can then open your document across a broad range of hardware and software, and it will look exactly as you intended—with layout, fonts, links, and images intact.

Applet (Source: Sun.com). An applet is a small program that can be included in an HTML page, just like an image is included. Java applets can perform interactive animations, immediate calculations, or other simple tasks without having to send a user request back to the server.

ASCII (Source: Learnthenet.com). ASCII is an acronym for American Standard Code for Information Interchange, a seven-bit code that represents the most basic letters of the Roman alphabet, numbers, and other characters used in computing. ASCII characters allow us to communicate with computers, which use their own language called binary, which is made up of zeros and ones. When we type ASCII characters from the keyboard (which look like words to us), the computer interprets them as binary so they can be read, manipulated, stored, and retrieved.

ASP (Source: ASPNews.com). Application Service Providers (ASPs) are third-party entities that manage and distribute software-based services and solutions to customers across a wide area network from a central data center. ASPs may be commercial ventures that cater to customers or not-for-profit or government organizations that provide service and support to end users.

Bandwidth (Source: Webopaedia.com). Bandwidth is the maximum amount of data that can travel a communications path in a given time, usually measured in seconds. For digital devices, the bandwidth is usually expressed in bits per second (bps) or bytes per second.

Banner (Source: SearchWebManagement.com). Depending on how it's used, a banner is either a graphic image that announces the name or identity of a site (and often is spread across the width of the Web page) or an advertising image. Advertisers sometimes count banner "views," or the number of times a banner graphic image was downloaded over a period of time.

Bookmark (Source: Whatis.com). Using a World Wide Web browser, a bookmark is a saved link to a Web page that has been added to a list of saved links. When you are looking at a particular Web site or homepage and want to be able to get back to it quickly later, you can create a bookmark for it. Netscape and some other browsers use the bookmark idea. Microsoft's Internet Explorer uses the term *favorite*.

Bounce (Source: Computeruser.com). An electronic mail message returned with a notice indicating the transmission failed, either because the message was misaddressed or a connection failed.

Browser (Source: Webguest.com). A software program that allows you to surf the Web. The most popular Web browsers right now are Netscape Navigator and Internet Explorer.

CGI (Source: Instantweb.com). Common Gateway Interface (CGI) is a standard for running external programs from a World Wide Web HTTP server. The CGI program can, for example, access information in a database and format the results as HTML. A CGI program can be any program that can accept command line arguments.

Cookie (Source: Webguest.com). A small piece of information that a Web server sends to your computer hard disk via your browser. Cookies contain information such as log-in or registration information, online shopping cart information, and user preferences. This information can be retrieved by other Web pages on the site so that the site can be customized.

CRM (Source: 1to1.com). Customer Relationship Management (CRM) is the same as one-to-one marketing. This customer-focused business model also goes by the names *relationship marketing, real-time marketing, customer intimacy,* and a variety of other terms. But the idea is the same: establish relationships with customers on an individual basis, and then use the information you gather to treat different customers differently. The exchange between a customer and a company becomes mutually beneficial, as customers give information in return for personalized service that meets their individual needs.

Digest (Source: Instantweb.com). A periodical collection of messages that have been posted to a newsgroup or mailing list. A digest is prepared by a moderator who selects articles from the group or list, formats them, and adds a contents list.

EDI (Source: Instantweb.com). Electronic data interchange (EDI) is the exchange of standardized document forms between computer systems for business use.

Encryption (Source: Learnthenet.com). A way of coding the information in a file or e-mail message so that if it is intercepted by a third party as it travels over a network it cannot be read. Only the person or persons that have the right type of decoding software can unscramble the message.

ePhilanthropy (Source: ePhilanthropyFoundation.Org). The building and enhancing of relationships with supporters of nonprofit organizations via an Internet-based platform, the online contribution of cash or real property, or the purchase of products or services to benefit a nonprofit organization, and the storage of and usage of electronic data or use of electronic methods to support fundraising activities.

Firewall (Source: Learnthenet.com). A firewall is a combination hardware and software buffer that many companies or organizations have in place between their internal networks and the Internet. A firewall allows only specific kinds of messages from the Internet to flow in and out of the internal network. This protects the internal network from intruders or hackers who might try to use the Internet to break into those systems.

FTP (Source: Instantweb.com). File Transfer Protocol (FTP) is a client-server protocol that allows a user on one computer to transfer files to and from another computer.

HTML (Source: Learnthenet.com). An acronym for Hypertext Markup Language, HTML is the computer language used to create hypertext documents. HTML uses a finite list of tags that describe the general structure of various kinds of documents linked together on the World Wide Web.

HTTP (Source: Learnthenet.com). HTTP stands for HyperText Transfer Protocol, the method used to transfer hypertext files across the Internet. On the World Wide Web, pages written in HTML use hypertext to link to other documents. When you click on hypertext, you jump to another Web page, sound file, or graphic.

Hyperlink (Source: Webguest.com). A highlighted word (or graphic) within a hypertext document (Web page). When you click a hyperlink, it will take you to another place within the same page or to another page.

IP Address (Source: About.com). An IP (Internet protocol) address is the thirty-two-bit numeric address that serves as an identifier for a computer; information is routed based on the IP address of the destination. The IP address is written as four numbers separated by periods. For example 207.158.192.40 could be an IP address. Each of the four numbers (which can be from zero to 255) is used in different ways to identify a particular network and a host on that network.

ISP (Source: Webopaedia.com). Internet Service Provider (ISP), a company that provides access to the Internet. For a monthly fee, the service provider gives you a software package, username, password, and access phone number. Equipped with a modem, you can then log on to the Internet and browse the World Wide Web and send and receive e-mail.

Listserv (Source: Searchvb.com). Listserv is a small program that automatically redistributes e-mail to names on a mailing list. Users can subscribe to a mailing list by sending an e-mail note to a mailing list they learn about; listserv will automatically add the name and distribute future e-mail postings to every subscriber. (Requests to subscribe and unsubscribe are sent to a special address so that all subscribers do not see these requests.)

NGO (Source: UN.org). A nongovernmental organization (NGO) is any non-profit, voluntary citizens' group that is organized on a local, national, or international level. Task-oriented and driven by people with a common interest, NGOs perform a variety of services and humanitarian functions, bring citizens' concerns to governments, monitor policies, and encourage political participation at the community level. They provide analysis and expertise, serve as early warning mechanisms, and help monitor and implement international agreements. Some are organized around specific issues, such as human rights, the environment, or health.

OPX (Source: OPXInfo.org). Open Philanthropy Exchange (OPX) is a specification for data transfer between institutions in the philanthropy industry. The purpose of the OPX standard is to help philanthropic institutions communicate in a common language. Through seamless transmission of data, OPX removes technical barriers and allows data to flow seamlessly from one organization to another.

Perl (Source: Instantweb.com). Practical Extraction and Report Language (Perl) is a general purpose language, often used for scanning text and printing formatted reports. The use of Perl has grown significantly since its adoption as the language of choice of many World Wide Web developers.

POP3 (Source: Instantweb.com). Post Office Protocol, version 3, is a publication that standardizes the way computers on the Internet send and receive e-mail messages. The computers that do the sending and receiving are called servers.

RGB (Source: Instantweb.com). Red, Green, Blue—the three colors of light that can be mixed to produce any other color. Colored images are often stored as a sequence of RGB triplets or as separate red, green, and blue overlays. The term is often used as a synonym for color, as in "RGB monitor" as opposed to monochrome (black and white).

Search engine (Source: Learnthenet.com). A search engine is a type of software that creates indexes of databases or Internet sites based on the titles of files, keywords, or the full text of files. The search engine has an interface that allows you to type what you're looking for into a blank field. It then gives you a list of the results of the search. When you use a search engine on the Web, the results are presented to you in hypertext, which means you can click on any item in the list to get the actual file.

SQL (Source: Instantweb.com). An industry-standard language for creating, updating, and querying relational database management systems.

SSL (Source: Instantweb.com). Secure Sockets Layer is a protocol designed by Netscape Communications to provide encrypted communications on the Internet.

TCP/IP (Source: Whatis.com). Transmission Control Protocol/Internet Protocol (TCP/IP) is the basic communication language or protocol of the Internet. It can also be used as a communications protocol in the private networks called intranets and in extranets. When you are set up with direct access to the Internet, your computer is provided with a copy of the TCP/IP program just as every other computer that you may send messages to or get information from also has a copy of TCP/IP.

Top-Level Domain (Source: NetworkSolutions.com). .COM, .NET, and .ORG are top-level domains in the hierarchical Internet Domain Name System. These top-level domains are just underneath the "root," which is the start of the hierarchy. Anyone may register Web Addresses in .COM, .NET, and .ORG.

URL (Source: Instantweb.com). Uniform Resource Locator, (previously "Universal"). A draft standard for specifying the location of an object on the Internet, such as a file or a news group. URLs are used extensively on the World Wide Web. They are used in HTML documents to specify the target of a hyperlink, which is often another HTML document (possibly stored on another computer).

WWW (Source: Webopaedia.com). A system of Internet servers that support specially formatted documents. The documents are formatted in HTML that supports links to other documents, as well as graphics, audio, and video files. This means you can jump from one document to another simply by clicking on hot spots. Not all Internet servers are part of the World Wide Web.

XML (Source: W3.org). Extensible Markup Language (XML) is a simple, very flexible text format. Originally designed to meet the challenges of large-scale electronic publishing, XML is also playing an increasingly important role in the exchange of a variety of data on the Web.

INDEX